Machine Learning and Data Science

Scrivener Publishing
100 Cummings Center, Suite 541J
Beverly, MA 01915-6106

Publishers at Scrivener
Martin Scrivener (martin@scrivenerpublishing.com)
Phillip Carmical (pcarmical@scrivenerpublishing.com)

Machine Learning and Data Science

Fundamentals and Applications

Edited by

Prateek Agrawal
Charu Gupta
Anand Sharma
Vishu Madaan
and
Nisheeth Joshi

Scrivener
Publishing

WILEY

This edition first published 2022 by John Wiley & Sons, Inc., 111 River Street, Hoboken, NJ 07030, USA and Scrivener Publishing LLC, 100 Cummings Center, Suite 541J, Beverly, MA 01915, USA
© 2022 Scrivener Publishing LLC
For more information about Scrivener publications please visit www.scrivenerpublishing.com.

Wiley Global Headquarters
111 River Street, Hoboken, NJ 07030, USA

For details of our global editorial offices, customer services, and more information about Wiley products visit us at www.wiley.com.

Limit of Liability/Disclaimer of Warranty

Library of Congress Cataloging-in-Publication Data

ISBN 9781119775614

Cover image: Pixabay.com
Cover design by Russel Richardson

Set in size of 11pt and Minion Pro by Manila Typesetting Company, Makati, Philippines

Printed in the USA

10 9 8 7 6 5 4 3 2 1

Contents

Preface

Machine Learning and Data Science: Fundamentals and Applications

Engineering high-quality systems requires mastering advanced machine learning and data science concepts and dealing with large and complex data. There is growing realization in the system development community that we can learn useful system properties from large data by analysis with machine learning and data science.

Machine learning and data science are currently a very active topic with an extensive scope, both in terms of theory and applications. They have been established as an important emergent scientific field and paradigm driving research evolution in such disciplines as statistics, computing science and intelligence science, and practical transformation in such domains as science, engineering, the public sector, business, social science, and lifestyle. Simultaneously, their applications provide important challenges that can often be addressed only with innovative machine learning and data science algorithms.

Those algorithms encompass the larger areas of artificial intelligence, data analytics, machine learning, pattern recognition, natural language understanding, and big data manipulation. They also tackle related new scientific challenges, ranging from data capture, creation, storage, retrieval, sharing, analysis, optimization, and visualization, to integrative analysis across heterogeneous and interdependent complex resources for better decision-making, collaboration, and, ultimately, value creation.

This book encompasses all aspects of research and development in ML and Data Science, including but not limited to data discovery, computer vision, natural language processing (NLP), intelligent systems, neural networks, AI-based software engineering, and their applications in the areas of engineering, business and social sciences. It also covers a broad spectrum of applications in the community, from industry, government, and academia. This book brings together thought leaders, researchers, industry practitioners, and potential users of machine learning, data science and analytics, to develop the field, discuss new trends and opportunities, exchange ideas and practices, and promote interdisciplinary and cross-domain collaborations.

Prateek Agrawal
Charu Gupta
Anand Sharma
Vishu Madaan
Nisheeth Joshi

Book Description

This book "*Machine Learning and Data Science: Fundamentals and Applications*" is providing the conceptual and fundamental research related to machine learning (ML) and data science (DS) domain. It also includes on demonstrating a wide range of interdisciplinary applications and innovative developments using ML and DS approaches that address latest findings and results regarding a wide variety of technological issues and developments to reform the scientific society.

The book contains 13 chapters. Chapter 1 titled "**Machine Learning: An Introduction to Reinforcement Learning**" highlights the fundamental concepts of Reinforcement learning methods procedures, techniques and reinforcement learning processes with particular focus on the aspects related to the agent-environment interface and how Reinforcement Learning can be used in various daily life practical applications.

Chapter 2 titled "**Data Analysis Using Machine Learning: An Experimental Study on UFC**" presents the experimental study to predict Ultimate Fighting Championship using proposed data analysis tool. This work opens new directions and investigation possibilities for further analyzing such unpredictable sports in a more efficient and effective manner.

Chapter 3 titled "**Dawn of Big Data with Hadoop and Machine Learning**" discusses several applications utilizing machine learning on the Hadoop platform for processing Big data.

Chapter 4 titled "**Industry 4.0: Smart Manufacturing in Industries - The Future**" explains how smart manufacturing can address entire regarding these opportunities of a holistic path then assist stakeholders together their respective desires extra effectively.

Chapter 5 titled "**COVID-19 Curve Exploration Using Time Series Data for India**" analyzes the real time trend patterns of COVID-19 cases in India with the help of different time series prediction models.

Chapter 6 titled "**A Case Study on Cluster Based Application Mapping Method for Power Optimization in 2D NoC**".

Chapter 7 titled "**Health Care A Case Study - Covid19 Detection, Prevention Measures and Prediction Using Machine Learning & Deep Learning Algorithms**".

Chapter 8 titled "**Analysis and Impact of Climatic Conditions on COVID-19 Using Machine Learning**" demonstrates the COVID-19 impact in various climate patterns and regions using machine learning models.

Chapter 9 titled "**Application of Hadoop in Data Science**" explains the key importance of Data science along with the utility of the Hadoop platform for processing data.

Chapter 10 titled "**Networking Technologies and Challenges for Green IOT Applications in Urban Climate**" provides informational and latest research guidance for green IOT based smart environment by examining the green IOT impacts.

Chapter 11 titled "**Analysis of Human Activity Recognition Algorithms using Trimmed Video Datasets**" summarizes some of the most frequently used algorithms on human activity recognition and suggests methods to improve them so that the researchers and readers may design and develop their own algorithms and tune the performances as per the application of these algorithms.

Chapter 12 titled "**Solving Direction Sense Based Reasoning Problems Using Natural Language Processing**" uses the images and NLP concepts and presents an application to solve direction and distance-based reasoning problems. This chapter concentrates on a directional relationship of objects, the distance between objects, and calculates the distance between the starting and ending travel point by the object.

Chapter 13 titled "**Drowsiness Detection Using Digital Image Processing**" demonstrates a machine learning method to detect the symptoms of driver fatigue farm or earlier which can prevent an accident by cautioning the driver by an alarm.

This book primarily covers all aspects of research and development in Machine Learning and Data Science starting from the fundamentals of machine learning approaches and ending with the computer vision applications. We feel that after reading this book, reader will have a thorough, well rounded understanding of machine learning and data science fundamentals.

Prateek Agrawal
Charu Gupta
Anand Sharma
Vishu Madaan
Nisheeth Joshi

Machine Learning: An Introduction to Reinforcement Learning

Sheikh Amir Fayaz[1], Dr. S Jahangeer Sidiq[2]*, Dr. Majid Zaman[3] and Dr. Muheet Ahmed Butt[1]

[1]Department of Computer Science University of Kashmir, Srinagar, J&K, India
[2]School of Computer Applications Lovely Professional University, Phagwara, Punjab, India
[3]Directorate of IT&SS University of Kashmir, Srinagar, J&K, India

Abstract

Reinforcement Learning (RL) is a prevalent prototype for finite sequential decision making under improbability. A distinctive RL algorithm functions with only restricted knowledge of the environment and with limited response or feedback on the quality of the conclusions. To work efficiently in complex environments, learning agents entail the capability to form convenient generalizations, that is, the ability to selectively overlook extraneous facts. It is a challenging task to develop a single illustration that is suitable for a large problem setting. This chapter provides a brief introduction to reinforcement learning models, procedures, techniques, and reinforcement learning processes. Particular focus is on the aspects related to the agent-environment interface and how Reinforcement Learning can be used in various daily life practical applications. The basic concept that we will explore is that of a solution to the Re-enforcement Learning problem using the Markov Decision Process (MDP). We assume that the reader has a basic idea of machine learning concepts and algorithms.

Keywords: Reinforcement learning, Markov decision process, agent-environment interaction, exploitation, exploration

*Corresponding author: jahangir.25453@lpu.co.in

Prateek Agrawal, Charu Gupta, Anand Sharma, Vishu Madaan, and Nisheeth Joshi (eds.) Machine Learning and Data Science: Fundamentals and Applications, (1–22) © 2022 Scrivener Publishing LLC

1.1   Introduction

1.1.1   Motivation

Many years ago, we started automating physical solutions with machines during the Industrial Revolution, replacing animals with machines. We kind of know how to pull something forward across a track and then we just implement those machines. We use the machines instead of humans and animals as laborers and, of course, if we want to make a huge boom in productivity, then after that, the second wave of automation occurred and is basically still happening. Now, we are in you could call the Digital Revolution, where instead of taking physical solutions, we took mental solutions as a canonical example. For example, if we have a calculator and we know how to do division, we can program that into a calculator and have the machine do the mental task in future operations. Though we automated its mental solutions, we still come up with the solutions by ourselves, i.e., we came up with what we want to do and how to do it and then we implemented it on the machine. The next step here is to define the problem, then have a machine solve for it itself. For this, we require learning, i.e., we require something in addition because if we do not put anything into the system, how can we know it. One thing we can put into a system is our knowledge. This is what was done with these machines either for mental or physical solutions, but the other thing we could put in there is some knowledge on how the machine could learn itself.

This chapter is structured as follows: the current section provides a brief introduction about machine learning and its types. The main focus in Section 1.1.3.3 has been put on Reinforcement Learning and its types, learning process, and RL learning concepts. Section 1.2 introduces a Reinforcement Learning Paradigm and its characteristics. Section 1.3 defines the Reinforcement Learning (RL) problem where the goal is to select the actions to make the most of the total rewards. Section 1.4 gives the basic algorithm which defines the solution of the reinforcement problem using the Markov Decision Process (MDP) with its mathematical Notation. Lastly, Section 1.5 briefly explains the applications of the Reinforcement Learning process in the current day to day learning environment.

1.1.2   Machine Learning

Machine learning is the science of getting computers to act by feeding them data and letting them learn a few trails on their own. Here, we are not actually programming the machine but feeding the machine lots of data so that it can learn by itself [15, 20].

Definition: *Machine learning is as subset of Artificial Intelligence (AI) which provides machines the capability to learn automatically and improve from experience without being explicitly programmed.*

Example:
As kids we would not be able to differentiate between fruits like apples, cherries, and oranges. When we first see how apples, oranges, and cherries look, we were not able to differentiate between them. This is because we have not observed them enough from what they look like, but as we grow up, we learn what apples, cherries, and oranges look like, i.e., we came to know the color, shape, and size of an apple and so on. Similarly, when it comes to a machine, if we input images of an apple or any fruit, initially it will not be able to differentiate between them. This is because it does not have enough data about them, but if we keep feeding the machine with a number of images about these (cherries, apples, and oranges), it will learn how to differentiate between the three. Just like humans learn by observing and collecting data, similarly machines also learn when we give a lot of data, i.e., when we input a lot of data to a machine it will learn how to distinguish between them. The machine will basically train in the data and try to differentiate between the various rules by using various machine learning algorithms.

1.1.3 How Machines Learn

There are three different types of machine learning:

1) Supervised Learning
2) Unsupervised Learning
3) Reinforcement Learning

1.1.3.1 Supervised Learning

This type of learning means to direct a certain activity and make sure it is done correctly. This is one of the popular machine learning methods. Several classification and regression applications were developed recently by researchers [52–58]. If we feed the model with a set of data, called training data, which contains both the inputs and the corresponding expected output, then the training data will teach the model for the correct output for a particular input [14, 17–19]. The data in supervised learning is labeled data. In supervised learning we have a joint distribution of data points and labels [47–49]. Our goal is to maximize the probability of the classifier as shown below:

$$Ds : (x, y) \sim p(x, y)$$

$$\in (x, y) \sim p(x, y) \left[logp \left(\frac{y}{x} \right) \right]$$

where "Ds" is the labeled data, and x (input) and y (output) are the samples from $p(x,y)$, which is a marginal response to the joint distribution from the labelled data set sample.

1.1.3.2   Unsupervised Learning

This type of learning acts without anyone's direction or supervision. In this method, the model is basically given a dataset which is neither labeled nor classified [22, 23], so the machine does not know how the output should look [31, 50, 51]. For example, if we input an image of a fruit, we are not going to label it as say "apple". Instead, we only give data and the machine is going to learn on its own.

$$Du : (x) \sim p(x)$$

where "Du" is the unlabeled data and x (input) is the sample from $p(x)$.

1.1.3.3   Reinforcement Learning

Is one of the types of machine learning which has been growing in the past few years. It has various applications like self-driving or automated cars and image processing techniques wherein we detect objects using reinforcement learning. This type of machine learning has become one of the most important types in the current world to establish or to encourage a pattern of behavior. It is a learning technique where an agent interrelates through its environment by generating actions and discovering errors or rewards. In other words, Reinforcement Learning is a type of a machine learning where an agent learns to act in an environment by carrying out actions and observing the results [1, 16].

Reinforcement Learning is all about taking a suitable action in order to make the most of the reward in a particular state or situation. In this learning there is no predictable output as in supervised learning; here, the reinforcement agent chooses which action to take in order to perform a specified task. In the absence of a training dataset, it is bound to acquire from its experience itself [2, 3].

Thus, Reinforcement Learning is the type of machine learning where machines learn from evaluation, whereas other learning algorithms (supervised learning) learn from instructions. So, Reinforcement Learning is essentially an interaction between the agent and the environment (Figure 1.1) in the fashion that the agent performs an action which makes some changes in the environment and based on that, the environment gives a reward (positive or negative) to the agent. If the reward is positive, that reinforces that particular action and if the award is negative that tends to prevent the agent from performing that same action again [21]. So, this process goes on for over many iterations until the agent has learned to interact with an environment in a meaningful way. This is an essence of reinforcement learning.

Let us try to understand the concept of reinforcement learning through an example of Tic-Tac-Toe which you are familiar with and might have played a lot in your childhood. This game (Figure 1.2) essentially consists of 9 places on the square board and you need to populate the 9 places with

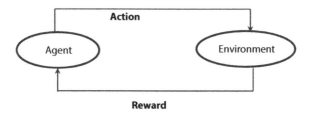

Figure 1.1 Action and reward process in reinforcement learning.

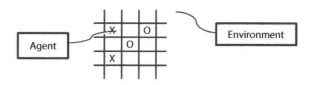

Figure 1.2 Tic tac toe.

two signs normally denoted with "X" (cross) and "O" (zero), i.e., it is a two player game where each player fills the squares with their chosen signs one by one.

Essentially this game consists of an environment where the entire board consists of 9 places with which the agent interacts and the objective of the agent is to learn to play the game well so that it can defeat the opponent as many times as possible. Then, you have different states or configurations, i.e., different combinations of X's and O's in the whole environment.

In order to change the state, you need to perform an action, i.e., whenever an agent puts an "X" sign at a particular place or the opponent puts an "O" sign at a particular place, that is called an action. The agent performs an action and it learns how to perform this action better and better. Initially, the agent does not have any experience in the environment. It performs actions randomly, but as it evolves the agent learns from this process and learns to perform actions in a better way rather than just doing it randomly.

To perform the actions in a better way, the agent needs to have a policy which is essentially based on two things: reward and value. Reward and value are kind of related to each other, but usually the reward is used for the last step of the game whether you win, lose, or the game ends in a draw. The value is the intrinsic value of each individual state or configuration, i.e., the higher the value of the configuration, the more likely it is to lead you to win or lose at the end of the game.

Each single place in the board can have either "X", "O", or a blank sign, so there are 3 possibilities for each place and there are total of 9 places in the environment.

Thus, the total number of states in this particular game is 3^9. Out of these 3^9 states there are various configurations which lead you to win, lose, or draw as shown below in Figure 1.3.

If a state leads you to a win we associate a value of +1 to that state and -1 and 0 for loss and draw situations, respectively. Here, we can use Apriori because we know exactly which states are winning or losing and which states end up in a draw.

The objective of a Reinforcement Learning Algorithm is to learn how to figure out the value for the intermediate states because assigning a value to an intermediate state is a more challenging task. In order to learn the value of intrinsic states we make the computer program to play against itself and keep track of the states that it went through while it played the game.

Now, let us say we take a particular state in which our system was where the agent needs to make a move, assuming that the agent was the one who started the game. The agent takes the value of the state at a particular time

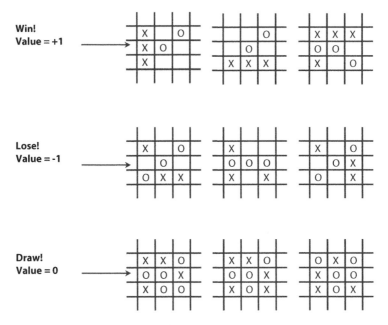

Figure 1.3 Various possible situations for win, loss, and draw.

instance t and then it takes the value of the state at the next time instance by which it updates the value of the current state by Equation 1.1.

$$V(S_t) = V(S_t) + \alpha \left[V(S_{t+1}) - V(S_t) \right] \qquad (1.1)$$

The difference between the value of the next state $V(S_{t+1})$ and the current state $V(S_t)$ is multiplied by the learning rate parameter, denoted by α, and the result is added with the current state by which the previous state value gets updated after every interval, thus, you get the learning value of all the intermediate steps which you have to go through before reaching the final state.

Let us take an example at a particular instance, say at step 4 of the game, as shown in Figure 1.4 and suppose the condition to be:

$$V(S_5) = 1$$

Initially, we assume the value of all the intermediate steps to be 0 and after making one move the value of the next state becomes 1. Thus, after updating the value from state 4 to state 5, it becomes Equation 1.2:

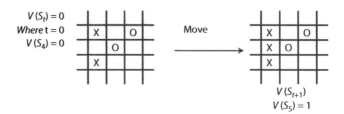

Figure 1.4a Instance of game at step 4.

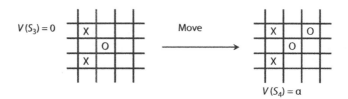

Figure 1.4b Instance of game at step 3.

$$V(S_4) = 0 + \alpha[1-0]$$
$$V(S_4) = \alpha \qquad (1.2)$$

Now, checking the value one step back, i.e., $V(S_3)$, it was assumed to be:

$$V(S_4) = \alpha$$

Earlier, $V(S_4) = 0$, but after making a move it was updated from 0 to α. Using this updated value of $V(S_4)$, we can calculate the value of $V(S_3)$ as shown below:

$$V(S_3) = 0 + \alpha[1-0]$$
$$V(S_4) = \alpha \qquad (1.3)$$

With this process we can keep updating the values of each state until we have either reached a saturation value of all the states or we have played the game a sufficient number of times [46]. So, if you make the computer play against another computer enough number of times you would have learned a value of every single intermediate state which you have to cross before reaching to the final state by winning, losing, or drawing the game.

Types of Reinforcement Learning
Fundamentally, Reinforcement Learning has been categorized into two types:

1. **Positive RL** can be defined only when the event occurs due to some particular behavior which can result in an increase in the strength and frequency of the behavior. This type of RL can help in the maximization of performance and effect sustaining the changes for longer periods of time. Too much positive RL can lead to a surplus of states which can lead to diminishing of the results by continuously increasing the positivity of the rewards [1, 7].

2. **Negative RL:** In distinction, negative reinforcement also makes a behavior more prospective to ensue; it is used for upholding a minimum performance standard rather than attainment of a maximum performance of the model. This type of RL can help to ensure that a model is kept away from adverse actions, but it cannot categorically make a model explore anticipated actions. This negative RL can lead to an increase in the behavior and it provides insolence to a minimum standard of performance [1, 7].

1.1.4   Analogy

In Reinforcement Learning we have an agent and a reward and there may be many track events in between. The agent is made to find the best possible path to grasp the reward [8, 9]. It may have a positive reward or negative reward, depending on whether the agent finds the best possible path or not.

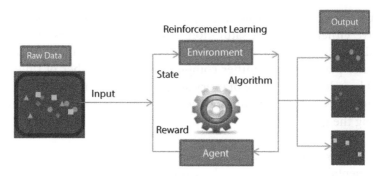

Figure 1.5 Reinforcement learning process.

1.1.5   Reinforcement Learning Process

Generally, Reinforcement Learning has two main components which include:

a) Agent
b) Environment

Here, the agent is defined as the representation for the Reinforcement Learning algorithm and the environment is the setting that the agent is acting on [8, 9].

The Reinforcement Learning process starts when the environment sends the state to the agent and then the agent will take some actions based on the observations (Figure 1.5). In turn, the environment will send the next state and the respective reward back to the agent. The agent will update its knowledge with the reward returned by the environment and it uses that to evaluate its previous actions. This loop keeps continuing until the environment sends a terminal state which means that the agent has accomplished all the tasks and finally gets the reward [10, 11].

1.1.6   Reinforcement Learning Definitions: Basic Terminologies

1. **Agent:** The Reinforcement Learning algorithm that learns from the trials and errors. The agent is responsible for taking actions in the environment.

2. **Environment:** The world through which the agent moves. The environment takes the agent's current state and actions as input. In turn, it returns the agent's reward and its next state as output.

3. **Reward (R):** An instant return from the environment to appraise the last action. Basically, a reward is given to an agent after it clears the specific stages.

4. **Policy (π):** The approach that the agent uses to determine the next action based on the current state. It is the strategy with which we approach the current state.

5. **Value (V):** The expected long term return with discount, as opposed to short term reward (R).

6. **Action value (Q):** This is a similar to value expect; it takes an extra parameter and the current action.

1.1.7   Reinforcement Learning Concepts

Reward Maximization: The basic aim of the reinforcement agent is to maximize the reward. The agent must be trained so that he takes the best action so that the reward is maximized [43].

Exploitation vs Exploration: When we are learning the game, we need to make choices to choose the next state with the highest value or to go to the next state randomly. Making choices randomly will lead to exploration and it is about exploring and capturing more information about an environment. Making a choice based on highest state value is called exploitation. Exploitation is about using the already known exploited information to heighten the rewards [44, 45].

1.2   Reinforcement Learning Paradigm: Characteristics

There are a few things which differentiate Reinforcement Learning (RL) from Supervised Learning (SL) in various aspects [33–35]:

1. No supervisor is present when we talk about Reinforcement Learning (RL). In RL no one knows what the right actions to take are. Instead, there are trial and error paradigms, [33] i.e., there are only reward signals.

2. In RL the feedback is delayed, i.e., the decision is not instantaneous.
3. Time really matters to optimize the rewards in Reinforcement Learning.
4. In RL, the agent needs to take actions and is influenced in the environment, i.e., the agent's actions affect the subsequent data that it receives.

1.3   Reinforcement Learning Problem

Reinforcement Learning rose with a lot of challenges, which includes the trade-off between exploitation. The main aim of RL is to gain a maximum number of rewards and for this the machine RL agent chooses actions that were tried in the past in which the results turn out to be more effective, but the actions should be naïve actions, i.e., these actions should be new and not selected before. The RL agent has to exploit what it previously recognizes in order to get a reward, but it also has to discover in order to make enhanced action choices in the upcoming tasks. The problem is that neither exploration nor exploitation can be followed completely without deteriorating at the task. The RL agent must try a range of actions and gradually indulge those that seem to be best.

One of the most fundamental quantities in Reinforcement Learning (RL) is a reward. A reward is basically a number, i.e., a reward (R_t) is a scalar feedback signal. It defines how well the agent is doing at the particular time stamp. The job of the agent is basically to get a sum of the rewards and many rewards in total. The RL problem is basically based on the reward hypothesis, which means that all goals can be described by the maximization of the expected cumulative reward.

Examples of Reward:

1. **Fly stunt maneuvers in a helicopter:** In this case a positive reward will be awarded in the case of preferred trajectory and a negative reward for crashing.
2. **Defeat the world champion at Backgammon:** Positive reward for winning and negative reward for losing the game.
3. **Playing games like Atari:** Positive rewards for increasing score and negative for decreasing.

4. Making a humanoid robot walk: Positive reward for the motion of the robot (forward or backward) and negative reward for falling over.

In all these examples the goal is to select the actions to make the most of the total rewards.

Solutions to Reinforcement Learning Problem: Algorithms Used in Reinforcement Learning

There are various algorithms which are used in Reinforcement Learning which include [42]:

1. Markov Decision Process
2. Q Learning Algorithm
3. Multi-Armed Bandit Problem
4. Thompson Sampling
5. SARSA Reinforcement Learning

Of the above listed algorithms, we have briefly described the most used algorithm in Reinforcement Learning, the Markov Decision Process.

Markov Decision Process

The Markov Decision Process (MDP) is a basic framework that can solve most Reinforcement Learning problems with a discrete set of actions. The Markov Decision Process provides us a way to validate sequential decision making. This reinforcement or formalization is the root for the organizing problems that are solved with Reinforcement Learning. MDP is a mathematical method for outlining modelling decisions. It provides a mathematical model to frame the decision building method where outcomes are partially haphazard and partially under the control of this decision maker. It is a discrete time control process which is basically used for providing a framework for creating the models. In MDP we mainly talk about finite processes where we assume that the states, rewards, and actions have a finite number of elements.

There are various Reinforcement Learning components which are involved in the Markov Decision Process, which include a decision maker called an agent that interacts with the environment that it is placed in. These interactions occur sequentially over time. At each time stamp the agent will get some representations of the environment state and based on these representations, the agent selects an action to take. The environment is then transitioned into some new state and the agent is rewarded as a consequence of the previous state [4, 5].

So, to summarize, the components of the Markov Decision Process (MDP) include the environment, agent, and all possible states of the environment, all the actions that the agent can take in the environment, and all the rewards that the agents can receive from taking actions in the environment [6]. This procedure of choosing an action from a certain state transitions to a new state and receiving rewards occurs sequentially in a repeated manner which generates a route that shows the classification of states and actions and maximizes the total amount of rewards that it receives from taking actions from given states of environment. This means that the agent wants to maximize not just the instantaneous reward but the cumulative rewards that it will receive overtime.

Markov Decision Process Mathematical Notation

- The Markov Decision Process consists of a set of the states S, a set of actions A and a set of rewards R.
- Here, we are assuming that all these states have a finite number of elements.
- The agent receives a representation at each time interval t from the environment state $S_t \in S$. After that, based on this state, the agent performs some action $A_t \in A$. This will result in a pair called a State-Action (S_t, A_t) pair.
- During the next time interval at $t + 1$, the environment receives the next transmitted state $S_{t+1} \in A$. At the same time interval, the agent will receive the reward $R_{t+1} \in R$ for the previous action A_t taken at time interval t from state S_t
- Thus, we can define the State-Action pair as function f to receive the rewards at time interval t as shown below:

$$f(S_t, A_t) = R_{t+1}$$

- Furthermore, we can then define the trajectory of the sequential process as:

$$S_t A_t R_{t+1}, S_{t+1} A_{t+1} R_{t+2}, S_{t+2} A_{t+2} R_{t+3} \dots S_n A_n R_{n+1}$$

where, $t = 0,1,2, \dots n, n+1$.

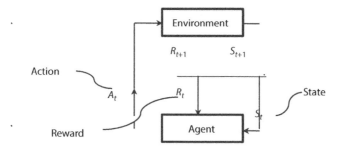

Figure 1.6 Environment-agent interaction between transition states.

Therefore, we have:

$$S_0 A_0 R_1, S_1 A_1 R_2, S_2 A_2 R_3 \dots S_n A_n R_{n+1}.$$

Illustration of MDP Notation

The stepwise illustration of the above idea is shown in Figure 1.6.

Step 1: At time t the environment is in state S_t.

Step 2: The agent observes the current state and selects an action at t.

Step 3: The environment transitions to state S_{t+1} and grants the agent with the reward R_{t+1}.

These same process steps are repeated for the next time interval $t + 1$ and the process goes on [7].

1.4   Applications of Reinforcement Learning

Reinforcement Learning can be defined as a type of Machine Learning (ML) approach which permits software agents and machines to automatically control the model actions within a precise framework so that it can maximize its performance. There are many applications of Reinforcement Learning and some of the practical applications are:

1. **It is used in the industrial automation of robotics with Reinforcement Learning**
   Robots are more efficient than humans. They can perform various difficult tasks in industries that are pretty much impossible for humans. These reinforcement agents can help in reduction

of energy spend and increasing the throughput [12, 13, 24]. For example, AI based agents are used by Deepmind to keep the Google data centers cool and reduce the energy consumption by 40%.

2. **Inventory Management Systems**
   One of the key concerns in supply chain inventory management systems is the organization of the inventory strategies that are implemented by different supply chain actors including suppliers, producers, traders, and distributors to smooth functioning of the material flow and minimalize costs while meeting consumer demand [40].

   Thus, RL algorithms in inventory systems can be implemented to decrease transfer time for supplying as well as recovering of the products in the depository for enhancing space application and other various operations [41].

3. **Delivery Management Systems**
   Split-delivery of vehicles is one of the main problems for vehicle routing. Q-Learning reinforcement is used to assist suitable customers with just one vehicle [39].

4. **Distributed Generation Sources**
   Reinforcement Learning is also used in power systems. It helps to develop a distributed regulator organization for a set of various distributed generation sources [38]. Graph topology is used in the exchange of material between these sources.

5. **Autonomous Microgrids**
   Reinforcement Learning is used in autonomous grids [32] to control the voltage level by using adaptive learning techniques.

6. Reinforcement Learning is also used in Machine Learning and data processing systems [26, 29].

7. It is also used to create training systems that provide the materials and custom instructions as per the prerequisite from the students [27, 28, 30].

8. **Reinforcement Learning in Healthcare**
   Patients can be handled from strategies learned from Reinforcement Learning systems. They are used to find ideal policies based on the earlier practices without the basic need for former information on the scientific approach of the biological systems [36]. RL makes this method more appropriate than other control-based systems in the healthcare sector [37].

Reinforcement Learning (RL) is still considered a very dynamic research area. Substantial progress has been made to develop the field and promote it in real life [25]. In this section, we have defined some application areas of Reinforcement Learning which are taken into consideration in the real life environment.

Conclusion

In recent years, Reinforcement Learning study has made development progress, but because of real world complication and convolution, currently, many problems need further study. Machine Learning is a developing area with an array of different methods to choose. In this chapter we have briefly described the concept of Reinforcement Learning. It provides an overview of Standard Reinforcement Learning (RL). Progressive decision-making relics a dynamic field of exploration with many hypothetical, organizational, procedural and experimental challenges still undeveloped. The significant improvements in the field of Reinforcement Learning (RL) have backed several new combined paths including deep learning. Reinforcement Learning (RL) is currently a hot topic with a wide variety of applications in every field, mainly in finance, robotics, health, and industries. Furthermore, exploration in artificial intelligence (AI) is heading for broad principles of learning, making decisions, and a wide range of other domains of knowledge. Research on Reinforcement Learning (RL) is a driving force towards easier and less general principles of (AI) artificial intelligence. Therefore, a fast and operative communication mode becomes an additional exploration emphasis of Reinforcement Learning (RL).

References

1. Sutton, R.S., Barto, A.G., 1998. Reinforcement Learning. An Introduction. MIT Press, Cambridge, MA.
2. Sutton, R.S., Precup, D., Singh, S., 1999. Between MDPs and semi-MDPs: a framework for temporal abstraction in reinforcement learning. Artif. Intell. 112, 181–211.
3. Ravindran, B., Barto, A.G., 2002. Model minimization in hierarchical reinforcement learning. In: Proceedings of the Fifth Symposium on Abstraction, Reformulation and Approximation (SARA 2002), Lecture Notes in Artificial Intelligence 2371. Springer-Verlag, pp. 196–211.

4. Ravindran, B., Barto, A.G., 2003b. SMDP homomorphisms: an algebraic approach to abstraction in semi-Markov decision processes. In: Proceedings of the Eighteenth International Joint Conference on Artificial Intelligence (IJCAI 2003). AAAI Press, Cambridge, MA, pp. 1011–1016
5. Parr, R., 1998. Hierarchical Control and Learning for Markov Decision Processes. University of California at Berkeley, Berkeley.
6. Bradtke, S.J., Duff, M.O., 1995. Reinforcement Learning Methods for Continuous-Time Markov Decision Problems. In: Advances in Neural Information Processing Systems. MIT Press, Cambridge, MA, pp. 393–400.
7. S. Russell and P. Norvig, Artificial Intelligence: A Modern Approach, 3rd ed. Pearson, 2009
8. R. S. Sutton and A. G. Barto, Reinforcement learning: an introduction, 2nd ed. Cambridge, MA: Mit Press, 2017.
9. D. Silver, "Deep reinforcement learning," in International Conference on Machine Learning (ICML), 2016.
10. V. Mnih et al., "Playing Atari with Deep Reinforcement Learning," in Conference on Neural Information Processing Systems, 2013, pp. 1–9.
11. P. Abbeel and J. Schulman, "Deep Reinforcement Learning through Policy Optimization," in Neural Information Processing Systems, 2016.
12. Kormushev, P., Calinon, S., Caldwell, D.G.: Reinforcement learning in robotics: applications and real-world challenges. Robotics 2(3), 122–148 (2013)
13. Guenter, F., Hersch, M., Calinon, S., Billard, A.: Reinforcement learning for imitating constrained reaching movements. Adv. Robot. 21(13), 1521–1544 (2007)
14. Khan E. Reinforcement control with unsupervised learning [A]. Int. Joint Conference on Neural Network [C] ,Beijing ,1992 ,88 –93
15. "How Machine Learning is Redefining Geographical Science: A Review of Literature", International Journal of Emerging Technologies and Innovative Research (www.jetir.org), ISSN:2349-5162, Vol. 6, Issue 1, page no. 1731-1746, January 2019, Available: http://www.jetir.org/papers/JETIRDW06285.pdf
16. Crites R H and Barto A G. Improving elevator performance using reinforcement learning [A]. In: Touretzky D S, Mozer M C, and M E H. Advances in Neural Information Processing Systems [M]. Cambridge, MA: The MIT Press, 1995, 1017–1023.
17. Majid Zaman, Sameer Kaul and Muheet Ahmed. "Analytical Comparison between the Information Gain and Gini Index using Historical Geographical Datal. (IJACSA)" International Journal of Advanced Computer Science and Applications, (pp. 429-440), Vol. 11, No. 5, 2020.
18. Razeef Mohd, Muheet Ahmed Butt and Majid Zaman Baba. "Grey Wolf Levenberg–Marquardt-based neural network for rainfall prediction", Data Technologies and Applications, Emerald Publishing Limited, ISSN: 2514-9288, accepted Dec., 2019.

19. Nasir Majeed Mir, Sarfraz Khan, Muheet Ahmed Butt and Majid Zaman, "An Experimental Evaluation of Bayesian Classifiers Applied to Intrusion Detection", Indian Journal of Science and Technology, Vol 9(12), DOI: 10.17485/ijst/2016/v9i12/86291, April 2016, ISSN (Print): 0974-6846 ISSN (Online) :0974-5645

20. Ashraf, Mudasir, Majid Zaman, and Muheet Ahmed. "An Intelligent Prediction System for Educational Data Mining Based on Ensemble and Filtering approaches." Procedia Computer Science 167 (2020): 1471-1483.

21. Waltz, M.D. & Fu, K.S. (1965). A heuristic approach to reinforcement learning control systems. IEEE Transactions on Automatic Control, AC-10, 390–398

22. Ashraf, Mudasir, Syed Mudasir Ahmad, Nazir Ahmad Ganai, Riaz Ahmad Shah, Majid Zaman, Sameer Ahmad Khan, and Aftab Aalam Shah. "Prediction of Cardiovascular Disease Through Cutting-Edge Deep Learning Technologies: An Empirical Study Based on Tensor Flow, Pytorch and Keras." In International Conference on Innovative Computing and Communications, pp. 239-255. Springer, Singapore, 2020.

23. Ashraf, Mudasir, Majid Zaman, and Muheet Ahmed. "To ameliorate classification accuracy using ensemble vote approach and base classifiers." In Emerging Technologies in Data Mining and Information Security, pp. 321-334. Springer, Singapore, 2019.

24. Kamei K Ishikawa M Determination of the optimal values of parameters in reinforcement learning for mobile robot navigation by a genetic algorithm [J] International Congress Series 2004, 1, 269, 193–196.

25. Mohd, Razeef, Muheet Ahmed Butt, and Majid Zaman Baba. "SALM-NARX: Self Adaptive LM-based NARX model for the prediction of rainfall." In 2018 2nd International Conference on I-SMAC (IoT in Social, Mobile, Analytics and Cloud) (I-SMAC) I-SMAC (IoT in Social, Mobile, Analytics and Cloud) (I-SMAC), 2018 2nd International Conference on, pp. 580-585. IEEE, 2018.

26. Holland, J.H. (1986). Escaping brittleness: The possibilities of general-purpose learning algorithms applied to parallel rule-based systems. In: R.S. Michalski, J.G. Carbonell, & T.M. Mitchell (Eds.), Machine learning, An artificial intelligence approach, Volume II, 593–623, Los Altos, CA: Morgan Kaufman.

27. Mudasir Ashraf, Dr. Majid Zaman, Dr. Muheet Ahmad "Performance analysis and different subject combinations: An empirical and analytical discourse of educational data mining" IEEE 8th International Conference Confluence 2018,11-12 January 2018, p. 79.

28. Ashraf, Mudasir, Majid Zaman, and Muheet Ahmed. "Using Ensemble Stacking C Method and Base Classifiers to Ameliorate Prediction Accuracy of Pedagogical Data." Procedia computer science 132 (2018): 1021-1040.

29. Barto, A.G. Bradtke, S.J. & Singh, S.P. (1991). Real-time learning and control using asynchronous dynamic programming (Technical Report 91–57). Amherst, MA: University of Massachusetts, Computer Science Department.

30. Majid Zaman, Muheet Ahmed Butt "Information Translation: A Practitioners Approach", World Congress on Engineering and Computer Science (WCECS), San Francisco, USA. October 2012.
31. Becker, S & Plumbley, M (1996). Unsupervised neural network learning procedures for feature extraction and classification. International Journal of Applied Intelligence, 6, 185 203.
32. Sheikh Amir Fayaz, Ifra Altaf, Aaqib Nazir Khan *et al.* A Possible Solution to Grid Security Issue Using Authentication: An Overview. Journal of Web Engineering & Technology. 2018; 5(3): 10–14p
33. Iglesias, A., Martínez, P., Aler, R., & Fernández, F. (2009). Learning teaching strategies in an adaptive and intelligent educational system through reinforcement learning. Applied Intelligence, 31(1), 89-106.
34. Brusilovsky P (1999) Adaptive and intelligent technologies for Web-based education. Kunstl Intell 4:19–25. Special Issue on Intelligent Tutoring Systems and Teleteaching.
35. Iglesias, A., Martínez, P., Aler, R., & Fernández, F. (2009). Reinforcement learning of pedagogical policies in adaptive and intelligent educational systems. Knowledge-Based Systems, 22(4), 266-270.
36. Gottesman, Omer, Fredrik Johansson, Matthieu Komorowski, Aldo Faisal, David Sontag, Finale Doshi-Velez, and Leo Anthony Celi. "Guidelines for reinforcement learning in healthcare." Nature medicine 25, no. 1 (2019): 16-18.
37. Yu, Chao, Jiming Liu, and Shamim Nemati. "Reinforcement learning in healthcare: A survey." arXiv preprint arXiv:1908.08796 (2019).
38. Mahmoud, M. S., Abouheaf, M., & Sharaf, A. (2019). Reinforcement learning control approach for autonomous microgrids. International Journal of Modelling and Simulation, 1-10.
39. Wang, Pengyue, Yan Li, Shashi Shekhar, and William F. Northrop. "A deep reinforcement learning framework for energy management of extended range electric delivery vehicles." In 2019 IEEE Intelligent Vehicles Symposium (IV), pp. 1837-1842. IEEE, 2019.
40. Giannoccaro, I., & Pontrandolfo, P. (2002). Inventory management in supply chains: a reinforcement learning approach. International Journal of Production Economics, 78(2), 153-161.
41. Kara, A., & Dogan, I. (2018). Reinforcement learning approaches for specifying ordering policies of perishable inventory systems. Expert Systems with Applications, 91, 150-158.
42. Szepesvári, C. (2010). Algorithms for reinforcement learning. Synthesis lectures on artificial intelligence and machine learning, 4(1), 1-103.
43. Schwartz, A. (1993). A reinforcement learning method for maximizing undiscounted rewards. In Proceedings of the tenth international conference on machine learning (Vol. 298, pp. 298-305).
44. Thrun, S. B. (1992). Efficient exploration in reinforcement learning.

45. Yogeswaran, M., & Ponnambalam, S. G. (2012). Reinforcement learning: exploration–exploitation dilemma in multi-agent foraging task. Opsearch, 49(3), 223-236.
46. Barto, A. G., & Sutton, R. S. (1995). Reinforcement learning. Handbook of brain theory and neural networks, 804-809.
47. Sidiq, S. J., & Zaman, M. (2020). A Binarization Approach for Predicting Box-Office Success. Solid State Technology, 63(5), 8652-8660.
48. Neha, K., & Sidiq, S. J. (2020). Analysis of Student Academic Performance through Expert systems. International Research Journal on Advanced Science Hub, 2, 48-54.
49. Sidiq, S. J., Zaman, M., Ashraf, M., & Ahmed, M. (2017). An empirical comparison of supervised classifiers for diabetic diagnosis. Int J Adv Res Comput Sci, 8(1), 311-315.
50. Ashraf, M., Zaman, M., Ahmed, M., & Sidiq, S. J. (2017). Knowledge discovery in academia: a survey on related literature. Int. J. Adv. Res. Comput. Sci, 8(1).
51. Sidiq, S. J., Zaman, M., & Butt, M. (2018). An empirical comparison of classifiers for multi-class imbalance learning. International Journal of Data Mining And Emerging Technologies, 8(1), 115-122.
52. Prateek Agrawal, Vishu Madaan, Aditya Roy, Ranjna Kumari, & Harshal Deore. (2021). "FOCOMO: Forecasting and monitoring the worldwide spread of COVID-19 using machine learning methods", Journal of Interdisciplinary Mathematics, pp. 1-25. DOI:10.1080/09720502.2021.1885812.
53. Anatoliy Zabrovskiy, Prateek Agrawal, Roland Matha, Christian Timmerer, and Radu Prodan, "ComplexCTTP: Complexity Class Based Transcoding Time Prediction for Video Sequences Using Artificial Neural Network", 6th IEEE Conference on Big data in Multimedia (BigMM'20), pp. 316-325, New Delhi, Sep 20, IEEEXplore.
54. Rupinder Kaur, Vishu Madaan, Prateek Agrawal, "Rheumatoid Arthritis anticipation using Adaptive Neuro Fuzzy Inference System", International Conference on Information Systems and Computer Networks (ISCON'19), pp. 340-346, Nov 2019, IEEEXplore.
55. Rupinder Kaur, Vishu Madaan, Prateek Agrawal, "Diagnosis of Arthritis Using k-Nearest Neighbor Approach", 3rd International Conference on Advances Informatics on Computing Research (ICAICR'19), pp 1601-171, Jul 2019, Springer CCIS.
56. Abhishek Sharma, Prateek Agrawal, Vishu Madaan and Shubham Goyal, "Prediction on Diabetes Patient's Hospital Readmission Rates", 3rd International Conference on Advances Informatics on Computing Research (ICAICR'19), pp. 1-5, Jul 2019, ACM-ICPS.
57. Charu Gupta, Prateek Agrawal, Rohan Ahuja, Kunal Vats, Chirag Pahuja, Tanuj Ahuja, "Pragmatic Analysis of Classification Techniques based on

Hyperparameter Tuning for Sentiment Analysis", International Semantic Intelligence Conference (ISIC'21), pp. 453-459, 2021, CEUR-WS.

58. Vishu Madaan, Aditya Roy, Charu Gupta, Prateek Agrawal, Anand Sharma, Christian Bologa, Radu Prodan, "XCOVNet: Chest X-ray Image Classification for COVID-19 Early Detection Using Convolutional Neural Networks", New Generation Computing, pp. 1-15. DOI: 10.1007/s00354-021-00121-7

Data Analysis Using Machine Learning: An Experimental Study on UFC

Prashant Varshney[1], Charu Gupta[1]*, Palak Girdhar[1], Anand Mohan[2], Prateek Agrawal[3]* and Vishu Madaan[4]

[1]*Department of Computer Science and Engineering, Bhagwan Parshuram Institute of Technology, Delhi, India*
[2]*L.N. Mithila University, Darbhanga, Bihar, India*
[3]*University of Klagenfurt, Austria & Lovely Professional University, Jalandhar, India*
[4]*Lovely Professional University, Jalandhar, India*

Abstract

In this study, a powerful prediction method based on machine learning is presented. The proposed work suggests the experimental study of the proposed data analysis tool to predict for the Ultimate Fighting Championship (UFC). In this work, UFC is particularly chosen to understand the overlapping of feature vectors and detection of outlier features as UFC prediction is a multidimensional problem. The proposed work focuses on the features of age and height of the fighter. The efficiency of the proposed work is presented with clear visualization.

Keywords: Data analysis, machine learning, python, ultimate fighting championship

2.1 Introduction

Data analysis is the process of finding useful answers from and patterns in data [1]. These patterns may be used for classification, prediction, and detecting anomalies, or simply to better understand the processes from which the data were extracted. In practise we often do not have

---

*Corresponding author: charu.wa1987@gmail.com

Prateek Agrawal, Charu Gupta, Anand Sharma, Vishu Madaan, and Nisheeth Joshi (eds.) Machine Learning and Data Science: Fundamentals and Applications, (23–46) © 2022 Scrivener Publishing LLC

any real control over what data is collected. There is often little room for experiment design and selection of measurements that could be useful for the intended application. We have to work with whatever data are already available. Fortunately, nowadays data is often already available. Companies often store details on all business transactions indefinitely and an industrial process may contain several thousands of sensors whose values are stored at least every minute. This gives us the opportunity to use this data to understand the processes and to create new data-driven applications that might not have been possible just a decade ago. However, the data sets are often huge and not structured in a way suitable for finding the patterns that are relevant for a certain application. In a sense, there is a gap between the generation of these massive amounts of data and the understanding of them. By focusing on extracting knowledge and creating applications by analysing data already present in databases, we are essentially performing what is often referred to as knowledge discovery and data mining [2].

In this chapter, for the purpose of data analysis, we will be using the Ultimate Fighting Championship's (UFC) data, which is an American Mixed Martial Arts organization based in Las Vegas, Nevada, is the largest MMA promotion in the world, and features the top-ranked fighters of the sport [3]. Based in the United States, the UFC produces events worldwide that showcase twelve weight divisions and abide by the Unified Rules of Mixed Martial Arts. This is a highly unpredictable sport.

The aim of this chapter is to understand the analysis of various dependent and independent features and visualize them for better understanding. These are as follows:

- How are age/height related to the outcome?
- Most popular locations in UFC
- Most popular way to win the fight
- Comparing techniques used by fighters

In this chapter, the proposed method validates the accuracy of the method with respect to the UFC dataset where prediction is a major concern.

2.2   Proposed Methodology

2.2.1   Data Extraction: Preliminary

To enable us to do any analysis, we have to get access to data required for this task. Most people would be able to only copy and paste it manually. However, this is not feasible for large websites with hundreds of pages. This is where web scraping comes into play. Web scraping is a process of

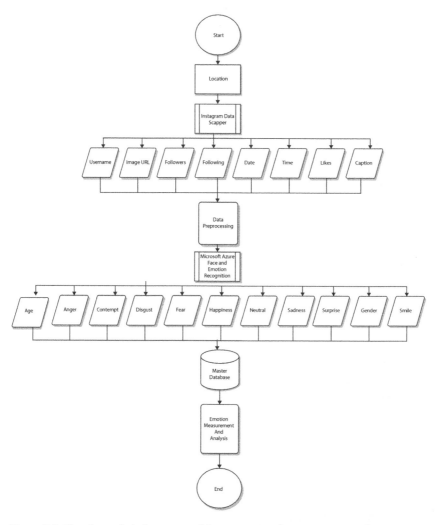

Figure 2.1 Flowchart of whole process of data extraction from instagram and pre-processing with face and emotion recognition.

automating the extraction of data in an efficient and fast way [4, 5]. With the help of web scraping, we can extract data from any website no matter how large the data on our computer. Moreover, websites may have data that we cannot copy and paste. Web scraping can help us extract any kind of data that we want. That is not enough. Let us say we copy and paste some data, how can we convert or save it in a format of our choice? Web scraping takes care of that too. When we extract web data with the help of a web scraping, we can save the data in a format such as CSV. We would then be able to retrieve, analyse, and use the data the way we want.

Web scraping simplifies the process of extracting data, speeds it up by automating it, and creates easy access to the scrapped data by providing it in a CSV format. In simple terms, web scraping saves us from the trouble of manually downloading or copying any data and automates the whole process. Here, in this experimental study, we have built our own web scrapper that scrapes data from Instagram and various other internet sources and stored that in a CSV format. Then after, we pre-process the extracted data, remove redundant data, and apply Face and Emotion Recognition algorithms (Figure 2.1).

2.2.2   Pre-Processing Dataset

Real-world data generally contains noise and missing values and may be in an unusable format which cannot be directly used for data analysis. Data pre-processing is a process of preparing the raw data and making it suitable for data analysis. It is the first and crucial step. When discovering knowledge from the dataset, it is not always the case that we come across clean and formatted data [6–9]. While doing any operation with data it is mandatory to clean it and put in a formatted way. For this we use the data pre-processing task.

a) Libraries and Packages Required

Data visualization is the discipline of trying to understand data by placing it in a visual context so that patterns, trends, and correlations that might not otherwise be detected can be exposed [10–12].

Python offers multiple great graphing libraries that come packed with lots of different features. No matter if you want to create interactive, live, or highly customized plots, Python has an excellent library for you.

To get a little overview, here are a few popular plotting libraries:

- **Matplotlib:** low level, provides lots of freedom

- **Pandas Visualization:** easy to use interface, built on Matplotlib
- **Seaborn:** high-level interface, great default styles
- **ggplot:** based on R's ggplot2, uses Grammar of Graphics
- **Plotly:** can create interactive plots

In this section, we will be using specific features of these libraries and tools.

b) Loading Libraries and Retrieving Data

In this chapter, Python is used for development with versions 3.6.X and 3.7.X (Jupyter Notebook) (Figure 2.2). Not all Python capabilities are loaded to your working environment by default. We would need to import every library we are going to use. We will choose alias names for our modules for the sake of convenience (e.g. NumPy - np, Pandas - pd).

1. import pandas as pd
2. import numpy as np
3. import matplotlib.pyplot as plt
4. import seaborn as sns
5. import warnings
6. warnings.filterwarnings('ignore')
7. from plotly.offline import download_plotlyjs,init_notebook_mode,plot, iplot
8. import cufflinks as cf
9. init_notebook_mode(connected = True)
10. cf.go_offline()
11. %matplotlib inline
12. from plotly import tools
13. import plotly.plotly as py
14. from plotly.offline import init_notebook_mode, iplot
15. init_notebook_mode(connected=True)
16. import plotly.graph_objs as go
17. import plotly.figure_factory as ff
18. import plotly.offline as offline
19. # Squarify for treemaps
20. import squarify
21. # Random for well, random stuff
22. import random
23. # operator for sorting dictionaries
24. import operator
25. # For ignoring warnings

	BPrev	BStreak	B_Age	B_Height	B_HomeTown	B_ID	B_Location	B_Name	B_Weight	B_Round1_Grappling_Reversals_Landed	B_Round1_Grappling_Standups_Landed	B_Round1_Grappling_Submissions_Attempts	B_Round1_
0	0	0	38.0	193.0	Hounslow England	808	Amsterdam The Netherlands	Allstair Overeem	120.0	NaN	NaN	NaN	NaN
1	0	0	36.0	172.0	Chicago, Illinois United States	1054	Chicago, Illinois United States	Ricardo Lamas	65.0	NaN	NaN	NaN	NaN
2	0	0	39.0	167.0	Isla Vista, California USA	959	Sacramento, California USA	Urijah Faber	61.0	NaN	NaN	NaN	NaN
3	0	0	33.0	167.0	San Diego, CA USA	1056	San Diego, CA USA	Danny Martinez	56.0	NaN	NaN	NaN	NaN
4	0	0	36.0	185.0	Southampton England	2005	Southampton England	Tom Watson	84.0	NaN	NaN	NaN	NaN
5	0	0	35.0	180.0	Amazonas Brazil	2101	Rio de Janeiro Brazil	Alan Patrick	70.0	NaN	NaN	NaN	NaN
6	0	0	26.0	175.0	Detroit, Michigan United States	2157	Las Vegas, Nevada United States	Kevin Lee	70.0	NaN	NaN	NaN	NaN
7	0	0	33.0	175.0	Dagestan Russia	2158	Coconut Creek, Florida United States	Rashid Magomedov	70.0	NaN	NaN	NaN	NaN
8	0	0	36.0	180.0	Zinzeli, Astrakhan Oblast Russia	2160	Zinzeli, Astrakhan Oblast Russia	Gasan Umalatov	77.0	NaN	NaN	NaN	NaN
9	0	0	33.0	162.0	Dagestan Republic Russia	2084	Dagestan Republic Russia	Ali Bagautinov	56.0	NaN	NaN	NaN	NaN

Figure 2.2 Snapshot of loaded dataset.

26. import warnings
27. warnings.filterwarnings('ignore')
28. df = pd.read_csv("../input/data.csv")
29. df.head(10)

c)   Understanding the Data

The dataset contains a list of all UFC fights since 2013 with summed up entries of each fighter's round by round record preceding that fight, created in an attempt to predict a UFC fight winner. Each row represents a single fight with each fighter's previous records summed up prior to the fight. Blank stats mean it is the fighter's first fight since 2013 which is where granular data for UFC fights begins (Figure 2.3). We have about 895 columns, a few important columns to note [16–18]:

- BPrev: Previous fights by 'Blue' fighter
- B_Age: Age of 'Blue' fighter
- B_Height: Height of 'Blue' fighter
- B_Weight: Weight of 'Blue' fighter
- B_Location: Location of 'Blue' fighter
- B_Hometown: Hometown of 'Blue' fighter
- RPrev: Previous fights by 'Red' fighter
- R_Age: Age of 'Red' fighter
- R_Height: Height of 'Red' fighter
- R_Weight: Weight of 'Red' fighter
- R_Location: Location of 'Red' fighter
- R_Hometown: Hometown of 'Red' fighter
- Date: Date of the fight
- winby: How the fighter wins the fight (decision, submission, KO, etc.)
- winner: Who was the winner of the fight?

Apart from this, the dataset contains all the techniques (punch, kicks, takedowns, etc.) attempted and landed by the fighters in each round. Pandas **describe()** is **used** to view some basic statistical details like percentile, mean, std, etc. of a data frame or a series of numeric values. Return type it the statistical summary of data frame.

	BPrev	BStreak	B_Age	B_Height	B_ID	B_Weight	B_Round1_Grappling_Reversals_Landed	B_Round1_Grappling_Standups_Landed	B_Round1_Grappling_Submissions_Attempts	B_Round1_Grappling
count	2318.000000	2318.000000	2301.000000	2318.000000	2318.000000	2306.000000	1647.000000	1647.000000	1647.000000	1647.000000
mean	2.391286	0.744607	31.776184	177.327249	2120.001726	73.699480	0.074681	1.103825	0.577413	
std	2.539978	1.145596	4.165267	8.807620	705.089725	15.425347	0.305691	1.537946	1.049758	
min	0.000000	0.000000	20.000000	152.000000	129.000000	52.000000	0.000000	0.000000	0.000000	
25%	0.000000	0.000000	29.000000	172.000000	1910.250000	61.000000	0.000000	0.000000	0.000000	
50%	2.000000	0.000000	31.000000	177.000000	2230.000000	70.000000	0.000000	1.000000	0.000000	
75%	4.000000	1.000000	35.000000	182.000000	2709.000000	84.000000	0.000000	2.000000	1.000000	
max	14.000000	10.000000	48.000000	213.000000	3196.000000	120.000000	3.000000	13.000000	8.000000	

Figure 2.3 Statistical summary of dataset loaded.

1. `df.describe()`

d) Missing Values

We observe that there are some missing values in our data. We know Age and Height are important features in any combat sport and they have a handful of missing values [19]. We will address the missing values in age and height. We can simply delete rows with missing values, but usually we would want to take advantage of as many data points as possible. Replacing missing values with zeros would not be a good idea, as age 0 will have actual meanings and that would change our data. Therefore, a good replacement value would be something that does not affect the data too much, such as the median or mean. The "fillna" function replaces every NaN (not a number) entry with the given input (the mean of the column in our case). Let us do this for both 'Blue' and 'Red' fighters.

```
1.  df['B_Age'] = df['B_Age'].fillna(np.mean(df['B_Age']))
2.  df['B_Height'] = df['B_Height'].fillna(np.mean
    (df['B_Height']))
3.  df['R_Age'] = df['R_Age'].fillna(np.mean(df['R_Age']))
4.  df['R_Height'] = df['R_Height'].fillna(np.mean
    (df['R_Height']))
```

2.3   Experimental Evaluation and Visualization

Data visualization is the discipline of trying to understand data by placing it in a visual context so that patterns, trends, and correlations that might not otherwise be detected can be exposed [13, 14].

Python offers multiple great graphing libraries that come packed with lots of different features. No matter if you want to create interactive, live, or highly customized plots, Python has an excellent library for you.

To get a little overview, here are a few popular plotting libraries:

- **Matplotlib:** low level, provides lots of freedom
- **Pandas Visualization:** easy to use interface, built on Matplotlib
- **Seaborn:** high-level interface, great default styles
- **ggplot:** based on R's ggplot2, uses Grammar of Graphics
- **Plotly:** can create interactive plots

Let us start by looking who is winning more from our dataset by plotting a pie chart of matches won by either red team or blue team (Figure 2.4):

```
1.    temp = df["winner"].value_counts()
2.    fig = {
3.      "data": [
4.        {
5.          "values": temp.values,
6.          "labels": temp.index,
7.          "domain": {"x": [0, 1]),
8.          "hole": .6,
9.          "type": "pie"
10.       },
11.
12.      ],
13.    "layout": {
14.        "title":"Winner",
15.        "annotations": [
16.          {
17.          "font": {
18.            "size": 17
19.          },
20.          "showarrow": False,
21.          "text": "Whos winning more",
```

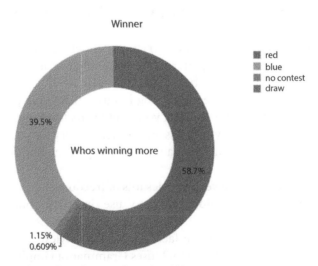

Figure 2.4 Pie chart of matches won by red and blue team.

```
22.                "x": 0.5,
23.                "y": 0.5
24.            }
25.
26.        ]
27.      }
28.  }
29.  iplot(fig, filename='donut')
```

Here, we follow our instincts and play around a bit with what I feel will matter.

Let us talk about Age, a critical factor in any sport. We will start by looking at the distribution of Age from our dataset:

```
1.  #fig, ax = plt.subplots(1,2, figsize=(12, 20))
2.  fig, ax = plt.subplots(1,2, figsize=(15, 5))
3.  sns.distplot(df.B_Age, ax=ax[0])
4.  sns.distplot(df.R_Age, ax=ax[1])
```

Age is a big factor in any sport, moreover in MMA where you must have a combination of strength, agility, and speed (among other skills). These skills peak at 27-35 and fighters fighting at this age should have a higher likelihood of winning the fight (Figures 2.5, 2.6 and 2.7). Let us validate by grouping age for blue fighters who have won the fight.

```
1.  BAge = df.groupby(['B_Age']).count()['winner']
2.  BlueAge=BAge.sort_values(axis=0, ascending=False)
3.  BlueAge.head(10)
```

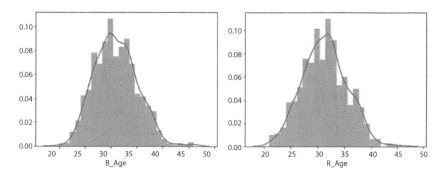

Figure 2.5 Distribution of age of fighters.

```
B_Age
30.0    164
33.0    138
29.0    134
32.0    128
27.0    120
31.0    112
28.0    106
34.0    106
26.0     72
35.0     67
Name: winner, dtype: int64
```

Figure 2.6 Top ten rows of dataset between ages of fighters and maximum matches won.

```
R_Age
24.000000    25
23.000000    17
40.000000    10
41.000000    10
22.000000    10
21.000000     5
43.000000     4
44.000000     3
46.000000     2
31.380081     1
Name: winner, dtype: int64
```

Figure 2.7 Bottom ten rows of dataset between ages of fighters and maximum matches Won46.000000 2.

Clearly, most fights have been won by fighters in their late 20's through early 30's, as they peak during this time and then lose strength, quickness, and cardiovascular capacity. On the other hand, younger fighters do not develop peak strength till 27-28, while older fighters are usually slower and more likely to lose. Let us check if this is true in our data. This time we will check for red fighters.

```
1.  RAge = df.groupby(['R_Age']).count()['winner']
2.  RedAge=RAge.sort_values(axis=0,ascending=False)
3.  RedAge.tail(10)
```

It looks like this is true. It makes me curious about the total number of red and blue fighters who are younger than 35.

```
1.  fig, ax = plt.subplots(1,2, figsize=(15, 5))
2.  above35 =['above35' if i >= 35 else 'below35'
    for i in df.B_Age]
3.  df_B = pd.DataFrame({'B_Age':above35})
4.  sns.countplot(x=df_B.B_Age, ax=ax[0])
5.  plt.ylabel('Number of fighters')
6.  plt.title('Age of Blue fighters',color = 'blue',
    fontsize=15)
7.
8.  above35 =['above35' if i >= 35 else 'below35'
    for i in df.R_Age]
9.  df_R = pd.DataFrame({'R_Age':above35})
10. sns.countplot(x=df_R.R_Age, ax=ax[1])
11. plt.ylabel('Number of Red fighters')
12. plt.title('Age of Red fighters', color = 'Red', fontsize=15)
```

Interestingly, most fighters are below 35. MMA is a brutal sport for older guys and can leave them with lifelong injuries (Figures 2.8 and 2.9). Lastly, let us look at the mean difference

```
1. df['Age_Difference'] = df.B_Age - df.R_Age
2. df[['Age_Difference', 'winner']].groupby('winner').mean()
```

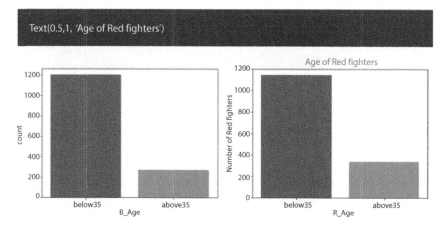

Figure 2.8 Bar chart of total number of fighters above and below age of 35 from red and blue team red fighters').

	Age_Difference
winner	
blue	-1.459711
draw	-1.555556
no contest	0.058824
red	0.273304

Figure 2.9 Mean difference of total number of fighters above and below age 35.

Age matters and youth is a clear advantage. Height is also a major advantage in MMA as it means greater reach, meaning a taller fighter can attack from a distance keeping themselves safe from the hitting zone (Figures 2.10, 2.11, 2.12 and 2.13). Let us start by looking at the distribution of height:

```
1. fig, ax = plt.subplots(1,2, figsize=(15, 5))
2. sns.distplot(df.B_Height, bins = 20, ax=ax[0])
#Blue
3. sns.distplot(df.R_Height, bins = 20, ax=ax[1]) #Red
```

```
1. fig, ax = plt.subplots(figsize=(14, 6))
2. sns.kdeplot(df.B_Height, shade=True, color='indi-
   anred', label='Red')
3. sns.kdeplot(df.R_Height, shade=True, label='Blue')
```

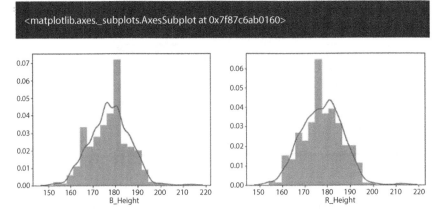

Figure 2.10 Distribution of height of blue and red team (respectively). Generated from above.

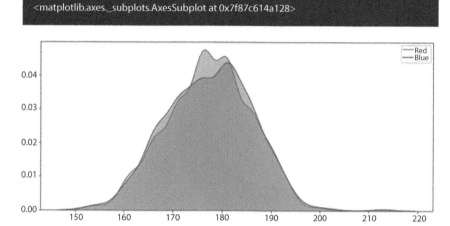

Figure 2.11 Shaded distribution of height of blue and red team (respectively).

	Height Difference
winner	
blue	0.118151
draw	2.444444
no contest	-1.411765
red	-0.052536

Figure 2.12 Height difference of fighters.

1. `df['Height Difference'] = df.B_Height = df.R_Height`
2. `df[['Height Difference', 'winner']].groupby('winner').mean()`

A taller fighter has an advantage and, on average, wins. Of course, *unless you are Rocky fighting Drago.* Now, let us talk about how the fighters are winning. The three most popular ways to win in an MMA fight are:

   1. **DEC:** Decision (Dec) is a result of the fight or bout that does not end in a knockout in which the judges› scorecards are consulted to determine the winner. A majority of judges must agree on a result. A fight can either end in a win for an athlete, a draw, or no decision.

How the fighter's are winning?

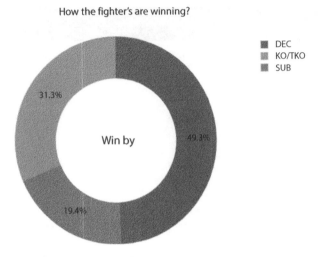

Figure 2.13 Donut chart of how fighters are winning match.

2. **SUB:** A submission, also referred to as a "tap out" or "tapping out", is often performed by visibly tapping the floor or the opponent with the hand, or in some cases with the foot, to signal the opponent and/or the referee of the submission.

3. **KO/TKO:** A knockout (KO) is when a fighter gets knocked out cold. (i.e. from a standing to not standing position from receiving a strike). A technical Knockout (TKO) is when a fighter is getting pummelled and is unable to defend him/herself further. The referee will step in and make a judgement call to end it and prevent the fighter from receiving any more unnecessary or permanent damage and call it a TKO.

```
1. temp = df["winby"].value_counts()
2. fig = {
3.   "data": [
4.     {
5.       "values": temp.values,
6.       "labels": temp.index,
7.       "domain": {"x": [0, 1]},
8.       #"name": "Types of Loans",
9.       #"hoverinfo":"label+percent+name",
10.      "hole": .6,
11.      "type": "pie"
12.    },
13.
```

```
14.       ],
15.    "layout": {
16.       "title":"How the fighter's are winning?",
17.         "annotations": [
18.            {
19.              "font": {
20.                "size": 20
21.              },
22.              "showarrow": False,
23.              "text": "Win by",
24.              "x": 0.50,
25.              "y": 0.5
26.            }
27.
28.         ]
29.       }
30.      }
31. iplot(fig, filename='donut')
```

Most fights go to the judges. The second most popular way is by Knockout or Technical KO. Let us check how this is distributed with respect to Age for red fighters (Figure 2.14).

```
1. g = sns.FacetGrid(df, col='winby')
2. g.map(plt.hist, 'R_Age', bins=20)
```

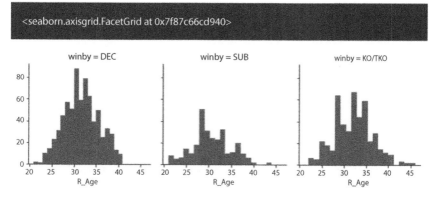

Figure 2.14 Age distribution of ways of winning among red team fighters.

MMA is a complex sport and, in a sense, it is the only sport where defense and offense could be done in the same movement. Hitting someone is a risk as it leaves you open for your opponent to counter. However, the *bigger the risk, the greater the reward*. More offensive attempts should mean you land more on your opponent (and with right skills and power, the greater chance you have to win the fight) (Figure 2.15). Let us see if this is true with our data.

```
1. sns.lmplot(x="B_Round1_Strikes_Body Significant Strikes_Attempts",
2.            y="B_Round1_Strikes_BodySignificantStrikes_Landed",
3.            col="winner", hue="winner", data=df, col_wrap=2, size=6)
```

Attempts and strikes landed are, as expected, perfectly linear. Now, let us look at the location and find the most popular countries (Figure 2.16).

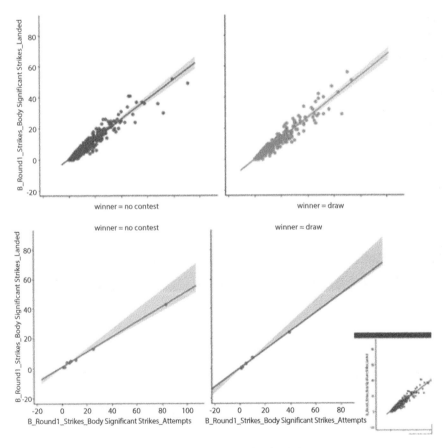

Figure 2.15 Line plot of offensive attempts and strikes landed.

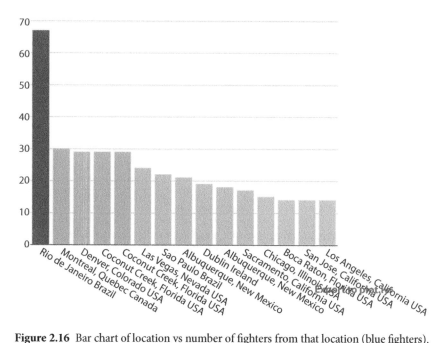

Figure 2.16 Bar chart of location vs number of fighters from that location (blue fighters).

```
1.  cnt_srs = df['R_Location'].value_counts().head(15)
2.
3.      trace = go.Bar(
4.      x=cnt_srs.index,
5.      y=cnt_srs.values,
6.      marker=dict(
7.        color=cnt_srs.values,
8.        ),
9.  )
10.
11. layout = go.Layout(
12.     title='Most Popular cities for Red fighters'
13. )
14.
15. data = [trace]
16. fig = go.Figure(data=data, layout=layout)
17. offline.iplot(fig, filename="Ratio")
```

MMA seems to be most prominent in Brazil and the USA. In fact, MMA is the second most popular sport after Soccer in Brazil. Now, let us look at the grappling reversals, grappling stand-ups, and grappling takedowns landed (Figures 2.17 and 2.18) in different weight categories in **Round 1:**

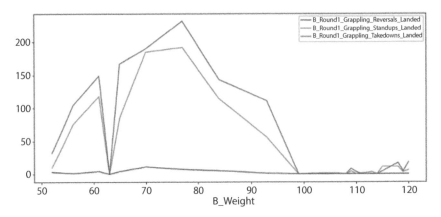

Figure 2.17 Line chart of grappling reversals, grappling standups, and grappling takedowns landed in different weight categories in Round 1.

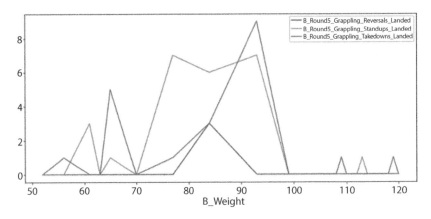

Figure 2.18 Line chart of grappling reversals, grappling standups, and grappling takedowns landed in different weight categories in Round 5.

```
1.  r1=df[['B_Weight','B__Round1_Grappling_Reversals_
    Landed', 'B__Round1_Grappling_Standups_Landed',
2.  'B__Round1_Grappling_Takedowns_Landed']].group-
    by('B_3Weight').sum()
3.
4.  r1.plot(kind='line', figsize=(14,6))
5.  plt.show()
```

There are very few grappling reversals, but a high amount of grappling takedowns that were landed. More specifically, weight classes between 70 - 80 prefer takedowns during Round 1.

Let us compare the same for Round 5.

```
1.   r5 = df[['B_Weight', 'B__Round5_Grappling_Reversals_Landed',
     'B__Round5_Grappling_Standups_Landed',
     'B__Round5_Grappling_Takedowns_Landed']].groupby('B_
     Weight').sum()
2.
3.   r5.plot(kind='line', figsize=(14,6))
4.   plt.show()
```

Interestingly, grappling reversals increase for fighters between weights 80-90, while takedowns have decreased in the lighter weight groups. Let us look for similar data for clinch head strikes, clinch leg strikes, and body strikes for Round 1 (Figures 2.19 and 2.20).

```
1.   clin_r1 = df[['B_Weight', 'B__Round1_Strikes_Clinch
     Head  Strikes_Landed',  'B__Round1_Strikes_Clinch
     Leg   Strikes_Landed',  'B__Round1_Strikes_Clinch
     Body Strikes_Landed']].groupby('B_Weight').sum()
2.
3.   #clin_r1.plot(kind='line', figsize=(14,6))
4.   plt.show()
```

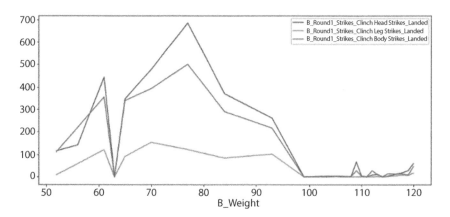

Figure 2.19 Line chart of clinch head strikes, clinch leg strikes, and body strikes for Round 1.

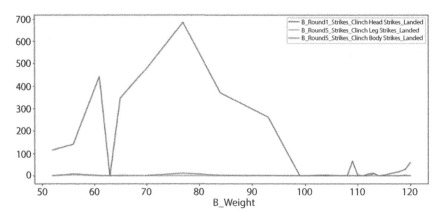

Figure 2.20 Line chart of clinch head strikes, clinch leg strikes, and body strikes for Round 5.

Fighters prefer to land more head strikes during Round 1. Let us compare this with what happens in Round 5:

1. ```
   clin_r5= df[['B_Weight', 'B__Round1_Strikes_Clinch
   Head  Strikes_Landed',  'B__Round5_Strikes_Clinch
   Leg   Strikes_Landed',  'B__Round5_Strikes_Clinch
   Body Strikes_Landed']].groupby('B_Weight').sum()
   ```
2.
3. ```
   clin_r5.plot(kind='line', figsize=(14,6))
   ```
4. ```
   plt.show()
   ```

By Round 5, fighters (who are now worn-out) are hardly landing any leg and body strikes. They are still landing a good amount of head strikes. This makes sense as the fight is coming to an end and instead of depending on the judges, they want to go for a Knockout.

2.4   Conclusion

In the present study, the proposed data analysis tool uses machine learning to study the prediction accuracy of UFC data. This sport particularly requires a lot of factors to be considered in order to have a correct prediction. Various factors like age, height, offensive attempts and strikes
   ```

landed, location, grappling reversals, grappling standups, and grappling takedowns, clinch head strikes, clinch leg strikes, and body strikes under various rounds have been considered to analyse and predict the efficacy of the proposed work. The present work opens new directions and investigation possibilities for further analysing, such as unpredictable sports, in a more efficient and effective manner.

References

1. De Silva, L. C., & Hui, S. C. (2003, December). Real-time facial feature extraction and emotion recognition. In *Fourth International Conference on Information, Communications and Signal Processing, 2003 and the Fourth Pacific Rim Conference on Multimedia. Proceedings of the 2003 Joint* (Vol. 3, pp. 1310-1314). IEEE.
2. Kaur, M., Vashisht, R., & Neeru, N. (2010). Recognition of facial expressions with principal component analysis and singular value decomposition. *International Journal of Computer Applications, 9*(12), 36-40.
3. Kartikay Sharma, Siddharth Bhasin, Piyush Bharadwaj (2019, September). A Worldwide Analysis of Cyber Security and Cyber Crime using Twitter. In International Journal of Engineering and Advanced Technology (IJEAT) ISSN: 2249 – 8958, Volume-8 Issue-6S3.
4. Waterloo, S. F., Baumgartner, S. E., Peter, J., & Valkenburg, P. M. (2018). Norms of online expressions of emotion: Comparing Facebook, Twitter, Instagram, and WhatsApp. *new media & society, 20*(5), 1813-1831.
5. Verma, A., Malla, D., Choudhary, A. K., & Arora, V. (2019, February). A Detailed Study of Azure Platform & Its Cognitive Services. In *2019 International Conference on Machine Learning, Big Data, Cloud and Parallel Computing (COMITCon)* (pp. 129-134). IEEE.
6. Jung, S. G., An, J., Kwak, H., Salminen, J., & Jansen, B. J. (2018, June). Assessing the accuracy of four popular face recognition tools for inferring gender, age, and race. In *Twelfth International AAAI Conference on Web and Social Media*.
7. You, Q., Luo, J., Jin, H., & Yang, J. (2016, February). Building a large-scale dataset for image emotion recognition: The fine print and the benchmark. In *Thirtieth AAAI conference on artificial intelligence*.
8. Khanal, S. R., Barroso, J., Lopes, N., Sampaio, J., & Filipe, V. (2018, June). Performance analysis of Microsoft's and Google's Emotion Recognition API using pose-invariant faces. In *Proceedings of the 8th International Conference on Software Development and Technologies for Enhancing Accessibility and Fighting Info-exclusion* (pp. 172-178).

9. Kang, Y., Jia, Q., Gao, S., Zeng, X., Wang, Y., Angsuesser, S., ... & Fei, T. (2019). Extracting human emotions at different places based on facial expressions and spatial clustering analysis. *Transactions in GIS, 23*(3), 450-480.

10. Schaeffer, S. E. (2007). Graph clustering. *Computer science review, 1*(1), 27-64.

11. Pardàs, M., & Bonafonte, A. (2002). Facial animation parameters extraction and expression recognition using Hidden Markov Models. *Signal Processing: Image Communication, 17*(9), 675-688.

12. Boy, J. D., & Uitermark, J. (2017). Reassembling the city through Instagram. *Transactions of the Institute of British Geographers, 42*(4), 612-624.

13. Rowley, H. A., Baluja, S., & Kanade, T. (1998). Neural network-based face detection. *IEEE Transactions on pattern analysis and machine intelligence, 20*(1), 23-38.

14. H. A. Rowley, S. Baluja and T. Kanade, "Rotation invariant neural network-based face detection," *Proceedings. 1998 IEEE Computer Society Conference on Computer Vision and Pattern Recognition (Cat. No.98CB36231),* Santa Barbara, CA, 1998, pp. 38-44.

15. Bhardwaj, P., Gautam, S., & Pahwa, P. (2018). A novel approach to analyze the sentiments of tweets related to TripAdvisor. Journal of Information and Optimization Sciences, 39(2), 591-605.

16. Bhardwaj, P., Gautam, S., Pahwa, P., & Singh, N. (2016). Characteristics and challenges of big data. Int. J. Recent Innov. Trends Comput. Commun, 5, 187-190.

17. Bhardwaj, P., Gautam, S., & Pahwa, P. (2017). Opinion Mining and Sentiment Analysis of Travel Websites through Twitter. International Journal of Applied Engineering Research, 12(22), 12431-12439.

18. Sharma, T., Kumar, S., Yadav, N., Sharma, K., & Bhardwaj, P. (2017, February). Air-swipe gesture recognition using OpenCV in Android devices. In 2017 international conference on algorithms, methodology, models and applications in emerging technologies (ICAMMAET) (pp. 1-6). IEEE.

19. Charu Gupta, Prateek Agrawal, Rohan Ahuja, Kunal Vats, Chirag Pahuja, Tanuj Ahuja, "Pragmatic Analysis of Classification Techniques based on Hyperparameter Tuning for Sentiment Analysis", International Semantic Intelligence Conference (ISIC'21), pp. 453-459, 2021, CEUR-WS.

Dawn of Big Data with Hadoop and Machine Learning

Balraj Singh[1,2*] and Harsh Kumar Verma[1]

[1]Department of Computer Science and Engineering, NIT, Jalandhar, India
[2]Department of Computer Science and Engineering, Lovely Professional University, Punjab, India

Abstract

Rapid data development by modern systems has changed the way we perceive the world. The data is growing fast and so are the expectations. The excessive growth of data has given a breakthrough to touch the new levels in technology and bring enhancements in every corner of life, but this enormous data has shown the limitations of the traditional systems in managing, storing, and processing large-scale data. As Big Data has gained momentum, different platforms and tools are made available to support it. Machine learning algorithms have become an integral part of Big Data analytics. Big Data without machine learning techniques is not a sufficient entity in itself. A right combination of machine learning algorithms and a proper underlying platform to process the data is a core requirement for the success of Big Data. The decision to opt for a particular algorithm and platform lies in the needs of the organization and the type of data being generated. Different platforms have their advantages and limitations. The right combination of platform and machine learning techniques for processing big data can bring many advancements and successes. This chapter discusses various applications utilizing machine learning on the Hadoop platform for processing Big Data. A broad view of the Hadoop platform's applicability in different domains, such as scientific research, healthcare, bioinformatics, sports, etc., is represented.

Keywords: Big Data, Hadoop, machine learning, applications

*Corresponding author: singh.balraj@hotmail.com

Prateek Agrawal, Charu Gupta, Anand Sharma, Vishu Madaan, and Nisheeth Joshi (eds.) Machine Learning and Data Science: Fundamentals and Applications, (47–66) © 2022 Scrivener Publishing LLC

3.1   Introduction

With the easy accessibility of high-performance computing platforms, the use of machine learning (ML) has seen a steep rise in different sectors and fields [1]. ML tools are now becoming an essential component of many business operations [2]. They help in learning from previous and current events and utilize this knowledge to perform predictions and make future decisions. At the core of the ML process is data that is used to power the machine learning models and algorithms [3]. The intelligent interpretations from the data are vital to the success of every domain and industry, but they need efforts and mechanisms beyond the traditional processing system. The striving competitive environment and changing needs have made necessary efficient processing and quicker results from the data [4]. To address these needs a large-scale data processing system with the support of machine learning techniques is needed. Machine learning with the right combination of a platform has revolutionized the technology and has given new dimensions of growth [5]. The rapid growth of data has challenged the machine learning techniques to efficiently process large-scale data. Basic toolkits such as R and Weka were not planned for such a scale of data. The proliferation of the data has made us rethink data processing platforms and ML algorithms [6]. The appropriate selection of a platform and a particular environment is one of the most challenging tasks as it is affected by the level of the project and the users working with the projects [7]. This has caused a great amount of disparity in selecting appropriate tools as no specific tool is sufficient to cover all the applications and their task. While selecting the appropriate environment and tools, one has to consider a tradeoff between the performance, application requirement, and suitability. In this scenario, [8] Hadoop is a popular choice as it supports distributed processing and has capabilities for both vertical and horizontal scalability. The Hadoop platform supports a wide range of machine learning algorithms and has supporting libraries [9]. The remaining part of the chapter is organized as follows: Section 3.2 discusses Big Data essentials, Section 3.3 discusses machine learning, Section 3.4 discusses Hadoop, Section 3.5 discusses the various applications of machine learning using Hadoop, and Section 3.6 is a conclusion.

3.2   Big Data

The fundamental advantages of big data are highly impactful and organizations are taking leading benefits from it [10]. It would not be wrong to say that data is everywhere now. Organizations are diving deep into the ever-expanding ocean of data which is extremely large in volume and highly unstructured to be analyzed by the traditional systems and processes. Big Data is simply much more than large-scale data. It is a combination of data, tools, platforms, and techniques to process the data to uncover meaningful patterns and information from it. The basic characteristics that govern Big Data are volume, velocity, variety, veracity, value, and variability [11]. The first three characteristics were initially considered and later, the organization proposed to expand the list of the characteristics with the remaining characteristics as given.

3.2.1   The Life Cycle of Big Data

Processes from loading to visualizing results involve a proper cycle in Big Data [12]. The following are the basic steps in the life cycle of Big Data.

I.   **Ingesting and loading data into the platform** is the process of loading data in the system. The complexity of the system is highly dependent upon the formats of the data being loaded. The data could be of structured and unstructured formats. The commonly used ETL (extract, transform, and load) process is associated with this phase of Big Data. The various tools that assist in this process of ETL are Apache Scoop, Apache Flume, Apache Chukwa, Apache Kafka, etc.

II. **Ensuring the persistence of the data in the storage system** refers to storing the data on the storage components of the system for permanent storage. Being Big Data, the complexity for storing and processing is high. The distributed file system is utilized to store the data across multiple nodes for better allocation of computing resources.

III. In **analysis of the data,** the actual process of extracting information from the data is done. The data is subjected to either batch processing or real-time processing depending upon the need of the application. In batch processing, data is divided into smaller units and processed across multiple processing units, while in real-time, the processing is done for continuous streams of data and produces results immediately. Apache Hadoop is a suitable platform for batch processing. For real-time processing, Apache Storm, Spark, Flink, etc. are suitable platforms.

IV. During **visualization of the output**, the trends and patterns in the data are analyzed for interpretation. Various tools are available for visualization. Jupyter and Apache are among the popular tools for visualization.

3.2.2 Challenges in Big Data

Big Data faces a lot of issues in processing, analyzing, and managing large-scale data [13]. The extraction of information with a proper application of the process and techniques is a most challenging task. Some of the challenges are:

I. **Data Processing:** Executing large-scale data on a single system or standalone platform will take an excessive amount of time to complete a job for Big Data. Moreover, the variation in resource demands of the jobs will make it technically non-feasible to complete on time. The solutions for such issues are given by the platforms which use parallel and distributed systems such as Hadoop.

II. **Data Storage Challenges:** Conventional storage systems do not go well with Big Data processing due to the diversity in the form of the data. The conventional systems are unable to process raw data that is semi-structured and un-structured. Moreover, continuous scalability requirements due to the extreme volumes of the data are another concern. Some systems are not easily scalable and bring a threshold for their suitability for Big Data platforms. To overcome these challenges, distributed file systems and NoSQL are better solutions and have higher scalability and performance.

III. **Performance:** The basic requirement of performance in extracting the information is a major challenge. The large-scale processing of data needs to be done efficiently and rapidly to bring a competitive edge. Distributed and parallel processing on a large-scale cluster is an appropriate option for processing large scale data efficiently.

IV. **Data Visualization:** One of the key challenges in Big Data interpretation is that the basic visualization tools are low in performance and have a poor response time. The recent advancements in visualization tools have assisted in better visualization and interpretations. Figure 3.1 shows the different sources of Big Data.

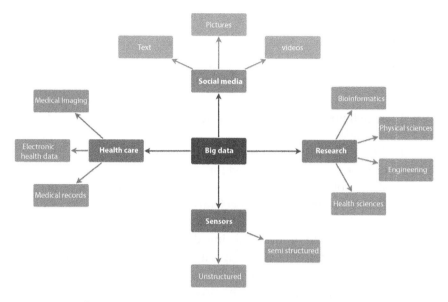

Figure 3.1 Different sources of big data.

3.2.3   Scaling in Big Data Platforms

A flexible platform can show elasticity to the changing needs of data processing. Different platforms respond to such requests differently [14]. Big Data platforms are broadly classified into two broad categories for scaling:

I. **Horizontal** is a scale-out technique. In these scenarios, multiple machines are added to enhance the computing power and typically the instances are running on separate machines. Examples of this are Peer to Peer Networks, Hadoop, Berkley Data Analytics Stack, etc.

II. **Vertical Scaling** is a scale-up technique and the demanded capabilities are added on a single system only. Examples of vertical scaling are high computing clusters, multicore CPU, graphic processing units, etc.

3.2.4   Factors to Understand Big Data Platforms and Their Selection Criteria

Various factors influence the choice of the big data platform. Table 3.1 shows the various tools and platforms for Big Data. The following section covers some of the points for selecting a platform:

Table 3.1 Major tools and platforms for big data.

Apache Hadoop	MongoDB	RapidMiner	Cassandra
Apache Spark	Kafka	Apache	Tableau

    I. Scalability: How a platform accommodates changes and upgrades

   II. I/O (input/output) Operations: Depends upon the job requirements and the speed for I/O

 III. Fault Tolerance: How does a system respond to cause of failure and the recovery mechanism?

 IV. Real-Time Processing: Capabilities of the system to perform iteratively and process real-time data streams

   V. Data Size Supported: The capacity of the platform to provide support for the Big Data

 VI. Iterative Tasks Support: The processing unit is more compute-intensive or data-intensive

3.2.5   Current Trends in Big Data

The following section covers some of the current trends of technology in Big Data:

    I. Increasing Streaming Analytics via Apache Flink and Spark Streaming: Promoting companies to opt for open source technologies.

   II. Increasing Data Analytics: Due to IoT as a new source of data, a need for higher data analytics is inevitable and in trend.

 III. Hadoop in Trend: Hadoop plays an important part in ingesting data in IoT scenarios.

 IV. Increasing Focus on Cloud-Based Data Analytics: Enterprises are considering cloud-based analytic platforms for storing and processing data.

   V. More Demand for Big Data and Analytical Skills: The need for a new Hadoop solution is in trend again as it provides support for analytics.

 VI. Achieving Maximum Business Intelligence With Data Virtualization: Business Intelligence

3.2.6   Big Data Use Cases

Big Data has vast applicability and can be used to address a range of issues [15]. In this section, some of the use cases of Big Data are discussed:

1) **Product Development:** Companies use Big Data platforms to understand customer requirements and develop models to forecast future needs.

2) **Predictive Maintenance:** Big Data can be used to plan contingency strategies for future failure by utilizing previous logs and other records. The predictions can be done using the old values.

3) **Customer Satisfaction:** Big Data tools can be used to review the sentiments of the customers using online logs such as their Tweets, Facebook comments, etc. for improving the service.

4) **Machine Learning:** Utilizing the available data, we have better implementation of the machine learning techniques. One of the biggest breakthroughs of Big Data is an application of machine learning techniques.

5) **Research and Innovation:** Big Data tools and applications are vastly utilized in research and development. Almost all the research domains have voluminous data for processing and interpretation. Big Data platforms have turned out to be some of the most useful platforms in research.

6) **Improving Operations:** The operational activities in different fields, such as transportation, healthcare, industry, etc., have seen tremendous improvement by utilizing the available data efficiently.

3.3   Machine Learning

Machine learning is a domain of artificial intelligence which helps in making predictions and decisions through machines by self-learning processes. It is a collection of techniques which helps to identify and understand the patterns in the data and makes intelligent decisions and predictions. A large amount of data developed through these multiple sources requires methods and strategies for proper processing. ML algorithms use patterns in the data to develop predictive models and utilize these models for prediction [16]. To efficiently process Big Data, machine learning is an appropriate option. The broad classification of machine learning is done in two categories:

a) **Supervised Learning:** These are used when the output is classified. In supervised learning users are aware of the input and the output. It utilizes the training datasets to learn from them and creates models using them [17]. Then, these models are used for performing predictions and decision making. Naïve Bayes and decision trees are examples of supervised learning. Applications are image classification, market prediction, etc.

b) **Unsupervised Learning:** In this, the users are only aware of the input but the information about the output variable is not there [18]. Unsupervised algorithms are used to create a function to find hidden and unlabeled data patterns. Their primary task is to build the class labels.

3.3.1 Machine Learning Algorithms

There are a lot of machine learning algorithms that can be used to develop predictive modes. Figure 3.2 represents the machine learning models. Depending upon the category of the type, machine learning algorithms can be divided into the following types:

1) Classification
2) Regression

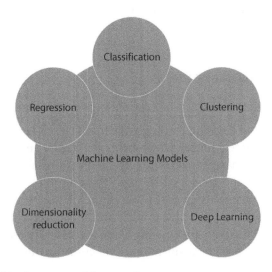

Figure 3.2 Machine learning model approaches.

3) Clustering
4) Dimensionality Reduction
5) Deep Learning

The details of these models are given below:

1) **Classification** is used to predict the type of an object within a limited set of options and the output variable is categorical. Some of the important models for classification are SVM, Decision Trees, Logistic regression, Nave Bayes, etc.
2) **Regression** is a basic technique that takes continuous values for performing predictions. Some of the basic techniques for the regression model are linear regression, Lasso regression, ridge regression, SVM regression, and decision tree regression.
3) **Clustering** is a model used to group similar objects. This belongs to unsupervised learning and identifies the object automatically without the need for user intervention. Some of the examples of clustering are statistical analysis, social network analysis, market analysis, etc. The basic clustering models are K means, K means++, K medoids, density-based clustering, hierarchical clustering, etc.
4) **Dimensionality Reduction** is a technique by which data from a high dimensionality space is transferred to a low dimensionality space. This technique involves lowering the number of features for improving the prediction process. Basic types of dimensionality reduction models are PCA, TSNE, SVD, etc.
5) **Deep Learning** is concerned with neural networks. Some of the basic models for deep learning are Convolution Neural Network (CNN), multi-layer perceptron, recurrent neural networks, etc.

3.4   Hadoop

Hadoop is a Big Data model that is efficient in batch processing of large-scale jobs [19]. It is an open-source model that allows distributed processing of large-scale jobs on commodity hardware. It is one of the popular and preferred platforms for Big Data processing. Its cluster is based on commodity hardware which provides high performance and throughput.

3.4.1   Components of the Hadoop Ecosystem

The Hadoop platform is a combination of multiple components. Each component on the Hadoop supports the processing of the job. These components are:

- **Hadoop Distributed File System (HDFS)** is a distributed file system of Hadoop for data storage [20]. HDFS distributes the data over different nodes to accommodate distributed processing. Data is divided into fixed-size blocks and saved on the nodes.
- **Yarn** provides the managerial activities to monitor and manage the resource on the Hadoop cluster [21]. Yarn is also responsible for the scheduling of jobs. It provides services such as resource negotiations with the resource manager to allocate the required services to the jobs.
- **Common** are a set of utilities that support cluster management.
- **MapReduce** is a programming module that is responsible for the parallel processing of the jobs [22]. It runs in the YARN cluster. The process of MapReduce is engaged in two phases: Map phase and Reduce phase. In the beginning the data is divided into splits and allocated to the Maps. After the intermediate processing of the data, which involves sorting and grouping, data is assigned to the reduce phase for final processing of the output. Figure 3.3 represents the abstract view of the MapReduce mechanism.

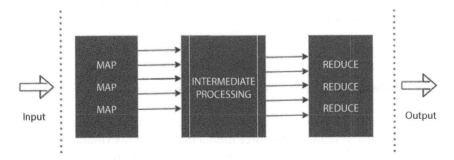

Figure 3.3 MapReduce mechanism.

3.4.2   Other Important Components of the Hadoop Ecosystem for Machine Learning

Along with the basic components, the following machine learning library is used in Hadoop:

- **Mahout:** Machine learning-based cluster algorithms and libraries are in high demand for utilizing the distributed platforms. Mahout is a Hadoop library to support machine learning algorithms for processing large-scale data [23].

3.4.3   Benefits of Hadoop with Machine Learning

Hadoop provides an abundance of benefits for processing large-scale jobs in a distributed environment. Some of the potential benefits of Hadoop are:

- **High-Performance Computing:** Hadoop provides high computing performance by utilizing a cluster of multiple nodes.
- **Machine Learning Libraries:** Hadoop has support for machine learning through its different supporting libraries.
- **Distributed Processing of the Data:** Hadoop distributes the data on multiple nodes and processes it in parallel on multiple nodes.
- **Fault Tolerance:** With a replication factor of 3, Hadoop provides fault tolerance. In case one of the nodes fails, the backup nodes continue.
- **Easy Scalability:** Hadoop supports both vertical and horizontal scalability. The up-gradation in the infrastructure is easily accommodated.

3.5   Studies Representing Applications of Machine Learning Techniques with Hadoop

In this section, we will touch on some of the studies depicting the use of machine learning techniques with Hadoop as an underlying mechanism. The spectrum of the applications is vast and covers different fields such as healthcare, agriculture, the entertainment industry, sports, network detections, transportation, etc. In [24], the authors utilized machine learning techniques on the Hadoop platform to predict diabetes in patients. They used Pima Indians Diabetes Database from the National Institute of Diabetes and Digestive Diseases data to process on the Hadoop cluster with the machine learning approach to predict diabetes. In [25], the authors worked on the national datasets to find the different patterns for diabetes using Hadoop and machine learning. It utilizes the patterns to identify potential risks and future treatment for the patients. In [26], the authors used Hadoop and machine learning algorithms to develop a model for heart stroke prediction. The authors used a genetic algorithm to experiment on the medical data to forecast the possibility of strokes. In [27], the authors prepared an analytics framework using open source software and tools. The proposed system is used for exploring the available datasets from hospitals for getting new insight and ratings for improving administration and patient management. In [28], the authors proposed a prediction-based model for assessing the readmission of a patient in the hospital. The proposed model helps in reduction of patient readmission in the hospital. The proposed model is generic and could be customized by different hospitals. In [29], the authors proposed a prediction model for predicting medical expenses and used a data mining approach and techniques to improve the process in the hospital. In [30], the authors used machine learning on Hadoop to analyze movie reviews. The Hadoop platform supported the efficient processing of data to understand the sentiments of the public. In [31], the authors utilized the machine learning approach to classify moods for song lyrics. The authors utilized a dataset of songs to perform sentiment analysis using different machine learning algorithms. In [32], the authors performed analysis of the sentiments using fuzzy classification on review data. In [33], an analysis of Facebook data is done with machine learning algorithms utilizing Hadoop as an underlying platform. In [34], the Hadoop platform is utilized for analyzing different data mining techniques. The authors used the University of California's machine learning repository with different classification techniques. They analyzed the time complexity and accuracy of the classifiers. In [35], the authors used Hadoop and a machine learning algorithm to predict the performance of the player. In [36], the authors performed a systematic review of the machine learning algorithms for recommender systems and discussed their suitability on the Big Data platform. In [37], the authors proposed PredictionIO, a machine learning server for software development. The proposed model supports horizontal scalability with Hadoop. [38] proposed a Google programming-based framework for forensics. It utilizes a set of matching learning techniques and Hadoop's supporting modules, such as Mahout and Hive, for performing the analysis. In [39], the authors represented machine learning and Big Data challenges for analyzing network traffic and solving classification issues. A drug combination is proposed by the authors in [40]. They utilized the MapReduce programming paradigm for efficient and scalable processing of data. The authors used a combination of Naïve Bayesian classifiers along with a support vector machine on the Hadoop to perform the prediction. In [41], the authors worked on neuroimaging using a machine learning approach on the Hadoop cluster. They used random forest classifiers to detect genetic variations. The analysis was done on Hadoop for processing the data. In [42], the advantage of Hadoop's low-cost implementation of MapReduce is utilized in bioinformatics. The authors used the Hadoop platform for next-generation sequencing. Similarly, in [43] a Hadoop implementation-based analytic kit is used for optimizing metagenomics applications. The authors utilized Hadoop's heterogeneous environment for both compute and data-intensive processing. In [44], analysis of the electrocardiogram is done using machine learning techniques to identify heart disease. The implementation of the whole process was done using Scala programming and Mi-lib of Spark. In [45], the authors worked on developing a solution for identifying early detection of heart disease. The random forest technique is utilized along with the Hadoop platform to perform the analysis. In [46], a predictive model for air pollution is proposed. The proposed technique uses Hadoop Spark for performing distributed processing for higher processing using a multimode cluster. An inverse-distance-weight is used for the prediction. The Hadoop cluster is preferred for its support for horizontal scalability. In [47], the authors proposed false alarm detection using machine learning implementation on the Hadoop platform. The authors proposed using distributed processing. Further, this paper proposes improved processing on the Hadoop file system and a reduction in the time taken while using machine learning algorithms. In [48], an e-commerce recommendation system is proposed. It uses a transaction database to identify the important rules in it. These rules are used to extract information related to customer behavior and preferences. The process is utilized in the Hadoop ecosystem. In [49], authors represented the recent trend of Big Data technology usage in biotechnology and plant science. The large-scale data is being processed using ML algorithms and a Hadoop distributed environment. [50] represents the use of the Big Data platform and ML in the agriculture irrigation system. The proposed solution is based upon IoT where information is sent to HDFS for processing using ML algorithms to provide recommendations. The received information is processed using K nearest neighbor and a neural network for providing a classification of different water levels. In [51], the authors performed an analysis of an agriculture park's data. Hadoop and Spark are used for analysis purposes to check the soil quality and process data for interpretations. In [52], the authors proposed a framework for adaptive learning. The proposed solution supports irrigation decisions by analyzing the soil features using ML algorithms. The underlying mechanism being used was Hadoop for processing the information. In [53], the authors proposed ML-based fault and abnormality detection in the wind turbine. The authors used a decision tree with large-scale data and processed it on the Hadoop platform. In [54], the authors represent ML-based predictive capabilities utilizing supervised classification on Twitter. It provides a case study for the integration of ML tools on Twitter and the extension of Pig on it. In [55], authors discussed the recent trends in Big Data platforms and machine learning. The different applications are discussed and their impact on knowledge management is represented by the authors. In [56], the authors addressed the issue of excessive data being developed through IOT devices for medical care devices. The proposed mechanism processes the collected data using the Hadoop platform to identify the health conditions. The proposed system uses various sensors, such as wearable devices, which are attached to the human body and measure health parameters and transmit them to a primary mobile device (PMD). The collected data is then forwarded to an intelligent building (IB) using the Internet where the data are thoroughly analyzed to identify abnormal and serious health conditions. In [57], the authors utilized the Hadoop framework to process large-scale data of images. It utilized the multimode computing infrastructure of the Hadoop for required processing power. In [58], the authors reviewed the various Big Data applications for the transportation and logistics industry. Further, the authors proposed the analytics-based containers code recognition approach. In [59], data is analyzed on the Hadoop cluster to correlate the customer's purchasing behavior with campaigns and browsing behavior. [60] used mining rules on customer behavior to understand customer behavior and buying patterns. The analysis was performed on the Hadoop platform. In [61], the authors used a clustering approach to analyze a banking data set on the Hadoop cluster. In [62], the authors used Hadoop's MapReduce platform to execute the public opinion dataset in text form. It used ML for analysis purposes. Machine learning is playing an important role in the health sector for predicting diseases and analyzing medical conditions [63–66]. The processing of excessively accumulated data on a Big Data platform provides deep insight to medical professionals to better understand the health condition of the patients. Many such applications of Big Data with appropriate platform and machine learning algorithms are there, which can improve the living standards of humans.

3.6   Conclusion

Technological advancements have resulted in an enormous amount of data. This data is from multiple sources and different formats. The traditional systems are not sufficient enough to manage and process this large-scale data. Big Data systems are the most suitable and feasible solution for processing this enormous data. The two essential requirements of the Big Data system are: 1) a platform that can store and process this data and 2) a mechanism for intelligent interpretations from the data. To address these requirements, Hadoop is a popular choice. It can store and process large-scale data through its resourceful cluster. To address the second need, Hadoop provides supporting libraries for machine learning algorithms to unfold the hidden information inside the data. A combination of a distributed processing platform along with machine learning algorithms is surely going to shape the future.

References

1. Lei, Yaguo, *et al.* "Applications of machine learning to machine fault diagnosis: A review and roadmap." Mechanical Systems and Signal Processing 138 (2020): 106587.
2. Ayodele, Taiwo Oladipupo. "Types of machine learning algorithms." New advances in machine learning 3 (2010): 19-48.
3. Dey, Ayon. "Machine learning algorithms: a review." International Journal of Computer Science and Information Technologies 7.3 (2016): 1174-1179.
4. Mohammed, Mohssen, Muhammad Badruddin Khan, and Eihab Bashier Mohammed Bashier. Machine learning: algorithms and applications. Crc Press, 2016.
5. Silver, Daniel L., Qiang Yang, and Lianghao Li. "Lifelong machine learning systems: Beyond learning algorithms." 2013 AAAI spring symposium series. 2013.
6. Zhou, Lina, *et al.* "Machine learning on big data: Opportunities and challenges." Neurocomputing 237 (2017): 350-361.
7. Manogaran, Gunasekaran, and Daphne Lopez. "A survey of big data architectures and machine learning algorithms in healthcare." International Journal of Biomedical Engineering and Technology 25.2-4 (2017): 182-211.
8. Erraissi, Allae, Abdessamad Belangour, and Abderrahim Tragha. "A Comparative Study of Hadoop-based Big Data Architectures." Int. J. Web Appl. 9.4 (2017): 129-137.

9. Asha, T., *et al.* "Building machine learning algorithms on Hadoop for big-data." International Journal of Engineering and Technology 3.2 (2013): 143-147.

10. Oussous, Ahmed, *et al.* "Big Data technologies: A survey." Journal of King Saud University-Computer and Information Sciences 30.4 (2018): 431-448.

11. Nguyen, Thuan L. "A framework for five big v's of big data and organizational culture in firms." 2018 IEEE International Conference on Big Data (Big Data). IEEE, 2018.

12. El Arass, M., I. Tikito, and N. Souissi. "An Audit Framework for Data Lifecycles in a Big Data context." 2018 International Conference on Selected Topics in Mobile and Wireless Networking (MoWNeT). IEEE, 2018.

13. Qi, Guo-Jun, and Jiebo Luo. "Small data challenges in big data era: A survey of recent progress on unsupervised and semi-supervised methods." IEEE Transactions on Pattern Analysis and Machine Intelligence 2020.

14. Cheng, Yingchao, Zhifeng Hao, and Ruichu Cai. "Auto-scaling for real-time stream analytics on HPC cloud." Service Oriented Computing and Applications 13.2 (2019): 169-183.

15. Oussous, Ahmed, *et al.* "Big Data technologies: A survey." Journal of King Saud University-Computer and Information Sciences 30.4 (2018): 431-448.

16. Bonaccorso, Giuseppe. Machine learning algorithms. Packt Publishing Ltd, 2017.

17. Osisanwo, F. Y., *et al.* "Supervised machine learning algorithms: classification and comparison." International Journal of Computer Trends and Technology (IJCTT) 48.3 (2017): 128-138.

18. Kassambara, Alboukadel. Practical guide to cluster analysis in R: Unsupervised machine learning. Vol. 1. Sthda, 2017.

19. Zeebaree, Subhi RM, *et al.* "Characteristics and analysis of hadoop distributed systems." Technology Reports of Kansai University 62.4 (2020): 1555-1564.

20. Hajeer, Mustafa, and Dipankar Dasgupta. "Handling big data using a data-aware HDFS and evolutionary clustering technique." IEEE Transactions on Big Data 5.2 (2017): 134-147.

21. Subbulakshmi, T., and Jisha S. Manjaly. "A comparison study and performance evaluation of schedulers in Hadoop YARN." 2017 2nd International Conference on Communication and Electronics Systems (ICCES). IEEE, 2017.

22. Glushkova, Daria, Petar Jovanovic, and Alberto Abelló. "Mapreduce performance model for Hadoop 2. x." Information systems 79 (2019): 32-43.

23. Anil, Robin, *et al.* "Apache Mahout: Machine Learning on Distributed Dataflow Systems." Journal of Machine Learning Research 21.127 (2020): 1-6.

24. Yuvaraj, N., and K. R. SriPreethaa. "Diabetes prediction in healthcare systems using machine learning algorithms on Hadoop cluster." Cluster Computing 22.1 (2019): 1-9.

25. Kalyankar, Gauri D., Shivananda R. Poojara, and Nagaraj V. Dharwadkar. "Predictive analysis of diabetic patient data using machine learning and Hadoop." 2017 international conference on I-SMAC (IoT in social, mobile, analytics and cloud)(I-SMAC). IEEE, 2017.

26. Sabibullah, M., V. Shanmugasundaram, and R. Priya. "Diabetes patient's risk through soft computing model." International Journal of Emerging Trends & Technology in Computer Science (IJETTCS) 2.6 (2013): 60-65.

27. Rao, A. Ravishankar, et al. "A framework for analyzing publicly available healthcare data." 2015 17th International Conference on E-health Networking, Application & Services (HealthCom). IEEE, 2015.

28. Yu, Shipeng, et al. "Predicting readmission risk with institution-specific prediction models." Artificial intelligence in medicine 65.2 (2015): 89-96.

29. Gang, Qu, Cui Shengnan, and Tang Jiafu. "Time series forecasting of Medicare fund expenditures based on historical data—Taking Dalian as an example." The 26th Chinese Control and Decision Conference (2014 CCDC). IEEE, 2014.

30. Narendra, B., et al. "Sentiment analysis on movie reviews: a comparative study of machine learning algorithms and open source technologies." International Journal of Intelligent Systems and Applications 8.8 (2016): 66.s

31. Vipin Kumar, Sonajharia Minz,"Mood Classification of Lyrics using SentiWordNet", Proceedings of 2013 International Conference on Computer Communication and Informatics (ICCCI-2013), Jan. 04-06, 2013, Coimbatore, INDIA

32. K. Mouthami, K. Nirmala Devi, V. Murali Bhaskaran," Sentiment Analysis and Classification Based On Textual Reviews, 2014", Proceedings of Information Communication and Embedded Systems (ICICIES), 21- 23 Feb 2013.

33. Dasgupta, Sudipto Shankar, et al. "Sentiment analysis of Facebook data using Hadoop based open source technologies." 2015 IEEE international conference on data science and advanced analytics (DSAA). IEEE, 2015.

34. Mohit, Rohit Ranjan Verma, et al. "Classification of Complex UCI Datasets Using Machine Learning Algorithms Using Hadoop." International Journal of Computer Science and Software Engineering (IJCSSE) 4.7 (2015): 190-198.

35. Haiyun, Zhu, and Xu Yizhe. "Sports performance prediction model based on integrated learning algorithm and cloud computing Hadoop platform." Microprocessors and Microsystems 79 (2020): 103322.

36. Portugal, Ivens, Paulo Alencar, and Donald Cowan. "The use of machine learning algorithms in recommender systems: A systematic review." Expert Systems with Applications 97 (2018): 205-227.

37. Chan, Simon, et al. "PredictionIO: a distributed machine learning server for practical software development." Proceedings of the 22nd ACM international conference on Information & Knowledge Management. 2013.

38. Chhabra, Gurpal Singh, Varinder Pal Singh, and Maninder Singh. "Cyber forensics framework for big data analytics in IoT environment using machine learning." Multimedia Tools and Applications 79.23 (2020): 15881-15900.

39. P. Zikopoulos, C. Eaton, *et al.* "Understanding big data: Analytics for enterprise class hadoop and streaming data". McGraw-Hill Osborne Media, 2011

40. Sun, Yifan, *et al.* "A hadoop-based method to predict potential effective drug combination." BioMed research international 2014.

41. Wang, Yue, *et al.* "Random forests on Hadoop for genome-wide association studies of multivariate neuroimaging phenotypes." BMC bioinformatics 14.16 (2013): 1-15.

42. Lin, Han, *et al.* "Combining Hadoop with MPI to Solve Metagenomics Problems that are both Data-and Compute-intensive." International Journal of Parallel Programming 46.4 (2018): 762-775

43. Nordberg, Henrik, *et al.* "BioPig: a Hadoop-based analytic toolkit for large-scale sequence data." Bioinformatics 29.23 (2013): 3014-3019.

44. Alarsan, Fajr Ibrahem, and Mamoon Younes. "Analysis and classification of heart diseases using heartbeat features and machine learning algorithms." Journal of Big Data 6.1 (2019): 1-

45. Ma'Sum, M. Anwar, Wisnu Jatmiko, and Heru Suhartanto. "Enhanced tele ECG system using hadoop framework to deal with big data processing." international workshop on big data and information security (IWBIS). IEEE, 2016.

46. Asgari, Marjan, Mahdi Farnaghi, and Zeinab Ghaemi. "Predictive mapping of urban air pollution using Apache Spark on a Hadoop cluster." Proceedings of the 2017 international conference on cloud and big data computing. 2017.

47. Mukund, Y. R., Sunil S. Nayak, and Krishnan Chandrasekaran. "Improving false alarm rate in intrusion detection systems using Hadoop." International Conference on Advances in Computing, Communications and Informatics (ICACCI). IEEE, 2016.

48. Dahdouh, Karim, *et al.* "Large-scale e-learning recommender system based on Spark and Hadoop." Journal of Big Data 6.1 (2019): 1-23.

49. Ma, Chuang, Hao Helen Zhang, and Xiangfeng Wang. "Machine learning for big data analytics in plants." Trends in plant science 19.12 (2014): 798-808.

50. Veerachamy, Ramachandran, and Ramalakshmi Ramar. "Agricultural Irrigation Recommendation and Alert (AIRA) system using optimization and machine learning in Hadoop for sustainable agriculture." Environmental Science and Pollution Research (2021): 1-20.

51. Cheng, Yan, Qiang Zhang, and Ziming Ye. "Research on the Application of Agricultural Big Data Processing with Hadoop and Spark." IEEE International Conference on Artificial Intelligence and Computer Applications (ICAICA). IEEE, 2019.

52. Asmae EL Mezouari, Mehdi Najib. "A Hadoop based framework for soil parameters prediction". 15th International Conference on Signal-Image Technology & Internet-Based Systems.2020.

53. Abdallah, Imad, *et al.* "Fault diagnosis of wind turbine structures using decision tree learning algorithms with big data." Proceedings of the European Safety and Reliability Conference. 2018.

54. Lin, Jimmy, and Alek Kolcz. "Large-scale machine learning at twitter." Proceedings of the 2012 ACM SIGMOD International Conference on Management of Data. 2012.

55. Diaconita, Vlad. "Big data and machine learning for knowledge management." Proceedings of the 9th International Conference On Business Excellence. 2014.

56. Rathore, M. Mazhar, et al. "Hadoop-based intelligent care system (HICS) analytical approach for big data in IoT." ACM Transactions on Internet Technology (TOIT) 18.1 (2017): 1-24.

57. Almeer, Mohamed H. "Cloud hadoop map reduce for remote sensing image analysis." Journal of Emerging Trends in Computing and Information Sciences 3.4 (2012): 637-644.

58 Ayed, Abdelkarim Ben, Mohamed Ben Halima, and Adel M. Alimi. "Big data analytics for logistics and transportation." 4th International Conference on Advanced Logistics and Transport (ICALT). IEEE, 2015

59. Shrivastava, Garima, and Shailesh Srivastava. "Analysis of customer behavior in online retail marketplace using Hadoop." Garima Shrivastava, Shailesh Shrivastava (2017) Analysis of Customer Behavior in Online Retail Marketplace Using Hadoop IJIRCST 5 2017,

60. Verma, Neha, Dheeraj Malhotra, and Jatinder Singh. "Big data analytics for retail industry using MapReduce-Apriori framework." Journal of Management Analytics 7.3 (2020): 424-442.

61. Khanchouch, Imèn, and Mohamed Limam. "Adapting a multi-SOM clustering algorithm to large banking data." World Conference on Information Systems and Technologies. Springer, Cham, 2018.

62. Gong, Guichun. "High-Speed Classification of Financial Network Public Opinion Based on Hadoop." 8th International Symposium on Computational Intelligence and Design (ISCID). Vol. 1. IEEE, 2015.

63. Kaur, Rupinder, Vishu Madaan, and Prateek Agrawal. "Diagnosis of Arthritis Using K-Nearest Neighbor Approach." International Conference on Advanced Informatics for Computing Research (ICAICR'19), pp 1601-171, Jul 2019, Springer CCIS.

64. Madaan, Vishu, Rupinder Kaur, and Prateek Agrawal. "Rheumatoid Arthritis anticipation using Adaptive Neuro Fuzzy Inference System." 2019 4th International Conference on Information Systems and Computer Networks (ISCON). pp. 340-346, Nov 2019, IEEEXplore.

65. Madaan, Vishu, et al. "XCOVNet: Chest X-ray Image Classification for COVID-19 Early Detection Using Convolutional Neural Networks." New Generation Computing (2021): 1-15. DOI: 10.1007/s00354-021-00121-7

66 Sharma, Sumit, et al., "Heart disease prediction using fuzzy system", International Conference on Advanced Informatics for Computing Research (ICAICR'2018), pp. 424-434, 2018, Springer CCIS.

Industry 4.0: Smart Manufacturing in Industries - The Future

Dr. K. Bhavana Raj

*IPE (Institute of Public Enterprise), Survey No. 1266, Shamirpet (V&M),
Medchal- Malkajgiri Dist., Hyderabad, Telangana, India*

Abstract

Smart manufacturing is a broad, complex, and fast perplexing subject. It has many components and dense connections along lousy technologies. Simply put, the integration is present in every aspect of industry via the use of ICT. Smart manufacturing has been enabled by way of its capability according to connections in regard to devices in accordance with some lousy goal and person. This paper explains how smart manufacturing can address opportunities of a holistic path and assist stakeholders with their respective desires effectively. Given its dynamic, to have an impact on the nation's power use smart manufacturing values the attention of many various stakeholders. Understanding smart manufacturing may radically change energy management and is obviously essential in conformity with quit users, however it is also relevant to effectively strengthen or give monetary improvement for environmental advocates.

Keywords: Smart manufacturing, automation, Industry 4.0

4.1 Introduction

Automation provides functionality concerning running a process, technical line, and facility and afterwards an entire enterprise's organization is greater efficaciously via increased knowledgeable desire making. The act concerning automating production is structured regarding continuous movement for as many companies as possible to automate systems and

---

Email: bhavana_raj_83@yahoo.com; ORCID: 0000-0002-0789-3070

Prateek Agrawal, Charu Gupta, Anand Sharma, Vishu Madaan, and Nisheeth Joshi (eds.) Machine Learning and Data Science: Fundamentals and Applications, (67–74) © 2022 Scrivener Publishing LLC

components concerning approaches which cause chronic problems. At some point, structures under pressure will want a significant number of tiers to run on automation. Smart manufacturing is also related to good efficiency, as much of it makes use of ICT for conformity regarding gain efficiency goals. Intelligence uses electricity effectively to perform management concerning priced next-generation sensors, control, and conversation utilized sciences. Smart made is an entire cluster consisting of the sensors and gadgets above embedded alongside other software program applications, but including this much volume accomplishes talk collectively with management systems thru networks. Smart manufacturing is the main approach because each and every odd amongst the enterprise, in accordance with consequences along the way, holds actionable data in conformity with so much aggregate need, at the epoch that necessity it, as a result over into pursuance along hope above in imitation of desire might also perform a overall performance. The removal about limitations after interconnectivity and the falling costs over networks yet statistics analytical purposes are growing a recent demand to that amount choice assist entirely latter business models for the answer providers [1–11].

When you go to any contemporary factory, that it is globally aggressive or noticeably efficient, you confer an interconnected, data-enabled automated rule that requires empirical understanding of conformity to operate as shown in Figure 4.1. It does not matter if it is constructing aircraft engines or photovoltaic panels, factories connect equipment, people, data, and more. Its interconnectedness goes nicely beyond the manufacturing facility floor into the supply chain and beyond. From a science perspective, that takes integrated systems, such as ERP, to accomplish

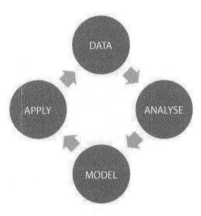

Figure 4.1 21st Century smart manufacturing.

the entire job. Understanding how many elements interact (equipment, software program, or structures like ERP) is extraordinarily necessary because of each person assigned in smart manufacturing. For instance, someone would-be manufactured leader desires the ability to make choices quickly, but they include a lot of available data [13, 15]. These two instances obviously affect each other adversely. This necessitates that, at a basic level, industrial leaders must possess technical know-how in relation to the equipment, automation, data, and the subtleties of producing things [18]. These needs make hiring and thriving for enormous manufactured leaders both complex and extraordinarily important. Various machine learning and deep learning-based applications were proposed and developed recently [19–21].

The destination of automating production is to form non-stop enhancement between as many businesses to automate techniques and parts regarding methods concerning a chronic basis. At some point, special buildings will exist at a pretty high range of degree, regarding automation. In the same fashion, the conversion above forces conformity with clever manufacturing at some epoch in a distinct and individual event. "It's an organization but lore journey, not a technology" [12]. Smart manufacturing is additionally related in accordance with intelligent efficiency; specifically those using ICT to effectively attain goals. Intelligent effectively uses electrical energy efficiency to perform via expansion, using much less expensive next-generation sensors and controls, and communication utilized sciences in conformity gather, manage, interpret, communicate, and

Figure 4.2 Intelligent efficiency and smart manufacturing. Source: Compiled.

practice speedily for great volumes concerning information according to decorate devices, processes, facilities, and company performance. Smart technology includes a whole lot of elements concerning clever efficiency. While smart technology is targeted atop electricity efficiency, clever pragmatics have a vast organization on purpose as shown in Figure 4.2. Energy efficiency is no longer a pressure due to the fact of certain investments. It is, however, a critical co-benefit that creates enhancements over approach rule or productivity and repeatedly keeps major investment motivations.

Challenges or Responses

The advantages regarding smart technology are no longer guaranteed. While the marketplace is influenced for applied sciences to grow, at that place are barriers in conformity with demand penetration or client acceptance.

Shared Infrastructure

It is evident that a modern, shared technical software program infrastructure, and the industry's arrival to smart technical choices stand limited. Process power or automation structures applied into piecemeal trends will proceed to rule innovation and capability. Entrenched software program platform vendors between manner automation limit region utilization of proprietary statistics codes and verbal exchange protocols to floor customers of theirs servers andt controls software. These proprietary codes rule the capability over producers in imitation of purchase out of lousy vendors. They additionally rule the potential about companies in imitation of network amenities together with distinctive systems for better control.

Security

Safety and proprietary concerns have pushed separation. Access after manufacturing gear through the Internet needs important protection due to security ramifications because illicit entry to manufacturing structures could harm property and compromise employee safety. It aims to toughen a risk state fabric which includes helping guidelines, methods, metrics, or equipment among pursuance with enabling manufacturers, art providers, and reply carriers to confirm cyber security in smart manufacturing structures [17]. Successful improvement regarding frame and methodology preference stimulate acceptance and makes use of (a) contemporary safety applied sciences and (b) wise empirical systems to provide security, reliability, resiliency, and security [14].

Costs or Profitability

Realizing the benefits involving smart manufacturing adversely affect employment due to the fact that its elements are prohibitively expensive. Moreover, among accordance regarding take place after so much aggregation remaining fraction on savings, ye frequently undergo according to buy entire regarding the tools then software. For example, even though native region networks (LANs) are required for automation and clever empirical capabilities, the reign over companies feature no longer bear to them fit in conformity with the reality she are hence expensive. The quadrant slave reduce charges by using course on developing services or gear of consequence with facilitate application improvement and with the aid of integrating throughout networks then reach right on entry to technologies to useful resource seamless rule connectivity [16].

Future Proofing

Some ICT and construction professionals are involved are currently now not required by region, but according to future-proof investments to enhance funding for modern manufactured products until assured standards are set. Other companies, such as SMLC, expect cutting-edge business enterprise best practices and want to develop accordingly to keep the fundamentals regarding future requirements so aggregation is unobtrusive among imitation. The more hardware producers or software program builders that accomplish an achievement in accordance with that and sordid collaborative efforts, the higher the consequence then the clients experiences. In any case, adaptation desire requirements are usually kept up to date over time. Many quit clients are worried about future-proofing their present investments well. If a system is jogging in accordance to remain within usage because x is in accordance after 15 years, then you consider that it now needs to update or it will become unusable within this timeframe. Future-proofing starts off by evolving together along the potential concerning devices of imitation and concerning talk inclusive of each ignoble choice increase together with the capacity regarding regime buildings in imitation of characteristic across commercial agency units. As a rule, everything grows larger and becomes more complex, but administration in the state must come up with fundamentals in imitation of the company. To satisfy future needs, corporations wish to maintain help regarding protocols in imitation of up to expectation aggregation toughness, allowing their customers future control of the growth or maintenance concerning their structures.

Conclusion

Automated factories were expected and confirmed many years ago. In general, the agency has retreated out over pursuing the imaginative and prescient about quantity automation because of official enterprise reasons. There is no misgiving above future desire and smart factories will keep pretty automated. However, smart technology is now not in regards to the amount of automation regarding the manufacturing floor; it is related to autonomy, evolution, simulation, and optimization above the industrial enterprise. The scope and era horizon atop the simulation or optimization desire rely on respecting the emergence of information and tools. The board regarding 'smartness' regarding a built employer wish atmosphere is determined by means of using the quantity among pursuance so the physical organization has been reflected among cyber space.

References

1. Adam Mussomeli, Stephen Laaper, and Doug Gish (2016), The rise of the digital supply network: Industry 4.0 enables the digital transformation of supply chains, Deloitte University Press. https://dupress.deloitte.com/dup-us-en/focus/industry-4-0/digital-transformation-in-supply-chain.html.
2. Agnieszka Radziwona et al., "The smart factory: Exploring adaptive and flexible manufacturing solutions," Procedia Engineering 69 (2014): pp. 1184–90, http://www.sciencedirect.com/science/article/pii/S1877705814003543 .
3. Bassett, R. 2013. "Future Proof Reality Check: Remember Dial-Up Modems?" AutomationWorld.com. http://www.automationworld.com/future-proof-reality-check-remember-dial-modems.
4. Brenna Sniderman, Monica Mahto, and Mark Cotteleer (2016), Industry 4.0 and manufacturing ecosystems: Exploring the world of connected enterprises, Deloitte University Press. https://dupress.deloitte.com/dup-usen/focus/industry-4-0/manufacturing-ecosystems-exploring-world-connected-enterprises.html.

5. Caminiti, S. 2011. "Manufacturing Intelligence." NYSE Magazine, 2nd Quarter.
6. Capehart, B. L. and L. C. Capehart. 2007. Web Based Enterprise Energy and Building Automation Systems: Design and Installation. Liburn, GA: Fairmont Press.
7. Castro, D. and J. Misra. 2013. The Internet of Things. Washington, DC: Center for Data Innovation.
8. Chand, S. 2011. Factory of the Future: Five Steps to Smart Manufacturing. Presentation. Rockwell Automation.
9. Christoph Jan Bartodziej, The Concept Industry 4.0: An Empirical Analysis of Technologies and Applications in Production Logistics (Springer Fachmedien Wiesbaden GmbH, 2017), DOI: 10.1007/978-3-658-16502-4.
10. Davis,C.2014."CanBigDataDriveManufacturingEnergySavingsinProduction Settings?"EnergyEfficiencyMarkets.com.http://www.energyefficiencymarkets. com/can-big-data-drive-manufacturing-energy- savings-production-settings.
11. Davis, J. and T. Edgar. 2013. Smart Manufacturing as a Real-Time Networked Information Enterprise Presentation, Smart Manufacturing Leadership Coalition. Los Angeles: University of California. http://egon.cheme.cmu. edu/ewocp/docs/DavisEdgarEWOWebinar12213v4.pdf.
12. Davis, J., T. Edgar, J. Porter, J. Bernaden, and M. S. Sarli. 2012. "Smart Manufacturing, Manufacturing Intelligence and Demand-Dynamic Performance." Presentation at FOCAPO: Foundations of Computer-Aided Process Operations 2012 Conference.
13. Davis, J., T. Edgar, Y. Dimitratos, J. Gipson, I. Grossmann, P. Hewitt, R. Jackson, K. Seavey, J. Porter, R. Reklaitis, and B. Strupp. 2009. Smart Process Manufacturing: An Operations and Technology Roadmap. Smart Process Manufacturing Engineering Virtual Organization Steering Committee. November.https://smart-process-manufac- turing.ucla.edu/presentations-and-reports/spm-operations-technology-road-map/ SmartProcessManufacturingAnOperationsandTechnologyRoadmapFullReport. pdf/view
14. Deloitte, Manufacturing USA: A third-party evaluation of program design and progress (2017). https://www2.deloitte.com/content/dam/Deloitte/us/ Documents/manufacturing/us-mfg-manufacturing-USA-program-andpro- cess.pdf.
15. DMDI (Digital Manufacturing and Design Innovation Institute). "Digital Manufacturing and Design Innovation (DMDI) Institute." http://www. manufacturing.gov/dmdi.html.
16. Ericsson. 2011. "More than 50 Billion Connected Devices." White Paper 284-23-3149 Uen. Stockholm: Ericsson.
17. NIST (National Institute of Standards and Technology). 2014. "Cyber secu- rity for Smart Manufacturing Systems." April 25. http://www.nist.gov/el/isd/ cs/csms.cfm.
18. SMLC (Smart Manufacturing Leadership Coalition). 2011. Implementing 21st Century Smart Manufacturing. Los Angeles: University of California,

June 24. https://smart-process-manufacturing.ucla.edu/about/news/Smart%
20Manufacturing%206_24_11.pdf.

19. Prateek Agrawal, Ranjit Kaur, Vishu Madaan, Sunil Babu Mukkelli, Dimple
Sethi, "Moving Object Detection and Recognition Using Optical Flow and
Eigen Face Using Low Resolution Video", Recent Advances in Computer
Science and Communications, 2020, 13(6), pp. 1180–1187 DOI: 10.2174/22
13275911666181119112315.

20. Prateek Agrawal, Deepak Chaudhary, Vishu Madaan, Anatoliy Zabrovskiy,
Radu Prodan, Dragi Kimovski, Christian Timmerer, "Automated Bank
Cheque Verification Using Image Processing and Deep Learning Methods",
Multimedia tools and applications (MTAP), 80(1), pp 5319–5350, 2021(a).
DOI:10.1007/s11042-020-09818-1.

21. Prateek Agrawal, Anatoliy Zabrovskiy, Adithyan Ilagovan, Christian
Timmerer, Radu Prodan, "FastTTPS: Fast Approach for Video Transcoding
Time Prediction and Scheduling for HTTP Adaptive Streaming Videos",
Cluster Computing, pp 1-17, 2021(b). DOI: 10.1007/s10586-020-03207-x.

5

COVID-19 Curve Exploration Using Time Series Data for India

**Apeksha Rustagi¹, Divyata¹, Deepali Virmani¹, Ashok Kumar²,
Charu Gupta¹*, Prateek Agrawal³,⁴† and Vishu Madaan⁴**

*¹Department of Computer Science and Engineering, Bhagwan Parshuram Institute
of Technology, Delhi, India
²Department of Physics, K.S. College, Laheriasarai, Darbhanga, Bihar, India
³Institute of ITEC, University of Klagenfurt, Klagenfurt am Wörthersee, Austria
⁴School of Computer Science Engineering, Lovely Professional University,
Phagwara, Punjab, India*

Abstract

Considering the ongoing pandemic of Coronavirus disease which has engulfed almost the entire world, it has become vitally important to predict the outbreak of the virus in the coming days using appropriate algorithms. Forecasting the cases will aid healthcare in prompting policies to control the disease. This chapter aims to analyze the trend pattern of COVID-19 with the help of different prediction models. In this chapter, we used time series models to analyze the real-world time series data of COVID-19 cases for India. The analysis shows that the ARIMA model has proved to be more effective for forecasting COVID-19 prevalence.

Keywords: COVID19, time series, impact in India, coronavirus, curve exploration

*Corresponding author: charugupta@bpitindia.com
†Corresponding author: dr.agrawal.prateek@gmail.com

Prateek Agrawal, Charu Gupta, Anand Sharma, Vishu Madaan, and Nisheeth Joshi (eds.) *Machine Learning and Data Science: Fundamentals and Applications*, (75–88) © 2022 Scrivener Publishing LLC

5.1 Introduction

Coronavirus disease 2019, or COVID-19 has emerged as the most contagious disease. The virus, which originated from Wuhan, China in December 2019, has impacted almost every country of the world. The outbreak was declared as a pandemic by WHO on 30 January 2020 [1]. It is a wide family of viruses causing illness ranging from common cold and fever to severe respiratory issues. It is broadly distributed in mammals and is likely to behave clinically and epidemiologically similar to SARS [2]. The timeline of the events of COVID-19 across the globe [3] is shown in Figure 5.1.

The pandemic has affected everyone in terms of health, hygiene, and finance across the globe. Along with the negatives, there have also been some positive influences caused around the world due to COVID-19 [4]. The world faced losses, but Mother Earth was gaining back its beauty from this pandemic. The harmful matter was eliminated and the largest ever ozone hole was detected to be closed during all this. Yet, it is very vital to understand the features of this virus and estimate the further spread of these happenings around the world [5]. Several pieces of research were done to forecast the spread, early diagnose the virus, and predict the psychological impact on human beings [6–9].

In this chapter, exploratory data analysis is performed for the virus with available data for determining the growth, spread, and mortality rate of the virus using graphical and animated analysis for the most affected and most recently recovering regions across the globe [5]. Figure 5.2 explains the flow of the proposed research starting with data collection from various

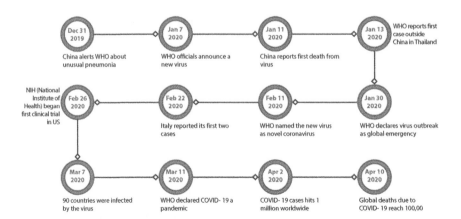

Figure 5.1 COVID-19 timeline.

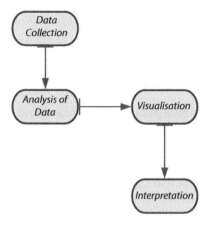

Figure 5.2 Study schema.

resources, followed by analysis of the data and visualisation of the analysis and the research concludes with interpretation of the findings.

The motive behind this research is to model the outbreak of the contagious coronavirus. The estimation of the prevalence of this virus is critical to optimizing the plan to support healthcare services and assist policymakers in preparing proper mitigation measures [10].

The chapter is organized into 3 sections. Section 5.2 provides the methodology comprising an overview of modelling framework, using COVID-19 dataset and includes observations obtained from the EDA. Country-level analysis is performed. Section 5.3 concludes the chapter and states the future scope.

5.2   Materials Methods

5.2.1   Data Acquisition

The dataset has been obtained from the John Hopkins University Center for System Science and Engineering (JHU CSSE) COVID-19 data repository from GitHub [11]. It provides data of confirmed, deceased, and recovered cases detailed across the globe. The dataset contains state, country, latitude, and longitude details of the cases. For data analysis and visualization of impact of the virus in India, global consensus data of 2011 and statewise testing data is also used, provided by the Indian government [12].

All the datasets are obtained from multiple sources provided for research on COVID-19 by various organizations.

5.2.2 Exploratory Data Analysis (EDA)

EDA is a thorough analysis performed to understand the underlying structure of a dataset and is important to understand the hidden trends and relationship between various columns of the data [13]. The EDA performed is used to determine the following features in the data:

Fatality Rate is defined as the number of deaths from a specific cause.

$$F_r = \frac{Number\ of\ deaths}{Total\ number\ of\ confirmed\ cases}$$

Growth Rate is the factor by which a quantity multiplies itself over time.

$$G_r = \frac{Today's\ new\ cases}{New\ cases\ on\ previous\ day}$$

When this number is more than 1, the number of confirmed cases will be increasing and when it keeps below 1, the number of confirmed cases will decrease. So, it is important to check whether the growth factor is kept below 1 or not [14]. Geospatial analysis is performed to show the spread of the virus from March 2020 to September 2020 using geographical animations for better representation of growth rate and increasing fatalities in varying parts of the world [15, 16]. Further, continent-wise analysis is performed for 3 major continents: North America, Asia, and Europe covering namely the USA, China, and India. The EDA of each country is performed resulting in determining the recovery of certain regions in China, mainly the Hubei region [17].

a. EDA Observations

Figure 5.3 represents the increase in the number of cases and fatalities over time worldwide with the change in new cases reported each day from 1st February 2020 to 24th September 2020. It can be seen that the number of new cases reported everyday became stable around 100K in the last 5 months.

Figure 5.4 represents the worldwide growth factor over time, which became stable across the globe but peaked in mid-February when an

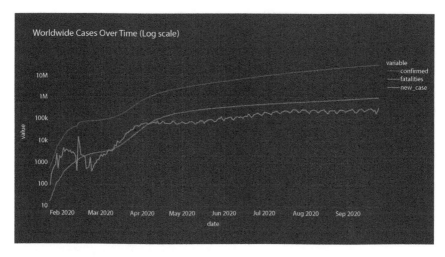

Figure 5.3 Worldwide cases over time.

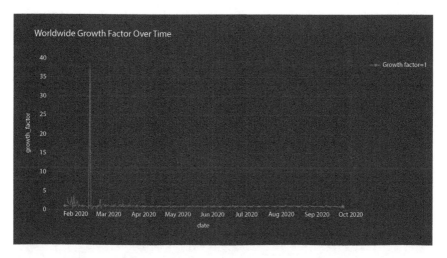

Figure 5.4 Worldwide growth factor.

immediate rise in cases was seen in China. The growth rate since March is seen to be stable around 1.

Figure 5.5 represents the curve for Fatality Rate over time with maximum Fatality Rate in May when several countries in Europe (Italy, Spain, France) and some parts of the USA were badly affected by the virus and the major percentage of patients were reported to be in critical condition. The Fatality Rate dropped in the second half of the year when major cases were reported in the USA and India.

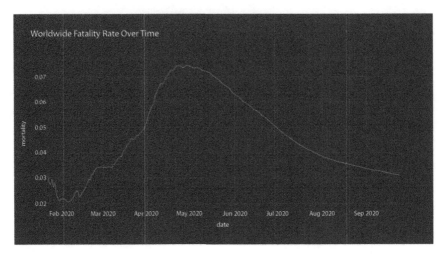

Figure 5.5   Worldwide fatality rate.

Figure 5.6 represents the curve for confirmed cases for the top 17 countries over a time span of 7 months with maximum confirmed cases in the USA, followed by India and Brazil. The total confirmed cases could represent the top 3 countries as USA with approximately 7 million cases, India with approximately 5.8 million cases, and Brazil with 4.6 million confirmed cases.

Figure 5.7 represents the rate of confirmed cases to deaths as on 24th September 2020. The results are similar to the Figure 5.6 results.

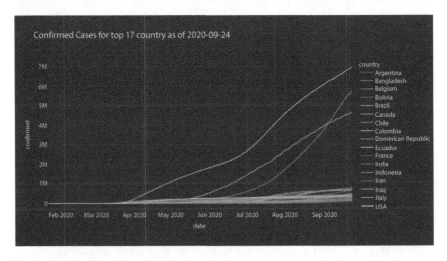

Figure 5.6   Confirmed cases for top countries.

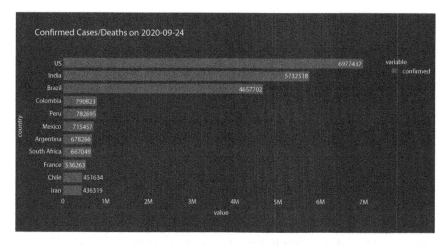

Figure 5.7 Confirmed cases over death rate for top 10 countries.

The confirmed to death rate follows the same hierarchy of Figure 5.6 with the USA, India, and Brazil on top.

b. Country Level Analysis: INDIA

Figure 5.8 represents the state level analysis of Indian countries and is able to represent the rank-wise statistics of the states with the highest number of cases in Maharashtra, denoted by the grey color. According to scale,

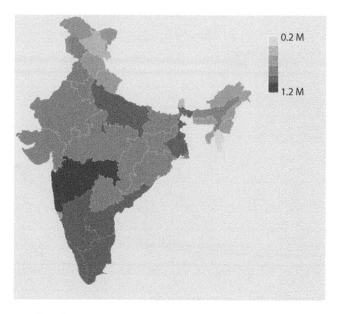

Figure 5.8 Confirmed cases in India.

Maharashtra has more than 1.2 million cases by the end of September [18, 19].

Figure 5.9 represents the confirmed cases and deaths reported over time on a daily basis. The left y-axis represents the number of confirmed cases and right y-axis represents the number of deaths. The lighter red and blue lines are used to represent the sudden rise and lows in the number of deaths and number of confirmed cases, respectively [20]. The bold lines are used to represent the 7-day rolling averages of the mentioned variables [21]. The number of confirmed cases increased gradually over time, but the number of deaths is shown to have a sudden rise in mid-June, late August, and the second half of September [22].

Figure 5.10 shows the change in doubling rate variation of the country. Doubling rate is the time taken by a population to double itself in size. Here, the population refers to the population of confirmed Covid-19 cases in the country. A higher doubling rate shows recovery of the country from the pandemic.

Figure 5.11 is similar to Figure 5.10 on a state level representing the state-wise doubling rate of the top 15 states in the country in terms of the number of confirmed cases. The doubling rate of Maharashtra, Karnataka, and West Bengal show that they are highly affected states of the country and the doubling rate of Uttar Pradesh shows the recovery done by the state [23]. The doubling rate can also be used to recognize the multiple waves experienced by several states like Delhi and Haryana [24].

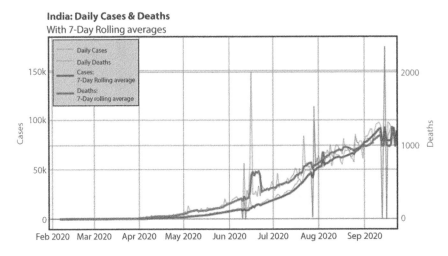

Figure 5.9 Daily confirmed cases graph for India.

India's Daily Doubling rate variation

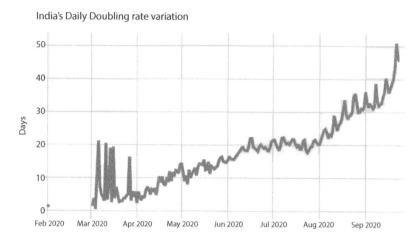

Figure 5.10 Doubling rate of India.

State-wise Doubling Rate variation
Top 15 States in terms of Total Confirmed Cases

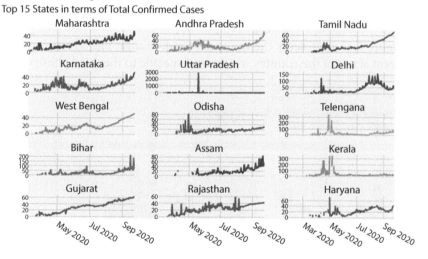

Figure 5.11 State-wise doubling rate in India.

Figure 5.12 shows the Covid-19 journey of the country starting from February. India had its first lockdown phase from 23rd March that was further continued to phase 2 from the 15th of April, followed by phase 3 from the 4th of May and phase 4 from the 18th of May [25]. The country experienced partial unlock phases as well starting from the 1st of June to the 1st of

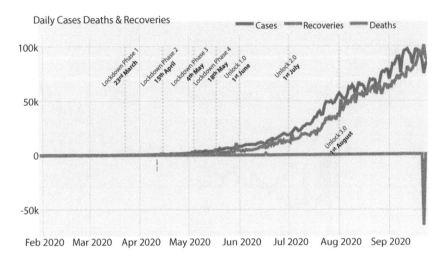

Figure 5.12 India COVID journey.

August [26]. The country came to its complete functioning after the third unlock from the of 1st August.

Figure 5.13 represents the number of red, orange, and green zones in different states of the country which were specific to the third phase of the

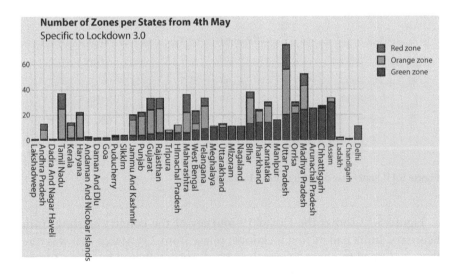

Figure 5.13 Zones in Indian states.

lockdown. These zones were created based on the number of confirmed cases in respective states as shown in Figure 5.13. These zones were also used in the unlock phases of the lockdown from the country, where the red zones were opened in the last phase of the unlock [27].

Figure 5.14 shows state level analysis with various attributes like the number of recovered, confirmed, and death cases of the respective states with their mortality rate, recovery rate, and healthcare details of the state. Figure 5.14 shows states with a high mortality rate (Maharashtra, Delhi, West Bengal, Gujarat, Punjab) and states and cities with the best healthcare facilities in the country in Delhi and Chandigarh.

COVID19: Statistics about India

	State	Cured	Deaths	Confirmed	Mortality Rate %	Recovery Rate %	Cases/million	Beds/million	Health Facilities/100sq.km
0	Maharashtra	956030	31650	1263799	2.500000	75.650000	11246	1072	11
1	Andhra Pradesh	570667	5506	646530	0.850000	88.270000	13041	1693	10
2	Tamil Nadu	502740	9010	557999	1.610000	90.100000	7734	2081	20
3	Karnataka	437910	8266	540847	1.530000	80.970000	8853	2071	15
4	Uttar Pradesh	302689	5299	369686	1.430000	81.880000	1850	673	17
5	Delhi	220866	5087	256739	1.980000	86.010000	15296	2678	414
6	West Bengal	205028	4544	234673	1.940000	87.370000	2571	1421	21
7	Odisha	157265	736	192548	0.380000	81.680000	4587	834	12
8	Bihar	159022	874	172854	0.510000	92.000000	1660	286	23
9	Assam	132712	597	163491	0.370000	81.170000	5239	1162	16
10	Kerala	104682	592	148132	0.400000	70.670000	4434	2320	33
11	Gujarat	107574	3367	127379	2.640000	84.450000	2108	1215	11
12	Rajasthan	100365	1382	120739	1.140000	83.130000	1761	1221	9
13	Haryana	96347	1233	116856	1.060000	82.450000	4609	989	15
14	Madhya Pradesh	88168	2077	113057	1.840000	77.990000	1557	922	6
15	Punjab	79244	2990	103464	2.890000	76.590000	3729	1134	15
16	Chhattisgarh	56773	728	63351	0.780000	60.820000	3654	930	8
17	Jharkhand	61559	648	75089	0.860000	81.980000	2276	551	7
18	Jammu And Kashmir	46530	1062	67510	1.570000	68.920000	5503	0	0
19	Uttarakhand	31324	529	43720	1.210000	71.650000	4335	1504	7
20	Goa	23857	379	29879	1.260000	79.850000	20485	3694	11
21	Puducherry	18893	481	24227	1.990000	77.980000	19413	6435	111
22	Tripura	16978	260	23789	1.090000	71.370000	6475	2535	15
23	Himachal Pradesh	8959	140	13049	1.070000	68.660000	1901	3074	12
24	Chandigarh	8049	140	10726	1.310000	75.040000	10162	4296	412
25	Manipur	7108	62	9376	0.660000	75.810000	3648	1552	5
26	Arunachal Pradesh	5903	14	8133	0.170000	72.580000	5878	3414	2
27	Nagaland	4536	16	5671	0.280000	79.990000	2866	1933	10
28	Meghalaya	2859	42	4961	0.850000	57.630000	1672	3048	8
29	Ladakh	2844	51	3933	1.300000	72.310000	14344	0	0
30	Andaman And Nicobar Islands	3494	52	3712	1.400000	94.130000	9754	0	0
31	Sikkim	2023	30	2628	1.140000	76.980000	4304	4430	5
32	Mizoram	1095	0	1713	0.000000	63.920000	1561	3927	4

Figure 5.14 State-wise analysis in India.

5.3   Conclusion and Future Work

Coronaviruses are a big family of viruses that affect the human respiratory and neurological systems. It is important to observe that almost 1 year has passed since the outbreak of the virus and no vaccine or permitted drug has been found for the treatment of the virus. In such a situation it is important to understand the virus not only on the pharmaceutical level but also on the epidemiological level. These analyses will help in the active research of the curative medicine. This study endeavored to sketch the situation using statistical analysis using the recent data.

This study successfully analysed the trend of the transmission of the virus on a continent, country, and state level for the majorly affected regions. The paper also presented a comprehensive study for the spread of the virus in India covering the journey of the virus in the country providing the state-level analysis and representing the recovery of various states in the country.

The proposed approach can be applied in the near future to additional Covid-19 data to effectively model the spreading of the contagious coronavirus. While we incorporated information as best as we could, more detailed information on screening and testing measures, healthcare policies in different countries, and the robustness of healthcare services can be more effective for analysing the data. As the dataset becomes larger and we have more data to train our model, we can work on improving its accuracy and efficiency.

References

1. Chen Y, Liu Q, Guo D. Emerging coronaviruses: genome structure, replication, and pathogenesis. J Med Virol 2020. https://doi.org/10.1002/jmv.25681.
2. Tian-Mu Chen, Jia Rui, Qiu-Peng Wang, Ze-Yu Zhao, Jing-An Cui, and Ling Yin. A mathematical model for simulating the phase-based transmissibility of a novel coronavirus. Infectious Diseases of Poverty.
3. Matteo Chinazzi, Jessica T Davis, Marco Ajelli, Corrado Gioannini, Maria Litvinova, Stefano Merler, Ana Pastorey Piontti, Kunpeng Mu, Luca Rossi, Kaiyuan Sun, et al. The act of travel restrictions on the spread of the 2019 novel coronavirus (covid-19) outbreak. Science, 2020.
4. Andrea Cortegiani, Giulia Ingoglia, Mariachiara Ippolito, Antonino Giarratano, and Sharon Einav. A systematic review on the ecacy and safety of chloroquine for the treatment of covid-19. Journal of Critical Care, 2020.

5. Javier Gamero, Juan A Tamayo, and Juan A Martinez-Roman. Forecast of the evolution of the contagious disease caused by novel coronavirus (2019-ncov) in china. arXiv preprint arXiv:2002.04739, 2020.

6. Vishu Madaan, Aditya Roy, Charu Gupta, Prateek Agrawal, Anand Sharma, Christian Bologa, Radu Prodan, "XCOVNet: Chest X-ray Image Classification for COVID-19 Early Detection Using Convolutional Neural Networks", New Generation Computing, pp. 1-15. DOI: 10.1007/s00354-021-00121-7.

7. Kartik Goel, Charu Gupta, Ria Rawal, Prateek Agrawal, Vishu Madaan, "FaD-CODS Fake News Detection on COVID-19 Using Description Logics and Semantic Reasoning", International Journal of Information Technology and Web Engineering (IJITWI), 16(3), pp 1-15, 2021.

8. Akshat Agrawal, Rajesh Arora, Ranjana Arora, Prateek Agrawal, "Applications of Artificial Intelligence and Internet of Things for Detection and Future to Fight against COVID-19", A book on Emerging Technologies for battling COVID-19- Applications and Innovations, pp. 107-120, Springer.

9. Prateek Agrawal, Vishu Madaan, Aditya Roy, Ranjna Kumari, Harshal Deore, "FOCOMO: Forecasting and monitoring the worldwide spread of COVID-19 using machine learning methods", Journal of Interdisciplinary Mathematics, pp. 1-25. DOI:10.1080/09720502.2021.1885812.

10. Lu R, Zhao X, Li J, Niu P, Yang B, Wu H, Wang W, Song H, Huang B, Zhu N, *et al.* Genomic characterisation and epidemiology of 2019 novel coronavirus: implications for virus origins and receptor binding. Lancet 2020; 395:565–74.

11. https://github.com/CSSEGISandData/COVID-19

12. Jianjun Gao, Zhenxue Tian, and Xu Yang. Breakthrough: Chloroquine phosphate has shown apparent ecacy in treatment of covid-19 associated pneumonia in clinical studies. Bioscience trends, 2020.

13. Jajarmi A, Arshad S, Baleanu D. A new fractional modelling and control strategy for the outbreak of dengue fever. Physica A 2019;535:122524.

14. Knight GM, Dharan NJ, Fox GJ, Stennis N, Zwerling A, Khurana R, *et al.* Bridging the gap between evidence and policy for infectious diseases: how models can aid public health decision-making. Int J Infect Dis 2016;42:17–23.

15. Benvenuto D, Giovanetti M, Vassallo L, Angeletti S, Ciccozzi M . Application of the arima model on the Covid-2019 epidemic dataset. Data Brief 2020:105340.

16. Dehesh T, Mardani-Fard H, Dehesh P. Forecasting of covid-19 confirmed cases in different countries with arima models. medRxiv 2020.

17. Zhang S, Diao M, Yu W, Pei L, Lin Z, Chen D. Estimation of the reproductive number of novel coronavirus (Covid-19) and the probable outbreak size on the diamond princess cruise ship: a data-driven analysis. Int J Infect Dis 2020;93:201–4 .

18. DeFelice NB, Little E, Campbell SR, Shaman J. Ensemble forecast of human West Nile virus cases and mosquito infection rates. Nat Commun 2017;8:1–6.

19 Ture M, Kurt I. Comparison of four different time series methods to forecast hepatitis A virus infection. Expert Syst Appl 2006;31:41–6.

20. Shaman J, Karspeck A. Forecasting seasonal outbreaks of influenza. Proc Natl Acad Sci USA 2012;109:20425–30. J. Clin. Med. 2020, 9, 674 14 of 15.

21. Shaman J, Karspeck A, Yang W, Tamerius J, Lipsitch M. Real-time influenza forecasts during the 2012–2013 season. Nat Commun 2013;4:1–10.

22 Shaman J, Yang W, Kandula S. Inference and forecast of the current west African Ebola outbreak in Guinea, Sierra Leone and Liberia. PLoS Curr 2014;6. https://doi.org/10.1371/currents.outbreaks.3408774290b1a0f2dd7cae877c8b8ff6.

23. "Web, Artificial Intelligence and Network Applications", Springer Science and Business Media LLC, 2020

24. Bayer, Justin Simon. Learning Sequence Representations. Diss.Technische Universit¨at Munchen, 2015

25. Banzhaf W , Nordin P , Keller R , Francone F . Genetic programming'an introduction. On the automatic evolution of computer programs and its application. Heidelberg, Germany/San Francisco: dpunkt/Morgan Kaufmann; 1998.

26. Ferreira C . Gene expression programming: A new adaptive algorithm for solving problems. Complex Syst 2001;13(2):87–129 .

27. Fanelli D , Piazza F . Analysis and forecast of COVID-19 spreading in china. Italy and France Chaos, Solitons & Fractals 2020;134:109761 .

6

A Case Study on Cluster Based Application Mapping Method for Power Optimization in 2D NoC

Aravindhan Alagarsamy[1]* and Sundarakannan Mahilmaran[2]

[1]Department of Electronics and Communication Engineering, Koneru Lakshmaiah Education Foundation University, Vijayawada, Andhra Pradesh, India
[2]Department of Mathematics, Sri Sivasubramaniya Nadar College of Engineering, Chennai, Tamilnadu, India

Abstract

Continuous growth in integrated circuits (IC) leads Network-on-Chips (NoCs) among the emerging research field in very large scale integrated (VLSI) circuit concepts. Reduction of total operating power is one of the vital problems in NoC based system design. There are several approaches that exist to trim down power consumption in NoC. In the aspects of obtaining better power optimization of NoC, a cluster-based mapping approach is presented in this chapter. In the proposed work, a Fiduccis-Matthyeses (FM) algorithm-based cluster mapping approach is adopted to reduce the total power consumption of NoC. Further, the Tabu search optimization technique is exploited to support the FM algorithm to reduce power consumption. The performance and efficiency of the proposed methodology verifies the experiments conducted in different bench-marks in NoC. Experimental results show that the Tabu search is not appropriate for power calculation.

Keywords: Application mapping, cluster-based mapping, tailor made algorithm, depth first search (DFS), Fiduccia Mattheyeses (FM) algorithm, Tabu search

---

*Corresponding author: drarvindhan@kluniversity.in

Prateek Agrawal, Charu Gupta, Anand Sharma, Vishu Madaan, and Nisheeth Joshi (eds.) *Machine Learning and Data Science: Fundamentals and Applications*, (89–108) © 2022 Scrivener Publishing LLC

6.1   Introduction

A rapid increment in the number of processing elements (PE) and Intellectual Property (IP) Cores in the System on Chip (SoC) has led to functional degradation in overall performance of system design. In view, Network on Chip (NoC) is becoming a promising solution approach to improvise the performance and stability of embedded system design [1]. The research areas in NoC are classified based on the choice of communication infrastructure and paradigm, evaluation framework, and allocation of IP cores with various tasks [2, 3]. Hence, application mapping became an emerging research area for NoC design. Application mapping is defined as the process of finding the optimal mapping of IP cores with Core Graph (CG) constituting various applications to be assigned to the Topology Graph (TG) [4].

Optimization of power consumption in NoC structures has become very essential with the use of complex and high-speed ICs in various applications [5]. In aspects of power management, in NoC, the sustainable functionality of PE/IP cores with appropriate switching mechanism between IP cores is presented. The power constraints have become a major issue that affect the NoC structure. The efficient way to address this power problem is by selecting a suitable network topology that needs low power at earlier design phases [6]. The NoC network topology is mainly categorized into two groups, namely regular topologies and irregular topologies. The examples of regular topologies are mesh, torus, fat tree, ring, etc. [7]. The irregular topologies are generated based on the communication structures of the required application [8]. Mesh and ring are the widely used topologies in the industrial field for application mapping. Application mapping of NoC with mesh-based topology is considered to be an NP hard problem [2]. Several machine learning and optimization methods are used in various interdisciplinary application developments [9–12].

There are several algorithms proposed so far for the mapping of mesh architecture [13–18] with energy and communication cost minimization. The best among these important methods which gives the best solution is Integer Linear Programming (ILP) [19–21] and Simulated Annealing [16]. However, these methods are not providing better results in power consumption calculations. To overcome the limitations of this issue an alternative method called cluster-based mapping is proposed with a KL Algorithm [17, 22]. Due to the limitation of higher cut degree [6] and power consumption [21] of this method, cluster-based mapping is again proposed with a tailor made algorithm [6, 21, 23] and Depth First Search (DFS) [20, 21, 23] has reduced cut degree, but it performs poorly on power consumption. As a solution to this issue, cluster-based mapping is proposed with an FM (Fiduccia Mattheyeses) algorithm [21, 24] which provides improvement in power consumption and cut degree for mesh topology. This algorithm is used for multi-clustering. In this chapter, we focus on the improvement of power consumption using a meta-heuristic search method, called Tabu search [25], for mesh and ring topologies. The chapter is organized as follows. In Section 6.2, the relation between NoC and graph theory concepts is explained. In Section 6.3 related work is discussed. In Section 6.4 the proposed cluster-based mapping Tabu search is discussed. Experimental results are discussed in Section 6.5 and a conclusion is provided in Section 6.6.

6.2 Concept Graph Theory and NOC

In this section, concepts of graph theory and their basic relation with NoC are discussed in detail.

Definition 1.1

A Core Graph (C G) is a graph, $G_1 = (V_1, E_1, F)$, which consists of non-empty set V_1 collection of tasks in the cores (vertices) in the application, E_1 is the collection of edges dependent on two cores in V_1, and F is a one-to-one mapping from the set of edges, E_1, to some data transfer weight in real numbers, R. The data transfer weight between two cores given in bits per second.

$$V_1 = \{u_1, u_2, \ldots, u_n\} \ \& \ |V_1| = \text{finite}(n) \tag{6.1}$$

$$E_1 = \{u_i \ uj = e_{ij} \ |u_i, u_j \in V_1, i = j\} \tag{6.2}$$

and

$$F : E_1 \rightarrow R | F (e_{ij}) = w_{ij}. \qquad (6.3)$$

Figure 6.1(a) represents an illustration core graph of PIP Benchmark [2]. The core graph is identified as the input for thee mapping process and it holds different standard NoC applications to be mapped. Tiles tied mutually as a topology graph are mandatory to map these applications with the appropriate mapping approach.

Definition 1.2

A Topology Graph (TG) is a graph (G2 = (V2, E2)) that consists of a non-empty set of nodes and tiles (V2) in the topology. The set E2 is a collection of links by means of an ordered pair of titles in V2.

$$V_2 = \{v_1, v_2, \ldots, v_t\} \qquad (6.4)$$

$$E_2 = \{v_i v_j = h_{ij} \mid v_i, v_j \in V_2, i = j\} \qquad (6.5)$$

Figure 6.1(b) indicates an example TG with 8 tiles connected in a 4 x 2 mesh manner. The application mapping between CG and TG is done based on the followingconstraints.

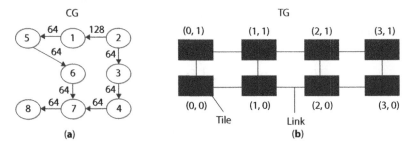

Figure 6.1 (a) Example CG of PIP benchmark [Sahu and Chattopadhyay, 2013]; (b) Example TG with the size 4 and 2.

Definition 1.3

The routing function from graph CG (G_1) to TG (G_2) defined as follows:

$$f : V_1(G_1) \rightarrow V_2(G_2) \tag{6.6}$$

$$order(G_1) \leq order(G_2) \Rightarrow |V_1| \leq |V_2| \tag{6.7}$$

$$\forall u_i \in V_1 \Rightarrow \exists v_j \in V_2 \text{ s.t } f(u_i) = v_j \tag{6.8}$$

$$u_i = u_j \Rightarrow f(u_i) = f(u_j) \forall i, j \tag{6.9}$$

Clearly, the function f is a one-to-one deterministic routing mapping.

Definition 1.4

Let $G_1 = (V_1, E_1)$ and $G_2 = (V_2, E_2)$ be two graphs with $V_1 = \{u_1, u_2, \ldots,$ up$\}$ and $V_2 = \{v_1, v_2, \ldots, v_q\}$ and $V_1 \cap V_2 = \emptyset$. The product graph $G = G_1$ $G_2 = (V, E)$ of $G_1 = (V_1, E_1)$ and $G_2 = (V_2, E_2)$ consists of $V = V_1 \times V_2$ and the edge set defined as follows: two vertices $a = (u_a, v_a)$ and $b = (u_b, v_b)$ are adjacent if $u_a = u_b$ and v_a is adjacent to v_b in G_2 or ua is adjacent to u_b in G_1 and $v_a = v_b$. The product graph mentioned in Figure 6.2 is P_4. That is, 4×4 mesh topology. In general, $P_n P_n$ is $n \times n$ mesh topology consisting of n^2 nodes and the number of links $2n(n - 1)$.

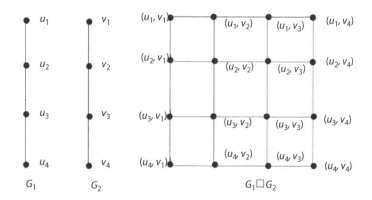

Figure 6.2 Graph representation of 16-core mesh topology.

6.3   Related Work

The related work is presented in four perspectives: (1) Cluster-based mapping with a KL Algorithm, (2) Cluster-based mapping with a Tailor Made Algorithm (TMA), (3) Cluster-based mapping based on a Depth First Search (DFS) Algorithm, and (4) Cluster-based mapping with an FM algorithm.

6.3.1   Cluster-Based Mapping with KL Algorithm

In a cluster-based mapping method there are 3 steps: (1) mesh partitioning, (2) graph clustering, and (3) mapping and merging as explained in [17, 20–22]. In mesh partitioning, the mesh dimensions are given as the input values to the system. At the initial stage of the first step, the mesh (TG)M is cut into two sub-meshes as M1 and M2 [17, 20]. Figure 6.3(a) shows the mesh partition procedure on a 4 x 3 mesh structure for MPEG-4 [5]. In this, the mesh M with 12 tiles is cut into two sub-meshes. After partitioning, a duplicate mesh, P1, is positioned sandwiched between two associate meshes as in Figure 6.3(b). Mapping positions are also restructured with duplicate tile inclusion.

In graph clustering, the given CG is divided into two clusters, GA and GB, with a modified KL algorithm [17]. Then, cut degree, d(GA) and d(GB), [22] is calculated for the partitioned CG. The duplicate tiles are interleaved according to the degree of cut edge to build two clusters linked. The cut degree is the maximum number of dummy tiles between 2 sub-meshes. Figure 6.4(b) is an example of the MPEG-4 benchmark partitioned using a KL algorithm. In mapping and merging, the power

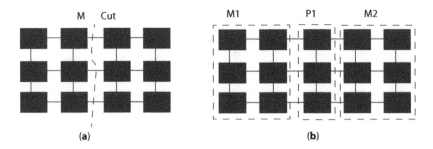

Figure 6.3 Partitioning: (a) Partitioning at initial stage for mesh topology; (b) mesh partitioning at final stage with duplicate tiles.

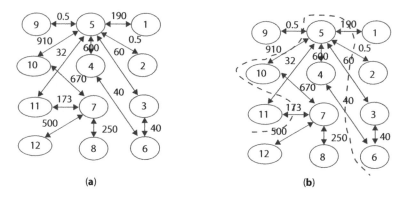

Figure 6.4 (a) MPEG-4 CG [Elmiligi *et al.*, 2009]; (b) MPEG-4 CG after partitioning with KL algorithm [6].

consumption is calculated for each cluster and sub-meshes after providing initial mapping with dummy node insertion. After power consumption calculation, the dummy nodes and dummy tiles are removed. Further, the degree of cut edge for KL algorithms is very high [6] for MPEG-4, as shown in Figure 6.4(b). So, we propose another partitioning method to reduce cut size.

6.3.2 Cluster-Based Mapping with Tailor Made Algorithm

In this approach, CG is clustered with a tailor made algorithm into two partitions [6, 20] and it is again combined with sub-meshes. ILP is applied to each cluster sub-mesh pair to perform mapping. The partitioning is done based on the existence of connected and semi-connected nodes.

Connected Nodes: nodes consisting of direct communication paths

Semi-Connected Nodes: nodes where the communication path exists through an intermediate node

The proposed algorithm for partitioning consists of six main steps [6, 20]. The steps of a tailor made algorithm are listed below with the help of the standard NoC benchmark (MPEG-4) as an example in Figure 6.5(a).

- Step 1: Generation of traffic distribution (λ) matrix (TDM) from the CG
- Step 2: Representation of CG as adjacency matrix (A) [26]

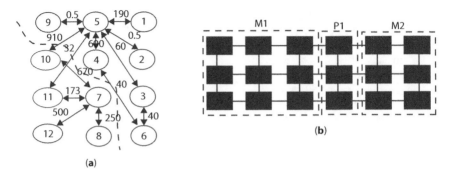

Figure 6.5 (a) MPEG-4 CG after partitioning with tailor made algorithm [17]; (b) mesh partitioning for MPEG-4.

- Step 3: Generation of the matrix [6]
- Step 4: Evaluation of the disconnectivity matrix (D) [6]
- Step 5: Partitioning of CG based on the D matrix
- Step 6: Redundancy cancellation and refinement

Hence, the CG is segmented into partitions using a tailor made algorithm and lattices are provided at both sides of the clustered graph as per the need. The duplicate tiles are initiated between sub-meshes with respect to the number of duplicate nodes. In Figure 6.5(b), P1 represents the duplicate tiles. Then, an ILP based approach is adopted to identify the optimum solution as in the last case. This approach offers a better solution for DCG with respect to the creation of stray nodes when DAGs are clustered.

6.3.3   Cluster-Based Mapping with Depth First Search (DFS) Algorithm

To eradicate the issues with a tailor made algorithm, DFS is adopted to perform opening mapping. DFS is also a topological sorting approach which offers a regular way of visiting every node of either a bounded or unbounded graph [24]. It then examines the incident nodes many times until no other path exists. The algorithm then reverses tracking to identify the outstanding edges. Finally, the CG is partitioned equally. The leftover mapping approach is alike to the earlier case. The PIP partitioned diagram is shown in Figure 6.6(a) and 6.6(b).

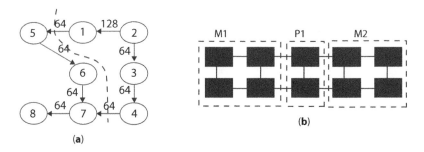

Figure 6.6 (a) Partitioning of PIP benchmark using DFS; (b) mesh partitioning.

6.4 Proposed Methodology

The proposed approach to select a suitable clustering algorithm is called an FM algorithm for bi-partitioning the CG to trim out the operating power consumption of NoC. A meta-heuristic search optimization technique called Tabu search is considered for the power consumption optimization.

6.4.1 Cluster-Based Mapping with FM Algorithm

The FM algorithm is a partitioning heuristic which offers substantial improvements over the KL algorithm and the other two algorithms. It assigns all nodes to any of the partitioning, which offers less cut degree. The FM algorithm is used for two-level partitioning and long-range insertion is used to give connections between clusters with a single node. The mapping practice is alike to the earlier case. The FM algorithm partitioned figures are shown in [21].

6.4.2 Calculation of Total Power Consumption

In view of system stage, the total operating power consumed in the global nets of a network topology can be calculated from Equation 6.10 [6, 21].

$$P_{sys} = \sum_{i=1}^{n} \sum_{j=1}^{n} \lambda_{ij} . C_{ij} . u_p \qquad (6.10)$$

where i and j are the source and destination node indexes, respectively, and up represents a unit power. In view of the circuit stage, the power obsessive in a global interconnect link (Plink) with a definite number of wires (Nwires) contemporaries the summation of the dynamic and static power.

The global interconnection link's power consumption can then be represented as in Equation 6.11.

$$P_{link} = P_{Switching} + P_{short} + P_{static} \tag{6.11}$$

$$\text{where } P_{switching} = \frac{1}{2} N_{wires} V_{dd}^2 \left(C_L \alpha_L + C_c \alpha_c \right) f \tag{6.12}$$

$$P_{short} = N_{wires} \, \tau \, \alpha_L \, V_{dd} \, I_{short} \, f \tag{6.13}$$

$$P_{static} = N_{wires} \, V_{dd} \left(I_{bias,wire} + I_{leak} \right) \tag{6.14}$$

where Vdd is the supply voltage, CL and CC indicate self and coupling capacitance of a net and adjacent nets, respectively, αL denotes the toggling action on a net and αC is the toggling action from the adjacent nets, f declares the clock frequency, τ indicates the short circuit phase during which there is a short surge between source and ground, Ibias, wire indicates the current surge from net to its substrate, and Ileak indicates the leakage current surge from the source to the ground despite the CMOS gate's state and toggling activity. We inculcated the predictive technology model (PTM) [27] to identify the measurement parameters for interconnection nets and devices using the BSIM3 models. The total power consumption of the global interconnection nets is given by Equation 6.15.

$$P_{gt} = \frac{P_{sys} \cdot P_{link}}{U_p} \tag{6.15}$$

To estimate the power utilization of the NoC router, a set of synthesized routers are modeled in VHDL. Then, they are implemented on silicon using 0.18μm technology. The power absorption for the entire network (Pt) together with global nets and routers could be given in Equation 6.16, where nr indicates the number of routers.

$$P_t = \sum_{i=1}^{n_r} P_{ri} + P_{gl} \tag{6.16}$$

6.4.3   Total Power Calculation by Using Tabu Search

Tabu search is a metaheuristic search approach proposed by Glover [22] that helps a heuristic search method search the solution space beyond local optimum. It also designs the solution for combinatorial optimization problems. A Tabu search inculcates adaptive memory and responsive exploration for efficient problem solving [22]. A Tabu search gets better efficiency from the exploration process by maintaining the present track of the current value of the objective function beside information related to the exploration process by regularized use of memory. A Tabu search holds data of the last results visited to limit the options of certain subsets in the neighborhood by omission moves to certain neighbor solutions which has been already visited [28]. Further, it drives the path of the search process by limiting the algorithm from getting from the rear to an earlier visited state. The best solution in the neighborhood is selected in every iteration. The pseudo-code for a Tabu search is presented below [29].

Algorithm 1 Tabu Search Process Pseudo-Code

Initiate $h = 1$
Generate initial solution
WHILE the stopping condition is not met
DO
Identify K (l) (Neighborhood set)
Identify J (l, h) (Tabu set)
Identify O(l, h) (Aspirant set)
Choose the best l^0
$l^0 \in K (l, h) = \{K (l) - J (l, h)\} + O(l, h)$
$l = l^0$
$h = h + 1$
END WHILE

After initial mapping of each node of CG to TG, the Tabu search algorithm is applied for power optimization. In this paper we mainly consider three different steps in the Tabu search for changing the position of the nodes.

1. Inversion-Rearranging two adjacent nodes between themselves
2. Transformation-Rearranging any two nodes between themselves
3. Transition-Shifting the position of one node

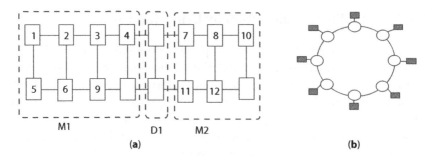

Figure 6.7 (a) MPEG-4 mesh partitioned with tabu search (b) general structure of ring topology.

The power analysis [30] is done as follows after a Tabu search is applied for ring and mesh topology, as shown in Figure 6.7(a) and (b) for MPEG-4 benchmark. For estimating the power, an entire system level and circuit level calculation for global physical interconnection links and NoC switches (routers) is to be carried out [30]. Further, every network architecture and a unique connectivity matrix is estimated, which represents the least number of nets a packet travels through during its data transition from the source tile to the destination tile.

6.5 Experimental Results and Discussion

To assess the performance of the proposed method, a set of experiments have been performed over power consumption and average number of hops between the cores [2] on standard NoC benchmarks like PIP, MPEG-4, and VOPD. The details of benchmarks are listed in Table 6.1. To validate the proposed approach, KL algorithm, Tailor Made Algorithm, DFS, and FM algorithm are implemented with and without Tabu search.

Table 6.1 Details of standard NoC benchmarks.

Benchmark	Nodes #	Edges #	2D mesh sizes
MPEG-4	12	26	4x4
VOPD	16	21	4x4
PIP	08	08	2x4

To evaluate the performance of 2D NoC, we used a cycle accurate network simulator MATLAB R2018b, Booksim 2.0 [31] and Orion 3.0 [31]. All experiments are run on a PC Intel core i7 − −8GBRAM 3.5 GHz processor.

6.5.1 Total Power Consumption in 2D NoC

The total power consumption in 2D NoC is estimated with the sum of global link power and router power [30], as shown in Equation 6.16. The global link power is evaluated through the number of power units consumed to transmit data packets given in a TDG between routers. To represent the router power in 2D NoC, a group of routers are modeled with various numbers of ports like 4, 5, 6, 7, and 8 ports using VHDL with 180nm technology. The result of a set of routers are validated with a group of experiments performed using a Synopsysr Design Compiler, VHDLSIM, and Power Compiler tools. Routers implemented in this work adopt a round robin scheduler to communicate the data one after another in a fixed order [30]. Router power with different operating frequencies is given in Table 6.2.

In this work, the router power consumption is adopted with the operating frequency of 500 MHz. For various topologies, an individual router power is calculated by adopting Equation 6.16. The number of routers present in topologies is varied according to the standard architecture. Table 6.3 represents the router power consumption for MPEG-4, VOPD, and PIP benchmarks for 500 MHz operating frequency.

Table 6.2 Router power with operating frequencies for 2D NoC.

Frequency	Router Power (Pr) in mW				
	4-Port	5-Port	6-Port	7-Port	8-Port
500 MHz	64.110	96.798	136.064	173.97	234.32
200 MHz	31.923	48.367	68.120	87.140	116.99
100 MHz	12.697	19.307	27.308	35.137	46.717
50 MHz	6.362	9.667	13.667	17.582	23.372
25 MHz	3.187	4.834	6.838	8.780	11.692

Table 6.3 Router power for standard NoC topologies with different numbers of ports.

| Parameter description | Topology | | | | | |
| | MPEG-4 | | VOPD | | PIP | |
	Mesh	Ring	Mesh	Ring	Mesh	Ring
2-Port	0	0	0	0	0	0
3–Port	4	12	4	16	4	8
4–Port	6	0	8	0	4	0
5–Port	2	0	4	0	0	0
8–Port	0	0	0	0	0	0
9–Port	0	0	0	0	0	0
12–Port	0	0	0	0	0	0
16–Port	0	0	0	0	0	0
No. of Routers	12	12	16	16	8	9
Router power (W)	0.835	0.769	1.156	1.025	0.513	0.513

Table 6.4 Total power consumption of 2D NoC for mesh topology without tabu search

Benchmark	KL algorithm	Tailor made algorithm	DFS	FM algorithm
MPEG4	0.978	1.385	-	0.914
VOPD	1.242	1.83	-	1.175
PIP	0.516	-	0.516	0.516

6.5.2   Performance of Tabu Search for Power Optimization with Mesh Topology

In this section, the performance of a Tabu search is estimated and analyzed over a KL algorithm, TMA, DFS and FM algorithm. To identify

Table 6.5 Total power consumption of 2D NoC for mesh topology with tabu search.

Benchmark	KL algorithm	Tailor made algorithm	DFS	FM algorithm
MPEG4	0.969	0.900	-	0.868
VOPD	1.229	1.231	-	1.175
PIP	0.516	-	0.516	0.516

the effectiveness of the Tabu search, the total power for MPEG-4, VOPD, and PIP is estimated with and without the Tabu algorithm. The adaptability of the FM algorithm for a mapping approach is also analyzed with the Tabu algorithm in comparison with the existing proven algorithm for 2D NoC mapping. The total power consumption values for mesh topology with and without Tabu search are shown in Tables 6.4 and 6.5.

Based on the obtained results from Tables 6.5 and 6.6, it is clear that the Tailor Made Algorithm shows 35% and 33% improvement in power consumption for MPEG-4 and VOPD, respectively, for the Tabu search compared to the other algorithm. However, the FM algorithm shows only 5% improvement in power consumption for MPEG-4 other than all the other methods. Nevertheless, the PIP benchmark has no improvement in power for mesh topology.

Table 6.6 Total power consumption of 2D NoC for ring topology without Tabu search.

Benchmark	KL algorithm	Tailor made algorithm	DFS	FM algorithm
MPEG4	0.941	1.2	-	0.843
VOPD	1.123	1.119	-	1.0441
PIP	0.516	-	0.516	0.516

Table 6.7 Total power consumption of 2D NoC for ring topology with tabu search.

Benchmark	KL algorithm	Tailor Made algorithm	DFS	FM algorithm
MPEG4	0.941	0.857	-	0.843
VOPD	1.123	1.119	-	1.0441
PIP	0.516	-	0.516	0.516

6.5.3 Performance of Tabu Search for Power Optimization with Ring Topology

In this section, the effectiveness of the Tabu search is analyzed for 2D NoC with ring topology. The total power consumption values for ring topology with and without Tabu search are shown in Tables 6.6 and 6.7. Based on the obtained results from Tables 6.6 and 6.7, it is clear that the tailor made algorithm offers 0.3% reduction in power consumption for MPEG-4 over the KL algorithm, DFS, and FM algorithm. On the other hand, the KL algorithm, DFS, and FM algorithm do not have further improvement in the power consumption.

6.5.4 Average Hop Counts for 2D NoC

In addition to the power consumption of 2D NoC, another important evaluation performance metric is the average hop counts between the cores among standard network topology. Table 6.8 represents the average number of hops among cores in mesh and ring topology for MPEG-4, VOPD, and PIP. The results of the comparison table show the efficiency of the KL algorithm, TMA, DFS, and FM algorithm over the average number of

Table 6.8 Average number of hops for mesh and ring topology.

Benchmark	KL algorithm	Tailor made algorithm	DFS	FM algorithm
MPEG4	2.75	2.75	-	2.75
VOPD	6.04	7	-	2.75
PIP	4	-	4	4

hops. The average number of hops (bavg) is a reference metric to measure the power consumption. It is given by

$$b_{avg} = \frac{C_a}{N_a}, \; C_a = \sum_{i=1}^{n} \sum_{j=1}^{n} \lambda_{ij} . C_{ij} . u_p \neq 0$$

where Na is the number of elements in the traffic distribution matrix. From Table 6.8, the FM algorithm shows a 60% reduction in the number of hops rather than the tailor made algorithm for the VOPD benchmark. Further, all other benchmarks have no improvement in their values.

6.6   Conclusion

In this chapter, we presented a new-fangled approach for cluster-based mapping for 2D NoC. The proposed mapping approach includes the analysis of power consumption and number of hops over mesh and ring topology. The competency of modified cluster-based mapping with an FM algorithm was assessed with a Tabu search for total power optimization. The experiment results prove that the Tabu search provides a reduction in power consumption only for MPEG-4 with mesh topology and VOPD and PIP benchmarks have identical values for the Tabu search. Further, the experiment proves that a Tabu search is not appropriate for power optimization with a cluster-based mapping approach.

References

1. Tobias Bjerregaard and Shankar Mahadevan. Bjerregaard, tobias and mahade- van, shankar. ACM Computing Surveys (CSUR), 38:1–es, 2006.
2. Pradip Kumar Sahu and Santanu Chattopadhyay. A survey on application mapping strategies for network-on-chip design. Journal of systems architecture, 59(1):60–76, 2013.
3. Radu Marculescu, Umit Y Ogras, Li-Shiuan Peh, Natalie Enright Jerger, and Yatin Hoskote. Outstanding research problems in noc design: system, microarchitecture, and circuit perspectives. IEEE Transactions on Computer- Aided Design of Integrated Circuits and Systems, 28(1):3–21, 2008.
4. Coskun Celik and Cuneyt F Bazlamacci. Effect of application mapping on network-on-chip performance. In 2012 20th Euromicro international

conference on parallel, distributed and network-based processing, pages 465–472. IEEE, 2012.

5. Brett H Meyer, Joshua J Pieper, JoAnn M Paul, Jeffrey E Nelson, Sean M Pieper, and Anthony G Rowe. Power-performance simulation and design strategies for single-chip heterogeneous multiprocessors. IEEE transactions on Computers, 54(6):684–697, 2005.

6. Haytham Elmiligi, Ahmed A Morgan, M Watheq El-Kharashi, and Fayez Gebali. Power optimization for application-specific networks-on-chips: A topology-based approach. Microprocessors and Microsystems, 33(5-6):343–355, 2009.

7. Partha Pratim Pande, Cristian Grecu, Michael Jones, Andre Ivanov, and Resve Saleh. Performance evaluation and design trade-offs for network-on-chip interconnect architectures. IEEE transactions on Computers, 54(8):1025–1040, 2005.

8. Reza Moraveji, Parya Moinzadeh, and Hamid Sarbazi-Azad. A general mathematical performance model for wormhole-switched irregular networks. Cluster Computing, 12(3):285–297, 2009.

9. Madaan, Vishu, Aditya Roy, Charu Gupta, Prateek Agrawal, Anand Sharma, Christian Bologa, Radu Prodan, "XCOVNet: Chest X-ray Image Classification for COVID-19 Early Detection Using Convolutional Neural Networks", New Generation Computing, pp. 1-15, 2021. DOI: 10.1007/s00354-021-00121-7.

10. Agrawal, Prateek, Ranjit Kaur, Vishu Madaan, Sunil Babu Mukkelli, Dimple Sethi, "Moving Object Detection and Recognition Using Optical Flow and Eigen Face Using Low Resolution Video", Recent Advances in Computer Science and Communications, 13(6), pp. 1180–1187, 2020. DOI: 10.2174/22 1327591166618111911215.

11. Prateek Agrawal, Deepak Chaudhary, Vishu Madaan, Anatoliy Zabrovskiy, Radu Prodan, Dragi Kimovski, Christian Timmerer, "Automated Bank Cheque Verification Using Image Processing and Deep Learning Methods", Multimedia tools and applications (MTAP), 80(1), pp 5319–5350, 2021(a). DOI:10.1007/s11042-020-09818-1.

12. Prateek Agrawal, Anatoliy Zabrovskiy, Adithyan Ilagovan, Christian Timmerer, Radu Prodan, "FastTTPS: Fast Approach for Video Transcoding Time Prediction and Scheduling for HTTP Adaptive Streaming Videos", Cluster Computing, pp 1-17. 2021 (b). DOI: 10.1007/s10586-020-03207-x.

13. Suleyman Tosun. New heuristic algorithms for energy aware application mapping and routing on mesh-based nocs. Journal of Systems Architecture, 57 (1):69–78, 2011b.

14. Majid Janidarmian, Ahmad Khademzadeh, and Misagh Tavanpour. Onyx: A new heuristic bandwidth-constrained mapping of cores onto tile-based network on chip. IEICE Electronics Express, 6(1):1–7, 2009.

15. Krishnan Srinivasan and Karam S Chatha. A technique for low energy mapping and routing in network-on-chip architectures. In Proceedings of

the 2005 international symposium on Low power electronics and design, pages 387–392, 2005.

16. César Marcon, André Borin, Altamiro Susin, Luigi Carro, and Flavio Wagner. Time and energy efficient mapping of embedded applications onto nocs. In Proceedings of the 2005 Asia and South Pacific Design Automation Conference, pages 33–38, 2005.

17. Suleyman Tosun. Cluster-based application mapping method for net-work-on- chip. Advances in Engineering Software, 42(10):868–874, 2011a.

18. Coşkun Çelik and Cüneyt F Bazlamaçcı. Evaluation of energy and buffer aware application mapping for networks-on-chip. Microprocessors and Microsystems, 38(4):325–336, 2014.

19. Suleyman Tosun, Ozcan Ozturk, and Meltem Ozen. An ilp formulation for application mapping onto network-on-chips. In 2009 International Conference on Application of Information and Communication Technologies, pages 1–5. IEEE, 2009.

20. A Aravindhan, S Salini, and G Lakshminarayanan. Cluster based application mapping strategy for 2d noc. Procedia Technology, 25:505–512, 2016.

21. S Salini, A Aravindhan, and G Lakshminarayanan. A case study on cluster based power aware mapping strategy for 2d noc. ICTCAT J. Microelectronics, 2(4):315–322, 2017.

22. Brian W Kernighan and Shen Lin. An efficient heuristic procedure for partitioning graphs. The Bell system technical journal, 49(2):291–307, 1970.

23. Charalampos Papamanthou. Depth first search & directed acyclic graphs. Review for the course, 2004.

24. Andrew B Kahng, Jens Lienig, Igor L Markov, and Jin Hu. VLSI physical de-sign: from graph partitioning to timing closure. Springer Science & Business Media, 2011.

25. Fred Glover, Manuel Laguna, and Rafael Marti. Principles of tabu search. Approximation algorithms and metaheuristics, 23:1–12, 2007.

26. Tero Harju. Lecture notes on graph theory. Wiley, 2014.

27. Yu Cao. Predictive technology model for robust nanoelectronic design. Springer Science & Business Media, 2011.

28. Anant Oonsivilai, Wichai Srisuruk, Boonruang Marungsri, and Thanatchai Kulworawanichpong. Tabu search approach to solve routing issues in communication networks 1. International Journal of Electrical and Computer Engineering, 3(5), 2009.

29. Fadi K Dib and Peter Rodgers. A tabu search based approach for graph layout. Journal of Visual Languages & Computing, 25(6):912–923, 2014.

30. Aravindhan Alagarsamy and Lakshminaraynan Gopalakrishnan. Sat: A new application mapping method for power optimization in 2dnoc. In 2016 20th International Symposium on VLSI Design and Test (VDAT), pages 1–6. IEEE, 2016.

31. William James Dally and Brian Patrick Towles. Principles and practices of interconnection networks. Elsevier, 2004.
32. Andrew B Kahng, Bill Lin, and Siddhartha Nath. Comprehensive modeling methodologies for NoC router estimation. Department of Computer Science and Engineering, University of California, 2012.

Healthcare Case Study: COVID19 Detection, Prevention Measures, and Prediction Using Machine Learning & Deep Learning Algorithms

Devesh Kumar Srivastava*, Mansi Chouhan and Amit Kumar Sharma

Manipal University Jaipur, Rajasthan, India

Abstract

In healthcare, COVID19 has been spreading in multiple forms across the entire world. Coronavirus, or COVID19, belongs to a large group of viruses that are the causes for mild respiratory tract infections in humans, varying from the common cold, or can be more severe like Severe Acute Respiratory Syndrome (SARS) and Middle Eastern Respiratory Syndrome (MERS). This work aims to provide information about symptoms of coronavirus, its detection, and its prevention. In this study, we proposed a model for predicting results. Predictions are made using patients' symptoms of having Covid19 or not by applying various machine learning and deep learning algorithms. The effectiveness of the proposed model is experimentally evaluated on patients' symptoms using 5000 rows of a data set. Many cases are highlighted as a group of problems related to the COVID19 pandemic and point out promising results.

Keywords: COVID19, coronavirus, machine learning, deep learning, classification, COVID19 symptoms, COVID19 precautions, COVID19 prevention

---

*Corresponding author: Devesh988@yahoo.com

Prateek Agrawal, Charu Gupta, Anand Sharma, Vishu Madaan, and Nisheeth Joshi (eds.) Machine Learning and Data Science: Fundamentals and Applications, (109–134) © 2022 Scrivener Publishing LLC

7.1   Introduction

Coronavirus comes from the family of RNA viruses of the Nidovirales order. The corona prefix comes from the Latin word for crown, named for the "crown-like" appearance of virus. The human coronavirus causes respiratory and gastrointestinal tract infections. Human epidemics can occur when it transmits from one species to another. There are various types of coronaviruses, including alpha, beta, gamma, and delta viruses. Human coronaviruses are alpha and beta coronaviruses. People who are suffering from an organ transplants, cancer, severe asthma, weak immune system, serious heart condition, old age, high blood pressure, diabetes, etc. are of high risk for COVID19. RT-PCR testing is the method for diagnosing COVID19 as positive or negative. HRCT (Chest City Scans) is a more reliable way to find and diagnose the COVID19 affected patient. The initial common symptoms of COVID19 shown in Figure 7.1 help to diagnose the COVID19 disease.

This chapter provides all the information regarding the COVID19 pandemic. The research provides whether the patient needs to go for the

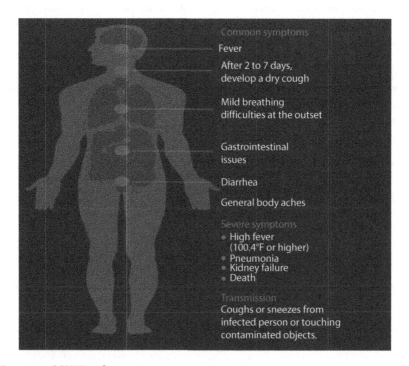

Figure 7.1 COVID19 diagnosis.

COVID19 test or not. The results are experimentally evaluated using the symptoms as inputs and applying various Machine Learning algorithms like Naive Bayes, random forest, j48 decision tree, logistic regression, and AdaBoost and deep learning algorithms like multilayer perceptron and voted perceptron for prediction. This paper will be a one-stop destination where people can get information about COVID19, its symptoms, avoidance methods, precautions, and prevention techniques. Also, for researchers, this paper will be helpful to study the COVID19 disease properly.

7.2   Literature Review

The Novel Corona-virus SARS-CoV-2 (COVID19) disease's first case was detected in the last month of 2019 in Wuhan City, China. It has spread worldwide and has created a major pandemic situation across the country. It is desirable to limit Human–to-Human broadcasts to scale back secondary infections among close contacts and healthcare-workers and to avoid transmission amplification events and further international spread from the country of China [1]. The new coronavirus, COVID19, developed a global-health-emergency owed to the very high-risk of spread and effect of COVID19. There are not any exact drugs or vaccines against COVID19, thus operative antiviral agents are still immediately needed to combat this virus. Herein, the FEP (Free Energy Perturbation)-based screening policy is freshly derived as a rapid protocol to accurately reposition potential agents against COVID19 by targeting the viral proteinase Mpro. This virus has also infected all the continents and over 180 other countries, including Italy, Spain, U.S.A., Germany, France, and Iran, gradually becoming a world pandemic because of the very high risk of spread and impact of COVID19 [2]. The paper [3] suggested the model of essential ingredients of COVID19 epidemics of very mild or no symptoms, mild symptoms, and severe symptoms. In this study, the researcher shows that the Disease-Free Equilibrium (*E0*) for the COVID19 coronavirus does not satisfy the criteria for a locally or globally asymptotic stability. This implies that, as a pandemic as declared by WHO (2020), the COVID19 coronavirus does not have a curative vaccine yet and precautionary measures are advised through quarantine and observatory measures [4]. The paper [6] has investigated the role in the spreading of COVID19 and finds the way that knowledge is often accustomed to arresting this fast-spreading virus/disease. The paper has highlighted that temperature and humidity both are extremely significant for transmitting the virus, with temperature being the stronger factor. The dry and cool environment is the most favorable state for the spreading of the coronavirus [6]. Society uses online measures like social media to get and share several forms of information at a historic and extraordinary scale. Only the situational information is appreciated for the general public and authorities to reply to the epidemic. Therefore, sharing accurate information through web apps or social media is very much important [7]. Authors used various machine learning approaches to predict the spread and early diagnosis of COVID-19 and its psychological impact on individuals [8–11].

7.3   Coronavirus (Covid19)

7.3.1   History of Coronavirus

- **229E:** One of the first strains of coronaviruses to be identified in the mid-60s, probably by D Hamre and JJ Procknow in their 1966 paper entitled 'A new virus isolated from the human respiratory tract,' published in Experimental Biology and Medicine

- **OC43:** Discovered in the Journal of Virology in 1967. A paper in the Virology Journal, however, identified this as the first human coronavirus to be discovered in 1965, citing a 1966 paper written by Tyrrell and Bynoe who worked with the nasal swab titled B814.

- **NL63 and HKU1:** First identified in 2004 in the Netherlands, possibly after being isolated from a seven-month-old infant with respiratory symptoms. There was an increase in human coronavirus studies during this period, which led to the discovery of NL63 and HKU1 in Hong Kong early in 2005.

- **SARS (Severe Acute Respiratory Syndrome):** From 2002 to 2003, SARS was found in the Guang Dong Province of China. It is one of the Beta coronaviruses that transmit from bats to civets cats to humans.

- **MERS (Middle Eastern Respiratory Syndrome):** In 2012 MERS was found in Saudi Arabia. It is one of the Beta coronaviruses that transmit from camels to humans. Saudi Arabia 2012 was transmitted by dromedical camels to humans.

- **2019-nCov (2019 Novel Corona Virus) or COVID19 (Coronavirus Disease):** In 2019, COVID19 is found in

Wuhan, Hubei Province, China. It is the 7th coronavirus found that causes illness in humans. It is the virus that is transmitted from bats or animals to humans and from humans to humans [12].

- The first discovery was that during its spread throughout China and the rest of the world, the coronavirus had developed into newer forms. Coronavirus can be categorized into several different forms O, A2, A2a, A3, B, B1, etc. There are currently 11 types, including type O which is the 'ancestral type' originating in Wuhan and by March-end, A2a started to dominate other forms around the world as the dominant form of SARS-CoV2 [13–16].

7.3.2   Transmission Stages of COVID19

The COVID19 pandemic has become a global health disaster creating problems for every individual from various countries in the world. The virus spreads over several countries in different stages of the COVID19 infection. The stages of the coronavirus are:

- **Stage 1:** In this stage, cases are caused by only coming in contact with the affected countries' infected person since only those who traveled to foreign countries tested positive. At this stage, the disease is not spreading.
- **Stage 2:** In this stage, there is only local transmission or spreading of the disease. Only the people who have close contact with the infected person like neighbors, friends, or relatives of the infected person have a chance of getting infected. In this stage, very few people are getting infected and contact tracing can easily be done.
- **Stage 3:** This is the stage of community transmission. In this stage, the person will test positive even not getting in contact with the affected person. In other words, people are helpless to recognize where they get infected by the virus.
- **Stage 4:** This is the most harmful stage where it takes the form of an epidemic. In this stage, a large number of people are infected and it is very challenging to control and hold the spread.

7.3.3   Restrictions of COVID19

To stop the spreading of coronavirus, the following restrictions are needed to be followed by people:

- Stay at home
- Leave the house for only the below reasons:
    a) Shopping for needs, for example medicine and food, must be as rare as possible
    b) One form of exercise a day like running, walking, or cycling, alone or with members of your family.
    c) Medical necessity or to provide care or support to a disabled person

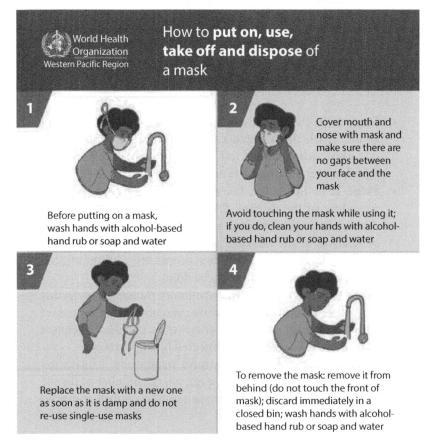

Figure 7.2 Direction for use of face mask.

d) Traveling to and from work, but only where this cannot be done from home
e) Social Distancing should be maintained
f) When leaving the house for any of the above stated reasons, use a face mask and hand sanitizer. The process of caring for yourself is shown in Figure 7.2.
g) Always wash food items and hands before touching your face and eyes.

7.3.4   Symptoms of COVID19

COVID19 symptoms vary from moderate to severe. It takes 2 to 14 days after exposure for symptoms to develop in any person. The major symptoms or signs may include fever, cough, shortness of breath, as shown in Figure 7.3, and other symptoms can be fatigue, diarrhea, aches and pains, sore throat, nausea, and runny nose. People having weak immune systems (majorly old age people or small kids) may develop serious symptoms like Pneumonia or Bronchitis. Some people may not even develop any symptoms suggested above after being unprotected from COVID19.

7.3.5   Prevention of COVID19

To stop the transmission of coronavirus, the following precautions and preventions should be observed:

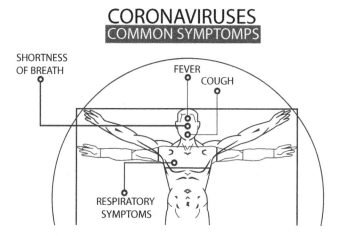

Figure 7.3 Symptoms of COVID19.

- Always wear a mask
- Maintain at least six feet distance when people are in close contact with each other
- Avoidance of social and mass gatherings
- The virus can be spread through respiratory droplets of coughs and sneezes or talking produced by a person who is already infected. Use a tissue to cover your cough and throw away the tissue. Sneeze in upper sleeves or elbow.
- These droplets may land in the face, mouths, or noses of other uninfected people who are nearby or can be inhaled into the lungs and get infected.
- Regularly wash your hands with soap for at least 20 seconds before eating food or touching your face, eyes, nose, etc.
- If your hands are not clean or looking dirty, then do not touch your eyes, nose, or mouth before washing your hands with soap.
- Disinfect or clean daily the surfaces you touch often
- Use hand sanitizer containing alcohol up to 70%

7.3.6   COVID19 Diagnosis and Awareness

The following awareness and diagnosis are required in COVID19 for the public:

- If any person feels like he/she has coronavirus or contains similar symptoms stated above, then he/she must contact the doctor instantly.
- Before going to the hospital or clinic for getting diagnosed ask your friends or relatives who live near that place to offer information and further guidance.
- The doctor may diagnose other similar infections that have common symptoms like COVID19.
- The doctor suggests the patient self-isolate or self-quarantine for 2 weeks to avoid the spread of coronavirus.
- RT-PCR testing is the method for diagnosing COVID19 as. positive or negative. HRCT (Chest city scans) is a more reliable way to find and diagnose the COVID19 affected patient.

7.3.7   Measures to Perform by COVID19 Patients

The positive patients are required to follow the guidelines that have been provided by the health departments. Some instructions also required to be followed strictly by COVID19 patients include:

- Avoid meeting others and visits to medical facilities
- Wear face masks and social distance
- Self-quarantine yourself for at least 14 days
- Eat food that enhances your immune system
- In critical or not handled situations, the patient is required to isolate in the hospital
- Regularly check their oxygen levels
- Isolate in a separate room
- Regular contact with a doctor

7.3.8   High-Risk People

The following people or patients are at high risk and are required to be more careful in this pandemic situation:

- Have/had an organ transplant
- Are under a certain type of cancer treatment
- Having blood or bone-marrow-cancer, such as Leukemia
- Having a severe lung-condition such as severe asthma or cystic fibrosis
- Having conditions that are more likely prone to infections
- Weak immune system due to undergoing medication
- Having pregnancy or a serious heart condition
- People 65 years or older and below 10 year old children
- People having diabetes, high blood pressure, cancer, or other medical issues are at high risk of getting COVID19 because of a weak immune system

7.3.9   Problem Formulation

In this pandemic situation, COVID19 transmission is spreading very fast in society. In this way, there is a problem with asymptotic or seasonal disease symptoms and people are not identifying that they are suffering from COVID19 and they are required to go for the COVID19 test. In this study, we are using different classifiers applied to different patients' symptoms for predicting if the COVID19 test is required or not. People having weak immune systems (majorly old age people or small kids) may develop serious signs like Pneumonia or Bronchitis. Some people may not even develop any symptoms, as suggested above, after being unprotected from COVID19. There also is no proof that kids are at greater risk of being infected by the virus. This coronavirus can be spread by getting in contact with any type of body fluid, like droplets in the cough. It might be caused by touching your hand to your mouth, nose, or eyes after meeting the person infected or something that is touched by the infected person.

7.4   Proposed Working Model

The proposed working model is based on machine learning algorithms for predicting the results. It has two major sections of the process: input the patients' details with their symptoms and apply machine learning algorithms on the input data and predict the results for patient need to take the COVID-19 test. The effectiveness of the proposed model is experimentally evaluated in 5000 patients' symptoms. We can see the working of the proposed model in Figure 7.4.

7.4.1   Data Selection

- The dataset is manually created by studying various papers on the disease and from there the symptoms of various patients are taken. By applying a decision tree algorithm, we predict the test set results.
- Data contains 5000 entries of different patients with 2500 entries for positive symptoms and 2500 entries for non-covid symptoms.
- In the dataset, if the patient has symptoms like cough, fatigue, etc., the inputs are either yes or no based on symptoms and the model will predict if he/she must go for the COVID19 test check-up.
- Data given as the input is: [1,1,1,0,1,1,0,1,1,1]. Here, 1 means yes the person has that symptom and 0 means no.

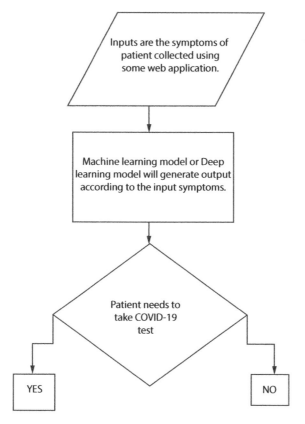

Figure 7.4 Working model.

Here, if the output is YES that means the patient has the symptoms like cough, fever, sore throat, sneezing, shortness of breath, diarrhea, headache, and body aches [Table 7.1].

• According to symptoms, the model will predict if the person has a chance of getting COVID19 or not. The data taken here are the symptoms which were common in some other diseases like a common cold, flu, pneumonia, etc., so the symptoms are taken to check the possibilities of a person having COVID19 or not.

Table 7.1 Patient symptoms.

Covid19	Cough	Fever	Sore throat	Fatigue	Sneezing	Shortness of breath	Nasal congestion	Diarrhea	Headache	Body ache
Covid	1	1	1	1	0	1	1	1	1	1
Covid	1	1	0	1	0	1	0	0	0	0
Covid	0	0	1	0	1	0	1	1	1	1
Covid	0	0	1	1	0	1	1	1	1	1
Covid	1	1	0	1	1	1	1	0	1	1
Covid	1	1	1	1	0	1	1	1	1	1
Covid	1	1	0	1	0	1	0	0	0	0
Covid	0	0	1	0	1	0	1	1	1	1
Covid	0	0	1	1	0	1	1	1	1	1
Covid	1	1	0	1	1	1	1	0	1	1
Covid	1	1	1	1	0	1	1	1	1	1
Covid	1	1	0	0	0	0	0	0	0	0
Covid	0	0	1	0	1	1	1	1	1	1
Covid	0	0	1	1	0	1	1	1	1	1

(Continued)

Table 7.1 Patient symptoms. (*Continued*)

Covid19	Cough	Fever	Sore throat	Fatigue	Sneezing	Shortness of breath	Nasal congestion	Diarrhea	Headache	Body ache
Covid	1	1	0	1	1	1	1	0	1	1
Covid	1	1	1	1	0	1	1	1	1	1
Covid	1	1	0	1	0	1	0	0	0	0
Covid	0	0	1	0	1	0	1	1	1	1
Covid	0	0	1	1	0	1	1	1	1	1
Covid	1	1	0	1	1	1	1	0	1	1
Covid	1	1	1	1	0	1	1	1	1	1
Covid	1	1	0	1	0	1	0	0	0	0
Covid	0	0	1	0	1	0	1	1	1	1
Covid	0	0	1	1	0	1	1	1	1	1
Covid	1	1	0	1	1	1	1	0	1	1
Covid	1	1	1	1	0	1	1	1	1	1
Covid	1	1	0	1	0	1	0	0	0	0

(*Continued*)

Table 7.1 Patient symptoms. (*Continued*)

Covid19	Cough	Fever	Sore throat	Fatigue	Sneezing	Shortness of breath	Nasal congestion	Diarrhea	Headache	Body ache
Covid	0	0	1	0	1	0	1	1	1	1
Covid	0	0	1	1	0	1	1	1	1	1
Covid	1	1	0	1	1	1	1	0	1	1
Covid	1	1	1	1	0	1	1	1	1	1
Covid	1	1	0	1	0	1	0	0	0	0
Covid	0	0	1	0	1	0	1	1	1	1
Covid	1	1	1	1	0	1	1	1	1	1
Covid	1	1	0	1	0	1	0	0	0	0
Covid	0	0	1	0	1	0	1	1	1	1
Covid	0	0	1	1	0	1	1	1	1	1
Covid	1	1	0	1	1	1	1	0	1	1
Covid	1	1	1	1	0	1	1	1	1	1
Covid	1	1	0	1	0	1	0	0	0	0

(Continued)

Table 7.1 Patient symptoms. (*Continued*)

Covid19	Cough	Fever	Sore throat	Fatigue	Sneezing	Shortness of breath	Nasal congestion	Diarrhea	Headache	Body ache
Covid	0	0	1	0	1	0	1	1	1	1
Covid	0	0	1	1	0	1	1	1	1	1
Covid	1	1	0	1	1	1	1	0	1	1
Covid	1	1	1	1	0	1	1	1	1	1
Covid	1	1	0	1	0	1	0	0	0	0
Covid	0	0	1	0	1	0	1	1	1	1
Covid	0	0	1	1	0	1	1	1	1	1
Covid	1	1	0	1	1	0	1	0	1	1
Covid	0	0	1	0	1	1	1	1	1	1
Covid	0	0	1	1	0	1	1	1	1	1
Covid	1	1	0	1	1	1	1	0	1	1
Covid	1	1	1	1	0	1	1	1	1	1
Covid	1	1	0	1	0	1	0	0	0	0

(*Continued*)

Table 7.1 Patient symptoms. (Continued)

Covid19	Cough	Fever	Sore throat	Fatigue	Sneezing	Shortness of breath	Nasal congestion	Diarrhea	Headache	Body ache
Covid	0	0	1	0	1	0	1	1	1	1
Covid	0	0	1	1	0	1	1	1	1	1
Covid	1	1	1	1	0	1	1	1	1	1
Covid	1	1	0	1	0	1	0	0	0	0
Covid	0	0	1	0	1	0	1	1	1	1
Covid	0	0	1	1	0	1	1	1	1	1
Covid	1	1	0	1	1	1	1	0	1	1
Covid	1	1	1	1	0	1	1	1	1	1
Covid	1	1	0	1	0	1	0	0	0	0
Covid	0	0	1	0	1	1	1	1	1	1
Covid	0	0	1	1	0	1	1	1	1	1
Covid	1	1	0	1	1	1	1	0	1	1
Covid	1	1	1	1	0	1	1	1	1	1

(Continued)

Table 7.1 Patient symptoms. (*Continued*)

Covid19	Cough	Fever	Sore throat	Fatigue	Sneezing	Shortness of breath	Nasal congestion	Diarrhea	Headache	Body ache
Covid	1	1	0	1	0	1	0	0	0	0
Covid	0	0	1	0	1	0	1	1	1	1
Covid	0	0	1	1	0	1	1	1	1	1
Covid	1	1	0	1	1	1	1	0	1	1
Covid	1	1	1	1	0	1	1	1	1	1
Covid	1	1	0	1	0	1	0	0	0	0
Covid	0	0	1	0	1	0	1	1	1	1
Covid	1	1	1	1	0	1	1	1	1	1
Covid	1	1	0	1	0	1	0	0	0	0
Covid	0	0	1	0	1	0	1	1	1	1
Covid	0	0	1	1	0	1	1	1	1	1
Covid	1	1	0	1	1	1	1	0	1	1
Covid	1	1	1	1	0	1	1	1	1	1

(*Continued*)

Table 7.1 Patient symptoms. (*Continued*)

Covid19	Cough	Fever	Sore throat	Fatigue	Sneezing	Shortness of breath	Nasal congestion	Diarrhea	Headache	Body ache
Covid	1	1	0	1	0	1	0	0	0	0
Covid	0	0	1	0	1	0	1	1	1	1
Covid	0	0	1	1	0	1	1	1	1	1
Covid	1	1	0	1	1	1	1	0	1	1
Covid	1	1	1	1	0	1	1	1	1	1
Covid	1	1	0	1	0	1	0	0	0	0
Covid	0	0	1	0	1	0	1	1	1	1
Covid	0	0	0	1	0	1	1	1	1	1
Covid	1	1	1	1	1	1	1	0	1	1
Covid	1	1	0	1	0	1	0	1	1	1
Covid	1	1	1	1	0	1	1	0	0	0
Covid	0	0	1	0	1	0	1	1	1	1
Covid	0	0	1	1	0	1	1	1	1	1
Covid	1	1	0	1	1	1	1	0	1	1

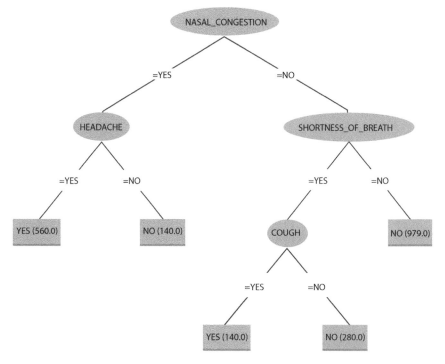

Figure 7.5 Symptoms for prediction.

7.4.2   Important Symptoms for Prediction

This section provides the important symptoms for prediction as shown in Figure 7.5.

7.4.3   Data Classification

7.4.3.1   *Logistic Regression*

LR is a statistical model that uses a logistic function to model a binary dependent variable in its basic form, though there are many more complex extensions. The logistic regression (or logic regression) estimates the parameters of a logistic model (a form of binary regression) in regression analysis. The logistic regression equation is shown by Equation 7.1:

$$Z = log\left(p\,/1-p\right) = \beta0 + \beta1X1 + \beta2X2...\beta kXk \qquad (7.1)$$

where
- ⇨   likelihood $p = (1\,/\,1 + e^{-z})$, takes log of likelihood and
- ⇨ $\beta0 + \beta1X1 + \beta2X2...\beta kXk$ are independent variables.

7.4.3.2   Naïve Bayes

This classifier is a family of simple "probabilistic classifiers" based on the application of Bayes ' theorem with strong (naïve) assumptions of independence among the features. They are among the simplest models of a Bayesian network. The Naive Bayes classifier equation is shown by Equation 7.2:

$$P(x) = P(c). \, P(c) / P(x) \qquad (7.2)$$

where

- ⇨ The posterior probability of the target-class given predictor (attribute) is indicated by $P(c|x)$
- ⇨ The prior probability of class is indicated by $P(c)$
- ⇨ The likelihood is the probability of the predictor given class is indicated by $P(x|c)$
- ⇨ The prior probability of the predictor is indicated by $P(x)$

7.4.3.3   Adaboost

AdaBoost, short for Adaptive Boosting, is a meta-algorithm of machine learning formulated by Yoav Freund and Robert Schapire who won the Gödel Prize 2003 for their work. It can be used to improve performance alongside many other types of learning algorithms. The Adaboost equation is shown by Equation 7.3:

$$H(x) = sign \sum_{t-1}^{T} \alpha_t h_t(x) \qquad (7.3)$$

where

- ⇨ for input x and weak classifier t, the output is $h_t(x)$
- ⇨ the weight assigned to the classifier is alpha_t
- ⇨ weight of the classifier is straight forward and it is based on the error rate E
- ⇨ alpha_t = 0.5 * ln((1 — E) / E).

7.4.3.4   Random Forest

Random forests or random decision forests are an ensemble learning method for classification, regression, and other tasks that work by building a multitude of decision trees at training time and outputting the class which is the class model (classification) or mean prediction (regression) of the individual trees. Random forest equation is shown by Equation 7.4:

$$RFfi_i = \frac{\left(\sum_{j\epsilon \text{ all trees}} normfi_{ij} \right)}{T}$$

(7.4)

where

⇨ From all trees in the Random Forest model the importance of a feature is calculated by RFfi sub(i)
⇨ The normalized feature importance in tree j is calculated by norm fi sub(ij)
⇨ The total number of trees is indicated by T

7.4.3.5 *Multilayer Perceptron*

An MLP consists of at least three layers of nodes: an input layer, a hidden layer, and an output layer. Except for the input nodes, each node is a neuron that uses a nonlinear activation function. MLP utilizes a supervised learning technique called back-propagation for training. The multilayer perceptron is shown by Equation 7.5:

$$y = \varphi \left(\sum_{i=1}^{n} w_i \, x_i + b \right) = \varphi \left(w^T x + b \right)$$

(7.5)

where

⇨ The vector of weights is denoted by w
⇨ The vector of inputs is denoted by x
⇨ The bias and the activation function are denoted by b and φ respectively

7.5.3.6 *J48*

The j48 algorithm is one of the best machine learning algorithms to examine the data categorically and continuously. When it is used for instance purposes, it occupies more memory space and depletes the performance and accuracy in classifying medical data. The j48 decision tree algorithm is shown by Equation 7.6:

$$H(x) = \Sigma_{j=1}^{k} \quad P_j \left(\frac{1}{p_j} \right) = -\Sigma_{j=1}^{k} P_j \ p_j \tag{7.6}$$

where

⇨   The system event Entropy is denoted by E
⇨   As an outcome, the probability of HEAD is denoted by p
⇨   As an outcome, the probability of TAIL is denoted by q

7.4.3.7   *Voted Perceptron*

The Voted Perceptron is a variant using multiple weighted perceptrons. The algorithm starts a new perceptron every time an example is wrongly classified, initializing the weights vector with the final weights of the last perceptron. The voted perceptron is an algorithm for learning a binary classifier called a threshold function which is shown by Equation 7.7:

$$f(x) = \{1 \ if \ (w.x + b) > 0 \ 0 \ otherwise \tag{7.7}$$

where

⇨   The vector of real-valued weights is denoted by w
⇨   The dot product is denoted by w.x, where:

$$w.x = \sum_{i=1}^{m} w_i x_i$$

⇨   The number of inputs to the perceptron is denoted by m
⇨   The bias is denoted by b

7.5   Experimental Evaluation

In this research, the model trained on 5000 patients' different symptoms, applied different classifiers for predicting the results and calculated the accuracy of different classifiers.

7.5.1   Experiment Results

Table 7.2 Accuracy and error rate of different algorithms.

Algorithms	Accuracy (%)	Error (%)	Time taken to build model (seconds)
Naive Bayes	73.7	26.3	0.03
Logistic Regression	89.32	10.68	0.13
Adaboost	89.32	10.68	0.11
Random Forest	99.94	0.06	0.34
Multilayer Perceptron	99.92	0.08	3.03
J48	99.86	0.14	0.05
Voted Perceptron	89.34	10.66	0.09

7.5.2   Experiment Analysis

The random database of patients having various symptoms is given as the input in the above seven classification models and each model is used to generate the output as "YES" or "NO", which determines if the patient needs to take the COVID19 test or not and calculates the accuracy of the model [Table 7.2]. The graphs Figure 7.6 and 7.7 depict the accuracy of various algorithms and Random Forest provides the highest accuracy (99.94%) for training the model in 0.34 second build time. J48 algorithms also provide

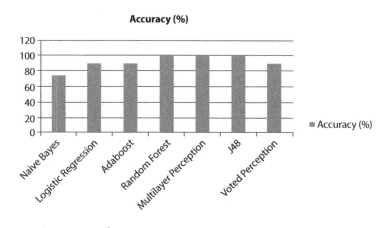

Figure 7.6 Accuracy graph.

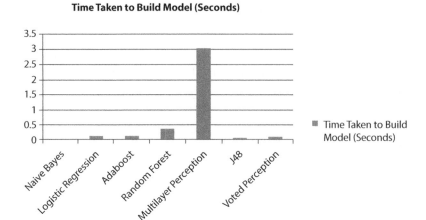

Figure 7.7 Time taken to build model.

99.86% accurate results in 0.05 seconds, the lowest build model time. Multilayer Perceptron also provides 99.92% accuracy of the model, but the build model time taken is high.

7.6   Conclusion and Future Work

This chapter aims to provide a source where the user can see information regarding coronavirus detection and prevention. It also displays various websites used to visualize the corona disease outbreak, facilities, government schemes for particular treatment, and symptoms, which are all available on various websites mentioned in this paper. This research has been evaluated with seven different classifiers. The random forest provides 99.94% accuracy for predicting whether patients should take a test for COVID19 or not. The j48 algorithm also classified better results in 0.05 seconds to build a model. This paper analyses the symptoms of a coronavirus-infected person where, according to the symptoms of the person, the model will generate output as to whether he/she has chances of having coronavirus and needs to get a test for COVID19. In this paper, the user can see the info about the virus and precautions against the virus. In this research, we have just 5000 random patients' datasets. The future of COVID19 analysis will be based on a time series dataset for finding the COVID19 influences in different countries and regions.

References

1. Chih-ChengLai, Tzu-PingShih, Wen-ChienKo, Hung-JenTang, Po-RenHsueh. *et al.* "Severe acute respiratory syndrome coronavirus 2 (SARS-CoV-2) and coronavirus disease-2019 (COVID19): The epidemic and the challenges" International Journal of Antimicrobial Agents DOI: https://doi.org/10.1016/j.ijantimicag.2020.105924 Volume 55, Issue 3, March 2020.

2. Zhe Li, Xin Li, Yi-You Huang, Yaoxing Wu. *et al.* "FEP-based screening prompts drug repositioning against COVID19" DOI: doi.org/10.1101/2020.03.23.004580 PP: 1-34 BioRxiv on March 25, 2020.

3. Pierre Magal; Glenn Webb -"Predicting the number of reported and unreported cases for the COVID19 epidemic in South Korea, Italy, France, and Germany" DOI: doi.org/10.1101/2020.03.21.20040154 BioRxiv on March 24, 2020.

4. Victor Alexander Okhuese -"MATHEMATICAL PREDICTIONS FOR COVID19 AS A GLOBAL PANDEMIC" DOI: doi.org/10.1101/2020.03.19.20038794 PP:1-16 BioRxiv on March 24, 2020.

5. Jian Lu -"A New, Simple Projection Model for COVID19 Pandemic" DOI: doi.org/10.1101/2020.03.21.20039867 PP: 1-10 BioRxiv on March 24, 2020.

6. Indrani Roy -"Combating Recent Pandemic of COVID19 -An Urgent Solution" DOI: DOI: 10.20944/preprints202003.0366.v1 PP:1-5 Preprints March 2020.

7. L. Li *et al.*, "Characterizing the Propagation of Situational Information in Social Media During COVID19 Epidemic: A Case Study on Weibo," in IEEE Transactions on Computational Social Systems DOI: 10.1109/TCSS.2020.2980007PP:1 -7 ISSN:2329-924X IEEE March 2020.

8. Prateek Agrawal, Vishu Madaan, Aditya Roy, Ranjna Kumari, Harshal Deore, "FOCOMO: Forecasting and monitoring the worldwide spread of COVID-19 using machine learning methods", Journal of Interdisciplinary Mathematics, pp. 1-25. DOI:10.1080/09720502.2021.1885812.

9. Vishu Madaan, Aditya Roy, Charu Gupta, Prateek Agrawal, Anand Sharma, Christian Bologa, Radu Prodan, "XCOVNet: Chest X-ray Image Classification for COVID-19 Early Detection Using Convolutional Neural Networks", New Generation Computing, pp. 1-15. DOI: 10.1007/s00354-021-00121-7.

10. Akshat Agrawal, Rajesh Arora, Ranjana Arora, Prateek Agrawal, "Applications of Artificial Intelligence and Internet of Things for Detection and Future to Fight against COVID-19", A book on Emerging Technologies for battling COVID-19- Applications and Innovations, pp. 107-120, Springer.

11. Kartik Goel, Charu Gupta, Ria Rawal, Prateek Agrawal, Vishu Madaan, "FaD-CODS Fake News Detection on COVID-19 Using Description Logics and Semantic Reasoning", International Journal of Information Technology and Web Engineering (IJITWI), 16(3), pp 1-15, 2021.

12. Dr. Niranjanamurthy M, Amulya M P: "Coronavirus – COVID19 before and after solution through web application and app". International Journal

of Advanced Science and Technology Vol. 29, No. 5s, (2020), pp. 27-41 ISSN: 2005 -4238 IJAST http://sersc.org/journals/index.php/IJAST/article/ view/7012/4180.

13. World Health Organization: Coronavirus disease (COVID19) outbreak. Web site: https://www.who.int/emergencies/diseases/novel-coronavirus-2019, accessed on 25/03/2020.

14. Joe Hasell, Esteban Ortiz-Ospina, Edouard Mathieu, Hannah Ritchie, Diana Beltekian, Bobbie Macdonald, and Max Roser. Statistics and Research Coronavirus (COVID19) Testing.

15. A. C. Ghani, C. A. Donnelly, D. R. Cox, J. T. Griffin, C. Fraser, T. H. Lam, L. M. Ho, W. S. Chan, R. M. Anderson, A. J. Hedley, G. M. Leung.Methods for Estimating the Case Fatality Ratio for a Novel, Emerging Infectious Disease. American Journal of Epidemiology, Volume 162, Issue 5, 1 September 2005, Pages 479–486, DOI: 10.1093/aje/kwi230.

16. Cleo Anastassopoulou, Lucia Russo, Athanasios Tsakris, Constantinos Siettos. Data-based analysis, modeling, and forecasting of the COVID19 outbreak. Plosone March 31, 2020 DOI: 10.1371/journal.pone.0230405.

8

Analysis and Impact of Climatic Conditions on COVID-19 Using Machine Learning

Prasenjit Das[1], Shaily Jain[1], Shankar Shambhu[2] and Chetan Sharma[3]*

[1]Chitkara University School of Computer Applications, Rajpura, Patiala, India
[2]Chitkara University Institute of Engineering and Technology, Rajpura, Patiala, India
[3]Chitkara University, Himachal Pradesh, Solan, India

Abstract

Coronavirus is a pandemic nowadays around the globe. This epidemic started from China and spread to the other countries of the world rapidly. The effect of this deadly disease is causing a huge number of deaths per day around the globe. Initially, it started spreading in the countries where the temperature is relatively low like Europe and North America. India also started witnessing cases in the month of February, which is by and large not that hot a month in the country. This created a belief in India that when the summers are set in the country, the virus would not have any or very little effect, but gradually this belief faded away and the coronavirus surrounded India and affected the regions which are comparatively hotter than other areas. In this paper, we have taken this temperature effect as one criterion for coronavirus and shown the relationship between coronavirus and temperature. Our result of r2 (r-squared), which is a measure of independence, has a value of +0.75 indicating that the factor of temperature has no significance in the rise in the number of Covid cases in India.

Keywords: Corona, Covid-19, transmission, temperature, variance, r-squared

*Corresponding author: chetan.sharma@chitkarauniversity.edu.in

Prateek Agrawal, Charu Gupta, Anand Sharma, Vishu Madaan, and Nisheeth Joshi (eds.) Machine Learning and Data Science: Fundamentals and Applications, (135–146) © 2022 Scrivener Publishing LLC

8.1 Introduction

The epic coronavirus, classified as 2019-nCoV, developed in Wuhan City, China in late 2019. As of January 24, 2020, 830 conditions were investigated from 9 nations of the world. Most of these nations were on the Asian continent, namely China, Japan, South Korea, Thailand, Singapore, Vietnam, Taiwan, Nepal, India, and United States. Twenty-six people died, mostly from patients who had primarily underlying illness [1]. Although hidden from the prevalence of infection in this way, its source and potential for transmission to humans, remain invisible and a major cause of increase in the number of cases across the world is from human transmission. As per the WHO, at the end of January a total 7818 cases were confirmed worldwide and out of them approximately 95% of cases were from China and only 82 cases were found in 18 countries other than China. At that time, the risk level was very high in China but later on with time it spread all over the world. The first occurrence of severe acute respiratory syndrome coronavirus (SARS-CoV) was detected in 2002 and after that, Middle East respiratory syndrome coronavirus (MERS-CoV) was detected in 2012. The third type of coronavirus, 2019-nCoV, appears in the human bodies, is transmitted from one human to another, and places the global health sector on high alert [2, 3].

The World Health Organization (WHO) was informed by China and the organization set out the task of organizing diagnostic tests and giving instructions for assessment and treatment. WHO was also active in giving out travel advisories and updated data, country-wise, related to number of cases and fatalities on day to day basis A few nations in the district, such as the United States, screened travellers from Wuhan or China for fever, planning to recognize 2019-nCoV cases before the infection spread further. Updates from Japan, Thailand, China, and Korea demonstrate that the difficulty related with 2019-nCoV is soft compared to SARS and MERS [4].

Coronavirus is the virus which has a huge family of viruses through which different birds and mammals are infected. It also infects humans as per the indication given by the World Health Organisation (WHO) [5]. All over the world, a number of outbreaks occurred for which these viruses are answerable, including the Severe Acute Respiratory Syndrome (SARS) pandemic of 2002-2003 and the Middle East Respiratory Syndrome (MERS) outbreak in South Korea in 2015 [6]. In December 2019, a coronavirus (SARS-CoV-2, otherwise called COVID-19) was launched in Wuhan City of China, starting universal concern. Different coronaviruses have different impacts on animals, as well as humans. Some viruses have caused shocking epidemics and some have modest respiratory infections whose symptoms are the common cold. In retrospect studies, the outbreak of Severe Acute Respiratory Syndrome (SARS) in Guangdong in 2003 gradually faded with the warming weather [7]. Our hypothesis germinates from the fact that COVID-19 also belongs to the family of SARS and, as previous research work has indicated, the effect of the virus dies with a rise in diurnal temperature. Research by [8] has concluded that the deadly SARS virus had faded its effect with warming temperature. It has been documented that the temperature and its variations might have affected the SARS outbreak [9]. A study in Korea found that the risk of influenza incidence was significantly increased with low daily temperature and a positive significant association was observed for diurnal temperature range (DTR) [10]. Few studies reported that the COVID-19 was related to meteorological factors, which decreased with the temperature increasing [11].

8.1.1 Types of Coronavirus

Coronaviruses have a place with the subfamily Coronavirinae in the family Coronaviridae. Various sorts of human coronaviruses change in how serious the subsequent malady becomes and how far they can spread. Specialists, as of now, perceive seven sorts of coronavirus that can infect people [12].
Common Types

1. 229E (alpha corona virus)
2. NL63 (alpha corona virus)
3. OC43 (beta corona virus)
4. HKU1 (beta corona virus)

Remote problems that cause the most serious complications include MERS-CoV, which causes Middle East Respiratory Syndrome (MERS), and SARS-CoV, a viral respiratory syndrome (SARS) virus. In 2019, a new lethal strain called SARS-CoV-2 began circulating, causing the disease COVID-19 [13].

8.1.2 Transmission of Virus

According to the different doctors and organizations, COVID-19 is transmitting from one person to another by a number of ways, but the amount of research available is very scarce as. to how HCoV is spreading from one another. Doctors and different researchers gave the theory that this virus can be transmitted from one body to another through fluids like mucus, sneezing, etc. [14].

Coronaviruses can spread in the following ways:

When any person has the problem of coughing and sneezing, they will cough or sneeze without any precaution or
without covering the mouth and it spreads into the air,
which becomes the spreading medium. The virus spreads
when any person comes into contact with an infected person by touching them or shaking their hand. If any person
touches the surface or items which are infected from virus
or contain virus and after that they touch their nose, eyes,
or mouth, they get infected from the virus. A study tells us
that coronavirus is different in humans and animals, but it is
not clear whether both viruses have any connection between
them. National Institutes of Health (NIH) recommend that
there is a group or category of people who have the highest
risk factor to get infected from the COVID-19.

Group of people having highest risk factor from COVID-19 [15]:

1. Infants or children age less than 10 years
2. Old people aged 65 years or older
3. Pregnant women
4. Persons having a habit of smoking and drinking
5. Asthma patients
6. Person suffering from a disease related to the respiratory
    system

Most of the people will be infected by the coronavirus in their lifetime.
Coronavirus can transform efficiently, which makes the virus communicable. The best way to prevent the viruses is people must stay in their home
and avoid gathering and meeting with people. People must avoid close
touch or contact with people. People should follow social distancing in
which they must maintain a gap of one meter from others. People should
wear masks or cover their mouth and nose. To avoid the spreading of the
virus among the people is to maintain hygiene in your home and society
and follow the rules strictly.

8.2   COVID-19

SARS-CoV-2 is the new coronavirus which Centers for Disease Control
and Prevention (CDC) started monitoring in the year 2019 and this virus
is responsible for the respiratory illness called COVID-19. This virus was
firstly identified by the authorities in Wuhan, China [16]. Approximately

one million people were infected by the virus in China as per the records and further health authorities of different countries identified that numbers of people are infected from COVID-19 around the world and spreading from one person to another very fast. According to analysis, it is shown that one infected person from COVID-19 can infect roughly 2 to 2.5 people. COVID-19 mainly has four stages of spreading between the people [1].

Stage 1: The disease does not spread locally. In this stage, only those people will be found infected who have any travel history to an already infected country.

Stage 2: Diseases are spreading locally when any infected person who brought the virus came into contact with their friends and family. In this case, it is very easy to trace the infected people and they can quarantine easily so as not to spread to society.

Stage 3: It is very difficult to trace infected people because we do not know the source of the infection. In this stage, infection is also found in the people who do not have any travel history or have come into the contact with any infected person. This stage is highly communicable and difficult to control.

Stage 4: It is practically impossible to control the spreading of disease because it makes clusters all over the country and until now China was only the country who experienced this.

When this disease is communicable from one person to another person by the end of January 2020, the World Health Organization (WHO) announced a public health emergency towards the COVID-19 in around 25 countries [17]. In consideration to this, almost all countries locked down their countries to prevent the people from spreading the global pandemic.

The very first case of COVID-19 was found that must have some connection to an animal and seafood market. This relation shows the world that initially maybe this virus was transmitted from animal to human. This creates panic in people, but later on studies confirm that this virus can be passed from human to human [12]. At present conditions, almost all countries suffer from COVID-19, which is very scary. As discussed earlier, SARS and MERS coronaviruses, which develop respiratory conditions in a person, can spread only through close contact with an infected person.

Common Symptoms of COVID-19

1. High Fever
2. Cough
3. Sneezing

4. Breathlessness
5. Person takes 2-14 days to get the symptoms of COVID-19

COVID – 19 symptoms can vary from person to person. People may have some symptoms or in some cases people have no symptoms. This virus can result in illness and even death [18].

Numerous theories are floating across the globe about how and when the pandemic will end and normalcy will prevail. These theories range from scientific reasoning to mythologies and superstitions. One such theory was that the coronavirus is not heat resistant and with the setting of summer across the globe or in the Indian subcontinent the virus will be gone.

In this chapter, we are working on this hypothesis to see if this theory holds in India. This theory was very much prevalent in India in the early days of the COVID-19 breakout. The reason provided for the same was that in the beginning of the year 2020 and end of 2019, China was the only country which was fighting against this virus. Now, China experiences sub-zero temperatures in winters (December-January) [18, 19]. The countries that were getting effected during that period and after January were European Countries (Italy, Spain) and the temperatures in those countries during that period were also experiencing similar weather conditions. In India though the cases of COVID19 started much later. The virus started showing its ugly side in the last week of February and early March 2020. Barring a few states, most of the nation is still not witnessing high temperatures. Figure 8.1 shows the number of active cases in the states until December 2020.

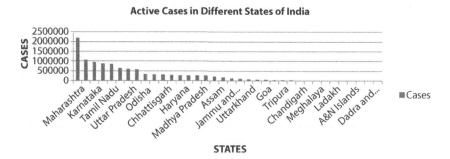

Figure 8.1 Number of active cases in different states of India.

8.3   Experimental Setup

The dataset comprises of the government of India website which showed the number of active cases in each state of India. The dataset has been taken from [19]. The dataset was taken from February 2020 when the cases of COVID-19 started trickling in India until 31st December, 2020. Figure 8.2 shows the active number of cases in each state and the average temperature during the period. It is widely believed that the number of cases increased across all the states very unevenly and after this event lead to a

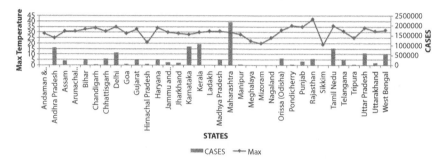

Figure 8.2   Active cases and average temperature in all states of India.

Table 8.1   Dataset used.

S. no.	State	Active	Max	Min
1	Maharashtra	2179185	34	28
2	Kerala	1067045	37	18
3	Karnataka	952565	36	22
4	Andhra Pradesh	890215	34	25
5	Tamil Nadu	852967	33	22
6	Delhi	639921	45	1
7	Uttar Pradesh	603788	42	4
8	West Bengal	575712	33	26
9	Odisha	337448	33	22
10	Rajasthan	320772	48	22

huge number of cases across the states of India. It has been documented and affirmed by Wang et. Al that COVID-19 is transmitted from humans who come in contact with each other [20]. The dataset comprises of the number of active cases in each of the states of India. To check the effect of temperature, we have taken the max and minimum temperature of each of these states from the government of India website [21].

We have considered the average of Maximum and Minimum temperature of all the states. A glimpse of the dataset is shown in Table 8.1.

8.4   Proposed Methodology

Our experiment is based on the hypothesis that the temperature has a significant effect in number of active cases of coronavirus in India. Authors in [22–24] have used different machine learning, CNN, and AI techniques for monitoring, early detection, and fighting mechanisms against this deadly disease. We know that the temperature of any state is an independent variable and the number of effective cases in the state is a dependent variable. In this chapter, we have taken the dataset from the website referring to WHO as mentioned earlier and then we select attributes from the given dataset. As we need only the number of cases state wise, we have selected only those attributes which contribute to our experiment. Then, we used Python in an Anaconda setup to evaluate our results. We calculated the R squared coefficient of determination to find linear regression between the two variables temperature and number of active cases in a state. In statistics, the coefficient of determination, denoted R2 or r2 and pronounced as "R squared", is the proportion of variance in the dependent variable that is predictable from the independent variable(s). Our aim is to check the hypothesis that temperature has an effect on the number of active cases.

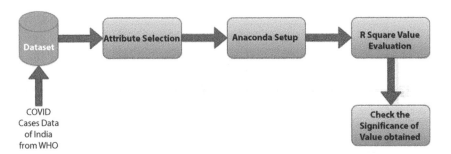

Figure 8.3 Proposed methodology.

```
                            OLS Regression Results
================================================================================
Dep. Variable:                    Deaths   R-squared:                     0.075
Model:                               OLS   Adj. R-squared:                0.042
Method:                    Least Squares   F-statistic:                   2.272
Date:                   Tue, 21 Apr 2020   Prob (F-statistic):            0.143
Time:                           14:04:22   Log-Likelihood:               41.281
No. Observations:                     30   AIC:                          -78.56
Df Residuals:                         28   BIC:                          -75.76
Df Model:                              1
Covariance Type:               nonrobust
================================================================================
                 coef     std err          t      P>|t|      [0.025      0.975]
--------------------------------------------------------------------------------
const          0.1225       0.063      1.950      0.061      -0.006       0.251
Max           -0.0029       0.002     -1.507      0.143      -0.007       0.001
================================================================================
Omnibus:                          39.967   Durbin-Watson:                 1.949
Prob(Omnibus):                     0.000   Jarque-Bera (JB):            142.573
Skew:                              2.721   Prob(JB):                   1.10e-31
Kurtosis:                         12.190   Cond. No.                       181.
================================================================================
```

Figure 8.4 Snapshot of Anaconda Execution output.

Finally, the value of R squared has been analysed. The proposed methodology is shown in Figure 8.3.

8.5   Results Discussion

The experimental setup on Anaconda is shown in Figure 8.3. We have imported some libraries like Numpy and Pandas for our experimentation. Figure 8.4 shows the snapshot of results obtained after running the steps and hence the value of R2. The value of R2 comes out as .075 or only 7.5%, which is not a significant value. It means that the temperature effect on COVID cases has only 7.5% impact, which is a very insignificant value, so to say it has no significance. This shows that our hypothesis that temperature effects the number of cases is not correct, i.e., temperature does not have any relationship with the increase and decrease in number of affected corona cases in the globe.

8.6   Conclusion and Future Work

Hence, we can conclude from the results of the R2 value that there is no linear relationship between two independent variables, i.e., temperature and active corona affected cases in different states in India. The .075 value of R2 leads to least significance and hence shows no relationship between temperature and corona cases. Our analysis will help medical practitioners to break this myth.

In the future, we can extend this work on determining the death rate comparison in terms of gender, age, and region. We can also take other factors like previous medical history and dietary habits into consideration for determining the correlation between these factors and COVID-19 deaths.

References

1. S. S. Unhale, Q. B. Ansar, S. Sanap, S. Thakhre, and S. Wadatkar, "a Review on Corona Virus (Covid-19)," World J. Pharm. Life Sci, vol. 6, no. 4, pp. 109–115, 2020.

2. P. C. Y. Woo, Y. Huang, S. K. P. Lau, and K.-Y. Yuen, "Coronavirus genomics and bioinformatics analysis," Viruses, vol. 2, no. 8, pp. 1804–1820, 2010.

3. J. F. Drexler *et al.*, "Genomic characterization of severe acute respiratory syndrome-related coronavirus in European bats and classification of coronaviruses based on partial RNA-dependent RNA polymerase gene sequences," J. Virol., vol. 84, no. 21, pp. 11336–11349, 2010.

4. Y. Yin and R. G. Wunderink, "MERS, SARS and other coronaviruses as causes of pneumonia," Respirology, vol. 23, no. 2, pp. 130–137, 2018.

5. "World Health Organization." https://www.who.int/emergencies/diseases/novel-coronavirus-2019/situation-reports (accessed Apr. 10, 2020).

6. J. S. M. Peiris *et al.*, "Coronavirus as a possible cause of severe acute respiratory syndrome," Lancet, vol. 361, no. 9366, pp. 1319–1325, 2003.

7. Y. Ma *et al.*, "Effects of temperature variation and humidity on the death of COVID-19 in Wuhan, China," Sci. Total Environ., p. 138226, 2020.

8. P. Wallis and B. Nerlich, "Disease metaphors in new epidemics: the UK media framing of the 2003 SARS epidemic," Soc. Sci. Med., vol. 60, no. 11, pp. 2629–2639, 2005.

9. J. Tan, L. Mu, J. Huang, S. Yu, B. Chen, and J. Yin, "An initial investigation of the association between the SARS outbreak and weather: with the view of the environmental temperature and its variation," J. Epidemiol. Community Heal., vol. 59, no. 3, pp. 186–192, 2005.

10. J.-E. Park, W.-S. Son, Y. Ryu, S. B. Choi, O. Kwon, and I. Ahn, "Effects of temperature, humidity, and diurnal temperature range on influenza incidence in a temperate region," Influenza Other Respi. Viruses, vol. 14, no. 1, pp. 11–18, 2020.

11. B. Oliveiros, L. Caramelo, N. C. Ferreira, and F. Caramelo, "Role of temperature and humidity in the modulation of the doubling time of COVID-19 cases," medRxiv, 2020.

12. S. Salehi, A. Abedi, S. Balakrishnan, and A. Gholamrezanezhad, "Coronavirus disease 2019 (COVID-19): a systematic review of imaging findings in 919 patients," Am. J. Roentgenol., pp. 1–7, 2020.

13. L. E. Gralinski and V. D. Menachery, "Return of the Coronavirus: 2019-nCoV," Viruses, vol. 12, no. 2, p. 135, 2020.

14. H. K. H. Luk, X. Li, J. Fung, S. K. P. Lau, and P. C. Y. Woo, "Molecular epidemiology, evolution and phylogeny of SARS coronavirus," Infect. Genet. Evol., vol. 71, pp. 21–30, 2019.

15. L. Wang, Y. Wang, D. Ye, and Q. Liu, "A review of the 2019 Novel Coronavirus (COVID-19) based on current evidence," Int. J. Antimicrob. Agents, p. 105948, 2020.

16. Z. Chen et al., "From SARS-CoV to Wuhan 2019-nCoV outbreak: Similarity of early epidemic and prediction of future trends," Cell-Host-Microbe-D-20-00063, 2020.

17. C. Sohrabi et al., "World Health Organization declares global emergency: A review of the 2019 novel coronavirus (COVID-19)," Int. J. Surg., 2020.

18. F. Jiang, L. Deng, L. Zhang, Y. Cai, C. W. Cheung, and Z. Xia, "Review of the clinical characteristics of coronavirus disease 2019 (COVID-19)," J. Gen. Intern. Med., pp. 1–5, 2020.

19. "India Covid 19." https://www.covid19india.org/ (accessed March 8, 2021).

20. C. Wang, P. W. Horby, F. G. Hayden, and G. F. Gao, "A novel coronavirus outbreak of global health concern," Lancet, vol. 395, no. 10223, pp. 470–473, 2020.

21. "India Meteorological Department." https://mausam.imd.gov.in/imd_latest/contents/departmentalweb.php (accessed Apr. 10, 2020).

22. Prateek Agrawal, Vishu Madaan, Aditya Roy, Ranjna Kumari, Harshal Deore, "FOCOMO: Forecasting and monitoring the worldwide spread of COVID-19 using machine learning methods", Journal of Interdisciplinary Mathematics, pp. 1-25. DOI:10.1080/09720502.2021.1885812.

23. Vishu Madaan, Aditya Roy, Charu Gupta, Prateek Agrawal, Anand Sharma, Christian Bologa, Radu Prodan, "XCOVNet: Chest X-ray Image Classification for COVID-19 Early Detection Using Convolutional Neural Networks", New Generation Computing, pp. 1-15. DOI: 10.1007/s00354-021-00121-7.

24. Akshat Agrawal, Rajesh Arora, Ranjana Arora, Prateek Agrawal, "Applications of Artificial Intelligence and Internet of Things for Detection and Future to Fight against COVID-19", A book on Emerging Technologies for battling COVID-19- Applications and Innovations, pp. 107-120, Springer.

Application of Hadoop in Data Science

Balraj Singh[1,2]* and Harsh K. Verma[1]

[1]Department of Computer Science and Engineering, NIT, Jalandhar, India
[2]Department of Computer Science and Engineering, Lovely Professional University, Punjab, India

Abstract

Continued growth and integration of information technology in every aspect of human life has given benefits, opportunities, and challenges. The benefits lie in improved living standards and advancements, while the major challenges are to understand the information lying deep inside the raw data. For getting insight into the raw data, the emergence of Data Science has a significant role. The extraction of data, preparation for analysis, and visualization are the core activities of the Data Science domain. It uses multi-disciplinary statistical methods and techniques to obtain meaningful information from the data. From small to large scale organizations, all are in pursuit of taking benefits from the available information to aggressively compete and thrive. With the diverse application of statistical logics, Data Science has emerged as a new standard for growth by utilizing state-of-the-art technologies and tools. Many software platforms and tools are contesting each other to provide advanced support and cutting-edge solutions for Data Science to dominate the market. "More is less", seems to be a new motto nowadays to investigate the options and availability of the platforms. Among the leading platforms, Hadoop has attained a distinction and a larger market share in the Data Science field. Hadoop provides versatility, flexibility, and simplicity while being enriched in processing data using commodity clusters. The associated economy and efficient processing of the data has made it a preferred choice for stakeholders from diverse backgrounds to adapt it. Hadoop is now a de facto and optimal choice for Data Scientists. Big Data and Data Science go hand-in-hand. The former is concerned with the challenges related to analyzing data in terms of velocity, variety, veracity, and volume, while the latter tends to provide solutions utilizing various

*Corresponding author: singh.balraj@hotmail.com

Prateek Agrawal, Charu Gupta, Anand Sharma, Vishu Madaan, and Nisheeth Joshi (eds.) Machine Learning and Data Science: Fundamentals and Applications, (147–168) © 2022 Scrivener Publishing LLC

mathematical approaches and computational research. This chapter discusses the key importance of Data Science along with the utility of the Hadoop platform for processing data.

Keywords: Big Data, Data Science, Hadoop, MapReduce

9.1   Introduction

Data has turned out to be one of the most important resources in today's world. Organizations have the option to cherish using data or perish. The exponential growth of data, if utilized scientifically and statistically with appropriate platforms, would bring wonders. An intelligent observation and analysis of the available data reflects the actual state of the business and its success [1]. The role of Data Science is paramount in such environments and organizations. The evolution of the methodologies and ease of working has given an opportunity to work closely with the data science and trending platforms. Large data provides larger opportunities. Data Science is turning out to be of extreme importance due to the dire need for understanding hidden information from the enormous data being produced. With the utility of software platforms and tools for managing large-scale data, the insurgence of Data Science for analysis is getting principal importance. To understand various relationships between the datasets, the scientists are taking advantage of machine learning techniques, statistical tools, and Big Data platforms. Big Data tools, such as Hadoop, have aided in various advancements in Data Science by facilitating the efficient processing of data and providing various utilities to Data Scientists. Data Science, in association with Big Data, has shaped a new paradigm in this modern world [2]. The basic organization of the chapter is as follows: Section 9.1 covers the details of Data Science and Big Data, Section 9.2 discusses the Hadoop platform, Section 9.3 discusses the use of Hadoop with Data Science, Section 9.4 discusses the studies representing the use of Data Science with the Hadoop platform, and the last section concludes the chapter.

9.1.1   Data Science

Data science is a multi-disciplinary approach that employs scientific techniques and procedures to draw meaningful understandings out of the raw data. It is an art of bringing hidden information from the data and uncovering important insights [3]. The advent of technology has resulted in the rapid development of enormous data. With the availability of large-scale data processing systems such as Hadoop, a combination of Big Data with

Data Science has given a breakthrough to society [4]. Data Science utilizes a diverse set of techniques to gather information and process it. It is a unified model of statistic methods, data analysis techniques, and machine learning to uncover the important information hidden in the data [5]. Data science helps in extracting, preparing, analyzing, and maintaining the data, as well as information extraction. It has a close relationship with machine learning, statistics, and data mining, which it employs to perform basic analysis [6]. Authors in [7] represented that the main work of Data Science is to disclose knowledge from the raw data and discussed that Data Science is a technical implementation of techniques from the field of Computer Science and Mathematics.

9.1.1.1   Life Cycle of Data Science Process

The basic life cycle of a process involved with the application of Data Science focuses on five important stages [8]. Figure 9.1 shows the life cycle of Hadoop. These include the initial step of data acquisition until the last step of decision making. These five stages are:

I)   **Capture:** The initial stage is associated with understanding the business need, acquiring and ingesting the data through different sources, and extracting it.

II) **Maintain:** This phase involves the process of maintaining the data which includes cleansing the data, warehousing, and data architecture.

III) **Process:** This phase involves identifying the clustering group, classification, and data modelling. Mathematical models are developed and applied in these phases.

IV) **Analyse:** This phase performs analysis on the data and evaluation of the models. Identification of the discrepancies and issues are identified in this phase. The outcomes are derived to analyse and compare them with the business needs.

V)   **Communicate:** In the final stage of the cycle, interpretations and visualizations are done to facilitate decision-making

Figure 9.1 Life cycle of Data Science project.

and business intelligence. Communication and recommendations are done in this phase to make use of information obtained.

9.1.1.2   Applications of Data Science

Data Science has started playing an important role in almost every industry now. It turns out to be popular in different domains and has impacted all the fields [9]. The following are a few examples of the industries that utilize Data Science:

- **Healthcare:** Data Science has given a breakthrough in the healthcare industry. Various sectors in healthcare, such as medical imaging, drug discovery, automated surgery, etc., are benefiting from Data Science.
- **Banking:** In this sector, Data Science assists in managing customers by analyzing the available in a superior way. Banks can make better decisions for risk modeling, improve fraud detection, etc.
- **E-commerce:** One of the major stakeholders of Data Science is the e-commerce industry. It has enormously benefited from Data Science by identifying potential customers and optimizing prices and buying options.
- **Academics:** Data Science has helped in improving students' learning, instructors' teaching quality, curriculum, and pedagogy. The information obtained from academics is utilized vastly to improve the overall learning process.
- **Entertainment Industry:** Recommendation systems on YouTube and other platforms are primarily based upon the application of Data Science. It is used to enhance the customer's experience.
- **Manufacturing Industry:** The quality of products is being improved. The overall manufacturing process and workforce can be optimized. Reinforcement learning is utilized for automating the manufacturing process.
- **Transport:** Data Science is playing a key role in improving the transportation industry. It is facilitating better customer service and providing safer driving conditions. Self-driving vehicles are taking advantage of Data Science for better vehicle behavior.

9.1.2   Big Data

Big Data analytics are becoming an essential requirement for every field [10]. The data scientist working on these analytics needs to access Big Data processing platforms. Big Data is an area that focuses on the ways to manage and process data which is of such a large scale that traditional data processing systems could not manage it. Big Data does not only refer to large-scale data but also includes platforms, technology, and tools. Scientists now have a wide range of choices to opt from different computing platforms [11, 12].

9.1.2.1   Benefits of Big Data

For an organization, it is imperative to understand the potential benefits of Big Data. Data could be taken from any source and utilized to understand the underlying issues. Table 9.1 represents some of the key benefits of Big Data applications [12].

9.1.2.2   Challenges in Big Data

Big data suffers from an ample number of challenges. It begins from the source of capturing the data, to further process it for obtaining useful information from it. Table 9.2 represents some of the challenges that are of prime concern in Big Data.

Table 9.1 Benefits of Big Data.

Improving business understanding	Competitive edge
Improve decision making Improving process and production	Calculate risk profiles Greater innovation

Table 9.2 Big Data challenges.

Capturing data	Data storage	Platform selection
Visualization	Data analytics	Data source
Querying	Importing/Exporting	Diversity of the data
Privacy and confidentiality	Sharing	Cost/Benefits

9.1.2.3   Characteristics of Big Data

Big Data has essential characteristics that influence it. Figure 9.2 shows the important characteristics of Big Data. The basic characteristics of Big Data that bring the actual challenge are given below [13]:

I.   **Volume:** It is the amount of data being generated. Enterprises capture data from multiple sources such as IoT sensors, commercial equipment, internet, etc. The quantity of data generated is among the initial characteristic of Big Data.

II. **Variety:** Variety represents the diversity of the data. The data exists in many forms such as structured, unstructured, and semi-structured. The Big Data platforms have to cope with the undefined types of data formats and convert them into their formats before processing them.

III. **Velocity:** A key characteristic of Big Data is the pace at which data is coming from different sources. It represents the rate of receiving and managing the data. The rapid data being generated by the live streaming portals such as Facebook, Twitter, etc. brings a real challenge and necessitates an organization to manage it for staying in the competition.
(Following are the new entries in Big Data characteristics)

IV. **Variability:** Another important factor is the flow of the data which is unpredictable. Sometimes, certain topics on social medial become trending and suddenly the flow of the data becomes very high, while on some occasions the data flow

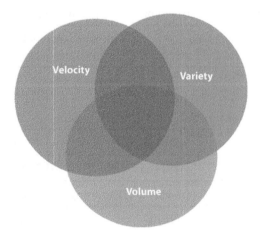

Figure 9.2 Big Data characteristics.

Table 9.3 Sources of Big Data.

Airplane Black Box	Social Media	Online Transactions	Research Data
Stock Exchange	Power Grids	Transport Data	Search Engine Data

becomes very low. Organizations have to understand such trends and plan out to manage them.

V. **Veracity:** This refers to the quality of the captured data. Since data is being generated and captured from multiple resources, it is not always feasible to clean and transfer it across multiple platforms. It is important to correlate the multiple linkages and hierarchies to manage the data effectively.

9.1.2.4   *Sources of Big Data*

Data is developed by multiple sources daily. The major contributors of Big Data [14] are given in Table 9.3. These develop an enormous amount of data every day.

9.2   Hadoop Distributed Processing

The large scale of data becomes a source of information that can provide a lot of insight into the current trends in business and different areas of the application. These data sets are structured, semi-structured, and unstructured. As Data Science has gained momentum, different platforms and tools are required to support it. The decision to opt for a particular tool or platform lies in the need of the organization and the type of data being generated. Different platforms have their advantages and limitations. The right combination of tools and infrastructure for processing Big Data can bring many fold advancements in an organization and provides an edge in the industry. However, the current scale of data makes it technically difficult to be processed on a single system. Distributed processing of the data becomes a viable solution where data is shared among multiple computing nodes to be processed in parallel [14]. One of the highly preferred choices for distributed processing of large-scale data is Hadoop. It has emerged as a platform of choice for empowering Data Science. Hadoop serves as a scalable platform and an engine for performing computations. It is capable of providing abstraction while performing the distributed processing with ease.

9.2.1   Anatomy of the Hadoop Ecosystem

Components of Hadoop are divided into major and supporting components. Figure 9.3 shows the basic architecture of Hadoop. Without major components, job processing cannot be accomplished while other components in Hadoop's ecosystem provide add-on services to facilitate job processing. The major components are:

- **Yarn:** Yarn is a managerial module of the Hadoop [15]. It takes care of the scheduling process, resource allocation, and utilization. In a distributed environment, the key challenge is to manage the resources. Yarn efficiently manages these resources in Hadoop. The resource manager negotiates the resources with the nodes to job demands. The node manager manages the node and facilitates the application with resources for job processing.
- **Hadoop Distributed File System (HDFS):** This is a principal component of the Hadoop to store data. Initially, data is loaded on the HDFS for processing [16].
- **MapReduce:** This is a programming model that processes the data on Hadoop [17]. It works on two phases: Map phase and Reduce phase. The Map phase converts the input into a Key-Value pair, while Reduce works on accepting the output

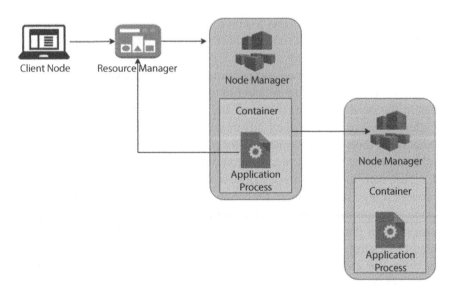

Figure 9.3 Hadoop architecture.

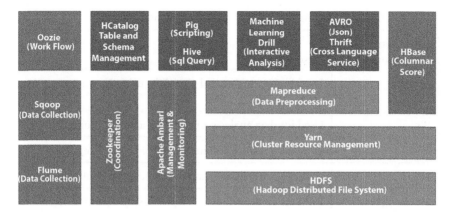

Figure 9.4 Hadoop ecosystem.

of the Map phase and aggregates the key bales for the final
output.
- **Hadoop Common:** Hadoop Common contains a set of
libraries and utilities required for working with the different
modules in Hadoop.

Different components of the Hadoop Ecosystem are shown in Figure
9.4.

9.2.2   Other Important Components of Hadoop Ecosystem

The name and descriptions of other components of the Hadoop, which
contains a suite of services, are given in Table 9.4 along with their basic
description [18].

9.2.3   MapReduce

MapReduce has integrated significant utilities inside it. MapReduce provides a programming model for job processing. Its applications run
in the Yarn cluster. MapReduce divides the process into the Map phase
and Reduce phase [19]. Initially, data is partitioned into multiple splits and
simultaneously assigned to the Maps. Intermediate values are sorted and
grouped according to the keys. Reducers take this data during the shuffle
period and combine it as a single sorted stream. Values with the same keys
are allocated to a single Reducer. Finally, the output of Reduce nodes is
written to HDFS. Figure 9.4 shows the basic structure of the MapReduce.

Table 9.4 Other important components of hadoop ecosystem.

Ecosystem component	Description
Spark	Used for processing real-time jobs using in-memory processing
Pig	Used for data analysis and writing analysis programs
Hive	Used for analytics and utilizes Hive Query Language
HBase	A NoSQL distributed database to retrieve small data
HCatalog	Used for creating tables and processing data of different formats
Thrift	Utilized for cross-language services
Flume	Utilized to ingest data into HDFS from multiple sources
Sqoop	Utilized for ingesting data from a relational database to HDFS
Oozie	Utilized for multiple jobs and managing them
Avro	Utilized for data exchange and serialization
Ambari	Utilized for managing and monitoring clusters
Zookeeper	Utilized for synchronization and coordination among nodes
Drill	Query engine for processing structured and semi-structured data
Mahout	Provides support for machine learning algorithms

Typically, the Map phase deals with the Map function created by the user which splits the job into intermediate sub-processes. The Reduce phase deals with the Reduce function which merges all the intermediate sub-processes. Figure 9.5 shows an illustration of MapReduce for the word count process. The data is initially given as an input for the Map phase where key-based segregation is done. After intermediate processing, an allocation is done to the Reduce phase where key-wise final data is organized for final output as shown in Figure 9.6.

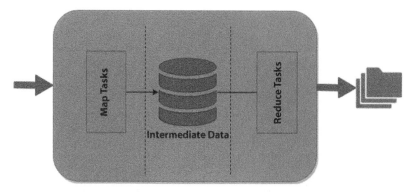

Figure 9.5 MapReduce mechanism.

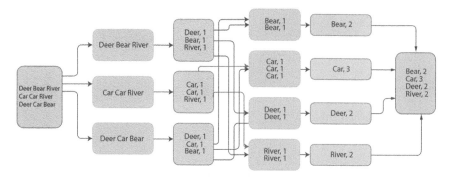

Figure 9.6 MapReduce process.

9.2.4   Need for Hadoop

Hadoop provides an abundance of benefits for processing large-scale jobs in a distributed environment [20]. Some of the potential benefits of Hadoop are shown in Figure 9.7.

Key capabilities which make Hadoop a highly capable distributed system are:

- **Scalability:** The size of the cluster can be increased and decreased without downtime. It supports both horizontal and vertical scaling.
- **Fault Tolerance:** With a replication factor of three, Hadoop saves data on multiple places and makes the system highly fault-tolerant.

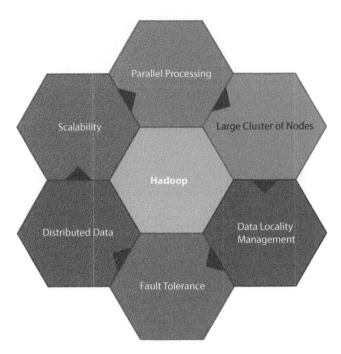

Figure 9.7 Benefits of hadoop.

- **Schema Independence:** It supports data in different formats which may be structured, semi-structured, and unstructured.
- **High Throughput:** The parallel processing mechanism of the Hadoop yields more processing per unit time and gives high throughput and low latency.
- **Share-nothing Architecture:** Nodes in the cluster are not dependent upon other nodes.
- **Data Locality:** In Hadoop, code is moved to the location where data resides and lowers the network traffic and cost associated with it.
- **Heterogeneous Clusters:** The cluster in Hadoop is formed of different types of resources.
- **Cost-Effective:** Upgrading of a cluster can be done with commodity hardware.

9.2.5   Applications of Hadoop

Hadoop has wide applications in multiple domains and fields [20]. Some of the applications are given in Figure 9.8. Hadoop is used in the retail industry to understand customer requirements. In the financial industry, it is used for forecasting and trading purposes. Trading plans and decisions are done using data processing through the Hadoop platform. Healthcare systems utilize the Hadoop platform to analyze public health data and quantify the improvements. The sports industry employs the Hadoop platform to process data collected through sensors to improve the performance of the players. Multi-disciplinary research is carried on Hadoop platforms for processing extremely large-scale data [21]. The banking sector is among the biggest sectors utilizing Hadoop. Below, are some of the applications. Hadoop is playing an important role in the majority of the important domains in the industry.

9.2.6   Use of Hadoop with Data Science

Hadoop is an important platform for Data Science for processing data efficiently [22]. It provides applications to work with a large number of computation nodes to perform distributed computing of the jobs and perform the Data Science activities effectively. Hadoop provides abstraction such that the data is shared across multiple nodes and the final output is

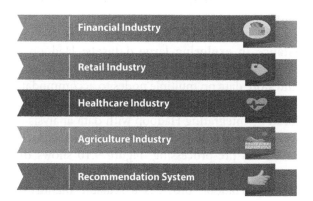

Figure 9.8 Applications of Hadoop.

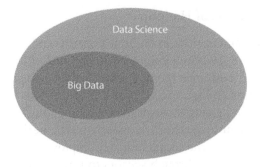

Figure 9.9 Representation of Big Data in Data Science.

received at a single place. Figure 9.9 shows Big Data in the sphere of Data Science.

9.3   Using Hadoop with Data Science

9.3.1   Reasons for Hadoop Being a Preferred Choice for Data Science

Hadoop is an ideal choice for data scientists. The following are some of the reasons [23]:

1) **Capability to store data in the unstructured form:** Hadoop can store data in a raw and unstructured form on HDFS. This makes it a better choice against others.
2) **Assistance in exploring large datasets:** Hadoop has the capability to provide exploratory data analysis. It can distribute and store data on multiple nodes to accommodate large-scale data processing. The larger data sets can be directly explored by integrating Hadoop with data analysis flow. To achieve this, simple statistics are used such as mean, median, quantile, and pre-processing. Figure 9.10 shows the basic process of data processing.
3) **Scalability:** Hadoop provides a scalable platform and is fault-tolerant. Two scalability options are supported in Hadoop: 1) Vertical scalability where more resources can be added to a single node to increase the overall capacity of the platform and 2) Horizontal scalability where more nodes

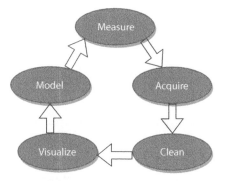

Figure 9.10 Basic process of data processing.

are added to the platform, i.e., more machines are added to enhance the computing capacity.

4) **Schema on reading:** Efficient in loading data, it initially stores the data and later performs the required analysis. Schema on read provides data agility by the application of schema-on-read and avoids the requirement for schema redesign. Figure 9.11 and Figure 9.12 shows schema on read and schema on write. It overcomes the barriers of traditional systems which use schema on write and suffer from slower processing and loading of the data.

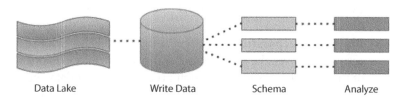

Figure 9.11 On read schema.

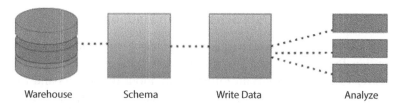

Figure 9.12 On write schema.

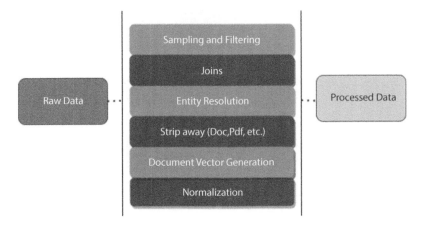

Figure 9.13 Data preparation process.

5) **Transparent parallelism:** Code deployment, storage, processing, and MapReduce capabilities make the Hadoop platform transparent in terms of implementation.

6) **Computing power:** With commodity hardware and easy scalability, Hadoop can achieve enormous computing power by utilizing multiple nodes.

7) **Mining large data sets:** The machine learning algorithms with large datasets suffer from memory availability and a longer period to learn. However, with Hadoop, these issues can be avoided by distributing the data across multiple nodes in the cluster.

8) **Big Data preparation:** A large amount of Data Science activity involves the preparation of the data. Hadoop is one of the suitable solutions for batch processing of the data and cleaning large data sets. Figure 9.13 depicts the data preparation process.

9.3.2   Studies Using Data Science with Hadoop

In [24], the author utilized the platform Hadoop to perform analysis of the Indian Premier League. The author performed analytics on the data of Twitter to extract important information about the players and trends going on on Twitter. Authors in [25] represented the concern of energy efficiency in Hadoop for performing Big Data analytics. The authors reviewed different studies on Hadoop concerning energy efficiency for processing large-scale data to perform Data Science activities.

In [26], authors reviewed different software platforms available to support Data Science activities. They classified the various platforms based on their attributes such as abstraction, supporting the underlying engine, and languages supported. The authors critically discuss the limitations and requirements for Big Data platforms to cater to the future needs of the Data Scientist. In [27], authors proposed an architectural framework to assist research in higher education. The authors utilized Hadoop as a part of the proposed solution to perform Data Science activities on the data. In [28], the use and applicability of Hadoop in bioinformatics is discussed by the authors. They represented the utility of Hadoop in the analysis of data in the bioinformatics field where massive data is being generated. As per the authors, Hadoop is a preferred choice in the bioinformatics community for performing scientific analysis. In [29], authors represented the significance of Data Science analysis for geographical problems. The authors represented that a lot of insight can be taken with the help of Data Science using large-scale platforms such as Hadoop to have a better understanding of the existing issues. In [30], the authors represented the use of Hadoop for analysis in the ongoing epidemic COVID-19. They discussed the benefits of Hadoop and work on modeling the problems using the Hadoop platform for performing analytics. In [31], authors represented the implementation of Hadoop for the Data Science platform for healthcare data. The authors demonstrated the use of healthcare applications on the open-source system Hadoop. In [32], authors used Data Science and the Hadoop platform in image processing. They proposed to lower the noise in the image with the help of applying adaptive filters. In [33], the authors utilized the Hadoop platform to index the documents for performing Big Data analytics. The authors represented the use of Apache Lucene with Hadoop to index the text data. In [34], the authors proposed an approach to process the raw tweets of the users to perform sentimental analysis and extract meaningful information from them. The authors used the Hadoop platform to perform the analysis of the data. In [35], the authors showed the utility of the Hadoop platform to perform the Data Science activities for extracting and analyzing the seismic attributes in the field of petroleum exploration. In [36], the authors showed the use of Hadoop for Big Data analytics. The authors performed an analysis of the temperature data set for showing the utility of Hadoop in the weather domain. In [37], the use of Hadoop for Data Science-based analysis in bioinformatics is discussed. The authors showed the utility of Hadoop in the analysis of next-generation sequencing in bioinformatics. In [38], the use of Hadoop for improving satellite imaging and its analysis are represented. The authors implemented Hadoop's MapReduce model to classify the data of remote sensing images. In [39], the authors implemented the healthcare data on the Hadoop platform for performing analysis. They loaded the data of healthcare on HDFS and simulated it as an entire healthcare data for performing analysis. In [40], the analysis of logs using the Hadoop platform is shown. The authors discussed the utility of Hadoop for performing analysis and extracting information about the different activities of the users. The authors in [41] discussed the analysis framework for geospatial data. Hadoop and its programming model MapReduce for performing analysis are used for the analysis. In [42], the authors performed sentiment analysis. The authors performed a semantic analysis of tweets by proposing a new formula to differentiate negative and positive words. The underlying platform for the analysis was Hadoop with MapReduce programming model. Some machine learning and Big Data analytics based medical applications [43–46] were also recently developed.

9.4   Conclusion

Data Science provides enormous scope for improving mankind and different industries. It has a vital role to play in every domain. A combination of Data Science with powerful platforms will take the information findings and interpretations to the next level. Hadoop is a promising platform and has turned out to be a comprehensive platform for performing analytics through its different tools. A majority of Data Science activities are processed on the Hadoop platform, owing to its capability of storing large amounts of data and providing distributed processing. To conclude, we will say that Data Science along with Hadoop has tremendous scope for the future and together these will achieve new heights in data extraction, information interpretation, and serving society.

References

1. Grus, Joel. *Data science from scratch: first principles with python.* O'Reilly Media, 2019.
2. Sun, Zhaohao, Lizhe Sun, and Kenneth Strang. "Big data analytics services for enhancing business intelligence." *Journal of Computer Information Systems* 58.2 (2018): 162-169.

3. VanderPlas, Jake. *Python data science handbook: Essential tools for working with data*. "O'Reilly Media, Inc.", 2016.
4. Berti, Alessandro, Sebastiaan J. van Zelst, and Wil van der Aalst. "Process mining for Python (PM4Py): bridging the gap between process-and data science." *arXiv preprint arXiv:1905.06169* (2019).
5. "Data Science," Wikepedia, Wikepedia Foundation, 21 Mar. 2020, en.wikepedia.org/wiki/Data_science
6. Concolato, Claude E., and Li M. Chen. "Data science: A new paradigm in the age of big-data science and analytics." *New Mathematics and Natural Computation* 13.02 (2017): 119-143.
7. Dhar, Vasant, Matthias Jarke, and Jürgen Laartz. "Big data." (2014): 257-259.
8. Brough, David B., Daniel Wheeler, and Surya R. Kalidindi. "Materials knowledge systems in python—a data science framework for accelerated development of hierarchical materials." *Integrating materials and manufacturing innovation* 6.1 (2017): 36-53.
9. Baesens, Bart. *Analytics in a big data world: The essential guide to data science and its applications*. John Wiley & Sons, 2014.
10. Concolato, Claude E., and Li M. Chen. "Data science: A new paradigm in the age of big-data science and analytics." *New Mathematics and Natural Computation* 13.02 (2017): 119-143.
11. Ovidiu-Cristian Marcu, Alexandru Costan, Gabriel Antoniu, and María S. Pérez-Hernández. "Spark Versus Flink: Understanding Performance in Big Data Analytics Frameworks". *s: 2016 IEEE International Conference on Cluster Computing*. 2016, pp. 433–442.
12. Parmita Mehta, Sven Dorkenwald, Dongfang Zhao, Tomer Kaftan, Alvin Cheung, Magdalena Balazinska, Ariel Rokem, Andrew J. Connolly, Jacob VanderPlas, and Yusra AlSayyad. "Comparative Evaluation of BigData Systems on Scientific Image Analytics Workloads". *In: PVLDB* 10.11 (2017), pp. 1226–1237.
13. Anuradha, J. "A brief introduction on Big Data 5Vs characteristics and Hadoop technology." *Procedia computer science* 48 (2015): 319-324.
14. Husain, Baydaa Hassan, and Subhi RM Zeebaree. "Improvised distributions framework of Hadoop: A review." *International Journal of Science and Business* 5.2 (2021): 31-41.
15. Yao, Yi, *et al.* "New scheduling algorithms for improving performance and resource utilization in hadoop YARN clusters." *IEEE Transactions on Cloud Computing* (2019).
16. Ouatik, Farouk, M. Erritali, and M. Jourhmane. "Comparative study of MapReduce classification algorithms for students orientation." *Procedia Computer Science* 170 (2020): 1192-1197.
17. Alarabi, Louai, Mohamed F. Mokbel, and Mashaal Musleh. "St-hadoop: A mapreduce framework for spatio-temporal data." *GeoInformatica* 22.4 (2018): 785-813.

18. Suneetha, N., *et al.* "Comprehensive Analysis of Hadoop Ecosystem Components: MapReduce Pig and Hive." (2017).

19. Khezr, Seyed Nima, and Nima Jafari Navimipour. "MapReduce and its applications, challenges, and architecture: a comprehensive review and directions for future research." *Journal of Grid Computing* 15.3 (2017): 295-321.

20. Haq, Hafiz Burhan Ul, *et al.* "The Popular Tools of Data Sciences: Benefits, Challenges and Applications." *IJCSNS* 20.5 (2020): 65.

21. Mishra, Pratik, Mayank Mishra, and Arun K. Somani. "Applications of hadoop ecosystems tools." *NoSQL: Database for storage and retrieval of data in cloud* (2017): 173-90.

22. Akil, Bilal, Ying Zhou, and Uwe Röhm. "On the usability of Hadoop MapReduce, Apache Spark & Apache Flink for data science." *2017 IEEE International Conference on Big Data (Big Data)*. IEEE, 2017.

23. Gorelik, Alex. *The enterprise big data lake: Delivering the promise of big data and data science*. O'Reilly Media, 2019.

24. Paul, Rajdeep. "Big data analysis of Indian premier league using Hadoop and MapReduce." *2017 International Conference on Computational Intelligence in Data Science (ICCIDS)*. IEEE, 2017.

25. Wu, WenTai, *et al.* "Energy-efficient hadoop for big data analytics and computing: A systematic review and research insights." *Future Generation Computer Systems* 86 (2018): 1351-1367.

26. Elshawi, Radwa, *et al.* "Big data systems meet machine learning challenges: towards big data science as a service." *Big data research* 14 (2018): 1-11.

27. Klašnja-Milićević, Aleksandra, Mirjana Ivanović, and Zoran Budimac. "Data science in education: Big data and learning analytics." *Computer Applications in Engineering Education* 25.6 (2017): 1066-1078.

28. Singh, Vikash Kumar, *et al.* "A literature review on Hadoop ecosystem and various techniques of big data optimization." *Advances in Data and Information Sciences* (2018): 231-240.

29. Singleton, Alex, and Daniel Arribas-Bel. "Geographic data science." *Geographical Analysis* 53.1 (2021): 61-75.

30. Azeroual, Otmane, and Renaud Fabre. "Processing Big Data with Apache Hadoop in the Current Challenging Era of COVID-19." *Big Data and Cognitive Computing* 5.1 (2021): 12.

31. Nazari, Elham, Mohammad Hasan Shahriari, and Hamed Tabesh. "BigData analysis in healthcare: apache hadoop, apache spark and apache flink." *Frontiers in Health Informatics* 8.1 (2019): 14.

32. Sharma, Nidhi, Sachin Bagga, and Akshay Girdhar. "Novel approach for denoising using hadoop image processing interface." *Procedia computer science* 132 (2018): 1327-1350.

33. Lydia, E. Laxmi, *et al.* "Indexing documents with reliable indexing techniques using Apache Lucene in Hadoop." *International Journal of Intelligent Enterprise* 7.1-3 (2020): 203-214.

34. Murthy, Jamuna S., G. M. Siddesh, and K. G. Srinivasa. "A real-time twitter trend analysis and visualization framework." *International Journal on Semantic Web and Information Systems (IJSWIS)* 15.2 (2019): 1-21.

35. Zhonghua, Ma. "Seismic data attribute extraction based on Hadoop platform." *2017 IEEE 2nd International Conference on Cloud Computing and Big Data Analysis (ICCCBDA)*. IEEE, 2017.

36. Ramachandra, A. C., M. N. Thippeswamy, and Ajith Bailakare. "Role of Hadoop in Big Data Handling." *International Conference on Intelligent Data Communication Technologies and Internet of Things*. Springer, Cham, 2018.

37. Taylor, Ronald C. "An overview of the Hadoop/MapReduce/HBase framework and its current applications in bioinformatics." *BMC bioinformatics* 11.12 (2010): 1-6.

38. Chebbi, Imen, *et al.* "A comparison of big remote sensing data processing with Hadoop MapReduce and Spark." *2018 4th International Conference on Advanced Technologies for Signal and Image Processing (ATSIP)*. IEEE, 2018.

39. Kuo, Alex, *et al.* "A Hadoop/MapReduce Based Platform for Supporting Health Big Data Analytics." *ITCH*. 2019.

40. Dhulipala, Laxman, *et al.* "Parallel batch-dynamic graphs: Algorithms and lower bounds." *Proceedings of the Fourteenth Annual ACM-SIAM Symposium on Discrete Algorithms*. Society for Industrial and Applied Mathematics, 2020.

41. Lage-Freitas, André, *et al.* "An Automatic Deployment Support for Processing Remote Sensing Data in the Cloud." *IGARSS 2018-2018 IEEE International Geoscience and Remote Sensing Symposium*. IEEE, 2018.

42. Madani, Youness, Mohammed Erritali, and Jamaa Bengourram. "Sentiment analysis using semantic similarity and Hadoop MapReduce." *Knowledge and Information Systems* 59.2 (2019): 413-436.

43. Kaur, Rupinder, Vishu Madaan, and Prateek Agrawal. "Diagnosis of Arthritis Using K-Nearest Neighbor Approach." International Conference on Advanced Informatics for Computing Research (ICAICR'19), pp 1601-171, Jul 2019, Springer CCIS.

44. Madaan, Vishu, Rupinder Kaur, and Prateek Agrawal. "Rheumatoid Arthritis anticipation using Adaptive Neuro Fuzzy Inference System." 2019 4th International Conference on Information Systems and Computer Networks (ISCON). pp. 340-346, Nov 2019, IEEEXplore.

45. Madaan, Vishu, *et al.* "XCOVNet: Chest X-ray Image Classification for COVID-19 Early Detection Using Convolutional Neural Networks." New Generation Computing (2021): 1-15. DOI: 10.1007/s00354-021-00121-7

46. Sharma, Sumit, *et al.*, "Heart disease prediction using fuzzy system", International Conference on Advanced Informatics for Computing Research (ICAICR'2018), pp. 424-434, 2018, Springer CCIS.

10

Networking Technologies and Challenges for Green IOT Applications in Urban Climate

Saikat Samanta[1]*, Achyuth Sarkar[2] and Aditi Sharma[2]

[1]Department of Computer Science and Engineering, National Institute of Technology, Arunachal Pradesh, India
[2]Department of Computer Science and Engineering, School of Technology, Quantam University, Roorkee, Uttarakhanda, India

Abstract

The Internet of Things integrates everything inside the intelligent universe and is an attractive field for study. Nearly half of the population lives in cities and this is a growing number. The future of the country rests in the urban climate. People are building possibilities, but there are also challenges. We want to live in even more areas which will cause more traffic and pollution and a need for more energy and water in the future. These issues should be discussed in an urban climate. A green IOT is proposed because it achieves low IOT power consumption. The intelligent atmosphere will have an intelligent grid, intelligent logistics, intelligent housing, intelligent harvesting, intelligent healthcare, and more. We address and analyze the green IOT techniques that can be used to minimize energy usage in IOT. We objectively examine green IOT techniques and propose that concepts should be put into action to impact green IOT on the smart world. Our aim is to provide informational and latest research guidance for a green IOT based smart environment. Finally, we discuss issues and challenges for an intelligent atmosphere.

Keywords: Green radio frequency identification, green wireless sensor network, green cloud computing, intelligent industrial technology, intelligent harvesting

**Corresponding author*: s.samanta.wb@gmail.com

Prateek Agrawal, Charu Gupta, Anand Sharma, Vishu Madaan, and Nisheeth Joshi (eds.) Machine Learning and Data Science: Fundamentals and Applications, (169–184) © 2022 Scrivener Publishing LLC

10.1   Introduction

The Internet of Things (IOT) is a connectivity idea that collaborates with sensors which collect and transmit important information from their surroundings using various types of sensors, such as Radio Frequency Identification (C. Sun, 2012). Over the last decade, energy usage levels have reached threatening peaks due to the massive size of digital context, the number of people, and the number of computers. The rise in the number of connected devices will be up to 100 billion by 2030 (Lopoukhine *et al.*, 2012). IOT is a wireless networking invention in which numerous intelligent agents share information, make communal decisions, and execute tasks in an optimized method. IOT regards data collection, data usage, and connectivity between devices and the environment. Big Data includes massive storage, cloud infrastructure, and broadcasting transmission bandwidth, making IOT omnipresent. High energy is required in the study of Big Data. Various energy needs, in fact, would place society and the environment into constant strain.

Green IOT has been launched in order to achieve intelligent planet growth and biodiversity to reduce emissions and electricity consumption. Green IOT application initiatives should be taken into consideration as a result of rising consciousness of environmental issues around the world. Green Ship IOT applies to technology that helps make the IOT world comfortable by using infrastructure and storage facilities to collect, process, view, and handle various information from users. The technology that allows green IOT is called the technology of Information and Communication (ICT). Green ICT technologies are equipment and storage for the processing, storage, access, and control of different information (Zhu *et al.*, 2015). ICT technology will affect climate change in the world (Zanamwe & Okunoye, 2013) because more and more energy will be used with the increasing use of ICT.

In this paper, we discuss and compare different Green IOT technologies as shown in Table 10.1. We analyze different issues and challenges of Green IOT in urban climates.

10.2   Background

In this section, we introduce some basic knowledge regarding the Internet of Things and Green Internet of Things.

Table 10.1 Overview of green IOT networking technologies.

Method	Technology
GRFID	A basic electronic device consisting of a small chip and an antenna that automatically recognizes and records tags attached to objects
GWSN	A network of spatially distributed, autonomous sensors that participate in the control of physical or environmental conditions
GCC	A modern computational paradigm for easy, on-demand access to a common pool of configurable resources. Integrating cloud computing into a handheld, mobile cloud computing environment would help unload a large array of data collection and retrieval operations from a mobile device
GCC	Archive for the compilation, maintenance, and distribution of data and information
GM2M	This technology allows wireless and wired devices to interact with other devices of the same nature

10.2.1 Internet of Things

IOT revolutionizes our everyday jobs by recording numerous items' intelligent policy formation and progress scenarios to protect our climate and our lifestyle. There is a variety of IOT applications in real life, as shown in Figure 10.1.

a. IOT in Smart Homes
IOT has multiple applications, but the Smart Home is one of the most critical frameworks. According to a report, the "Smart House" keyword is searched every month by 60,000 individuals. There are nearly 256 companies and start-ups in the Smart Home IOT insights platform project. In conjunction with other IOT games, Smart Home start-ups have absolute funding and financing of about $2.5 billion. These start-up firms include AlertMe, Philips, Haier, Belkin, and so forth.

b. IOT in Smart Wearables
Wearables are also an IOT program. Examples of these are Apple's mobile watch, the LookSee bracelet, and so forth. Wearable builder Jawbone has

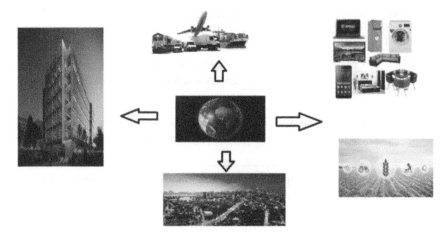

Figure 10.1 IOT and its application.

the greatest volume of funding for all IOT Start-ups and is worth more than half a billion dollars.

c. IOT in a Smart City

The Smart City is putting a lot of problems ahead of researchers, as well as start-up firms, with a wide range of user cases, from the water delivery scheme to traffic management, waste management, and so on. Its success is due to IOT's promising strategy. The IOT works to relieve the actual challenges of urban cities including traffic congestion issues, noise, and emissions control.

d. IOT in Industrial Intranet

The manufacturing internet has already submitted an invitation. Since it does not have as much success as Smart Homes or Wearables, there is little industry research, which includes Gartner or Cisco. Application of the IOT contributes to the best total potential. Its popularity does not hit the masses at present. They are retrieved after the unstructured text has been pre-processed.

e. Digital Health

The health industry has an important potential IOT application. This is defined by the need for a linked health care system and intelligent medical instruments also have a lot of promise.

f. Smart Agriculture

Smart agriculture has the most potentially explored uses of IOTs. This technology will transform the paradigm of farming as remote faming positions can be controlled and livestock can be tracked. This would become one of the most important applications in the dominant agricultural countries.

10.3   Green Internet of Things

In recent years, IOT has seen tremendous growth. This influenced the performance of an IOT device's network infrastructure and energy infrastructure. The introduction of energy effective processes and methods at both the hardware and the device level aims to accomplish these characteristics. The use of electricity, carbon dioxide, and greenhouse gases affects the current IOT technologies, software, and services. IOT models are not designed for energy efficiency and waste energy because they are still available, even if they are not needed. This requires a lot of energy to be used during transmission and sends data all the time. In Green IOT, the computer is only allowed when needed. Green IOT focuses on the intelligent role of energy-reduced machines. Adequate heat ventilation generated from servers and data centers and energy conservation through smart IOT technology are numerous energy conservation strategies via Green IOT implementation.

10.3.1   Green IOT Networking Technologies

Green Internet Technologies includes special hardware and software particularly intended to consume less resource without sacrificing efficiency while maximizing power consumption. The green IOT's networking technologies is shown in Figure 10.2 and includes Green RFID (Namboodiri & Gao, 2010), Green WSN, Green CC (Lin *et al.*, 2015) and Green DC (Farahnakian *et al.*, 2015), Green M2M (Wang *et al.*, 2014) for the computer, and Green DC (Shuja *et al.*, 2016).

a. Green Radio Frequency Identification

RFID tags may stock up information or information at a tiny level for any entity for which they are connected. RFID transmission requires a variety

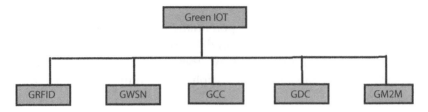

Figure 10.2 Green IOT networking technologies.

of RFID systems within a few meters. Active Tags have incorporated batteries for continuous propagation of their own signal, while Passive Tags do not have an active battery source. Reducing the size of the RFID tag will help minimize the volume of non-degradable content.

b. Green Wireless Sensor Network
A WSN has several sensor nodes but features a large number of sensor nodes with limited power and energy. The Green WSN may be an combination of techniques including the Green Energy Conservation technique, Radio Optimization technique, and Green Routing techniques. Smart data algorithms reduce storage space requirements and data size and switch sensors on and off as necessary.

c. Green Cloud Computing
Since we already know that we have IaaS, PaaS, and SaaS in cloud computing, hardware and applications in the green framework can be used to reduce electricity consumption. Energy-efficient measures must be implemented. Green cloud-based infrastructure such as networking, connectivity, etc. can also be used.

d. Green Data Center
Data Centers are responsible for the collection, management, handling, and distribution of all data forms and applications. Data centers focused on green energy resources should be planned. In addition, the routing protocol should be configured to be sensitive to them and disable idle devices in the network and to provide the energy parameter for their packet routing.

e. Green M2M
Since no significant number of devices is involved in M2M communication, there should be energy saving dependent on transmitting capacity and streamlined communication protocols, as well as routing algorithms. Passive nodes can be tested so that resources can be saved.

10.3.2 Green IOT Applications in Urban Climate

Significant improvements have taken place in our world and thanks to developments in IOT, many changes will quickly occur. Even then, the expense of innovation is theoretically important due to an increase in e-waste, chemical emissions, and energy use. It is predicted that Green IOT will lead to a green environment and add significant changes to our future life. Mostly, in the future we will see in our daily lives a lot of robots, machines, sensors, drones, and things that work and communicate with each other to perform their tasks intelligently in the green world, as seen in Figure 10.3.

Green IOT supports IOT in its discovery of different energy sources, environmental sustainability, and minimization of environmental harm for the IOT. Numerous uses of green IOT are also meaningful for political, environmental, and social sustainability, as well as for protecting natural resources and enhancing human health.

10.3.3 Intelligent Housing

The green IOT allows home-produced heating, illumination, and electrical equipment to be remotely operated by a computer and smart phone. The

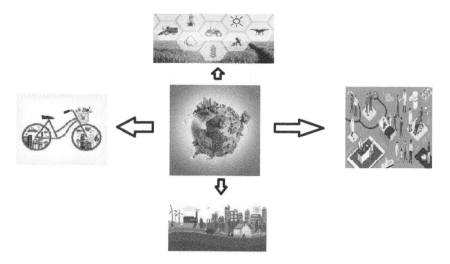

Figure 10.3 Green IOT applications in Urban climate.

life cycle of green IOT consists of green architecture, green use, green development, and ultimately, green disposal. Recycling should be considered in order to reduce environmental effects. Aslam *et al.* (2016) formulated a QOS model in a smart house for the intended supply of heterogeneous IOT devices using the allocated optimization networks.

10.3.4   Intelligent Industrial Technology

Factories have become automated with computers that can run entirely automatically with little or no human interference depending on the Internet.

10.3.5   Intelligent Healthcare

A connection is made to the use of biometric system sensing devices in patients for the capture, control, and monitoring of the human body. IOT innovations in the healthcare industry include the implementation of new and advanced Internet-connected sensors for the collection of vital data in real time. As a result, successful health insurance services increase the quality of care, enhance access to care, and reduce time and cost.

10.3.6   Intelligent Grid

Intelligent grid reliability is about justice, just like IOT. It refers to the capacity of the grid to constantly adapt and adjust to deliver power at the highest output and lowest possible cost. The smart grid provides customers with the opportunity to invest in the solution. The deployment of IOT-based touch sensor networks and smart grids is discussed. Yang *et al.* (2015) suggested a low-cost remote memory permit for the smart grid. In addition, Liu *et al.* (2017) proposed many approaches to boost the data validity of IOT level technology loss in smart cities. The new smart grid will quantify and swap power use and build full-energy solutions.

10.3.7   Intelligent Harvesting

IOT will encourage farmers to face the massive challenges that they are facing. The industry should consider ways and strategies for dealing with water shortages, cost management, and limited access to property. Green IOT applications for agriculture have been proposed by Nandyala and Kim (2016).

10.4 Different Energy-Efficient Implementation of Green IOT

In this section, we include a crucial literary analysis of all models recently proposed for the energy-efficient implementation of IOT, which are briefly illustrated in Table 10.2. We categorize energy-efficient models on the basis of technology. The detailed taxonomy used in them is seen in Table 10.2.

Green IOT is a very hot issue in ICT markets, as conventional energy supplies are increasingly dwindling and energy consumption is exponentially growing. Miorandi *et al.* (2012) addressed various technology and techniques for energy performance in IOT and did not address the device models specifically designed for Green IOT.

Table 10.2 Comparative study of multiple approaches to green IOT.

Paper	Technology	Type	Mechanism
(Foteinos *et al.*, 2013)	Mobile Phone/ Sensor	Recycling Type	Unused components are recycled to make them productive again
(K. Sun & Ryoo, 2015)	Sensor	Software Type	MAC and wireless intelligent sensor combination to reduce inter-node communications
(Zamora-Izquierdo *et al.*, 2010)	Information Management	Policy Type	Data from multiple building components to improve energy conservation policies
(Sample *et al.*, 2007)	Cloud Computing	Software Type	Use the Access Pointer to minimize contact and traffic dynamic packet download
(Moreno *et al.*, 2014)	Smart Building	Policy Type	Energy usage reduction approaches and techniques
(Caragliu *et al.*, 2011)	Processor	Hardware Type	Allocation by schedule of specific task

Baliga *et al.* (2011) compared cloud and PC computing energy usage across a number of scenarios and found that model selection would be the better choice in those circumstances. In addition, the issues surround quality of service (QOS), which in some cases could further increase energy consumption, are not discussed.

Green technologies for integrating IOT were developed (Kiourti *et al.*, 2016) and centered specifically on solutions for Green IOT while retaining QOS across multiple domains. The data center and cloud storage networks and their green solutions were not addressed and they are the backbone of the IOT network.

Diverse energy saving techniques by IOT-collected data using smart buildings have been developed by Akkaya *et al.* (2015). The mentioned systems have demonstrated that energy can be saved when heating, ventilation, and air conditioning strategies are applied. For all the discussions of current frameworks, there has been no debate about the comparative energy conservation study of the models.

A key aspect of IOT implementation is wireless sensor networks (WSN). The techniques which can be used to extract energy using various environmental resources in WSN were outlined by Karakus *et al.* (2013). However, this can contribute to improved energy efficiency if another medium is used to store energy instead of batteries, therefore thorough study in this field is needed.

10.5   Recycling Principal for Green IOT

The application of recyclable content for system output in an IOT network will help to ensure that it is environmentally safe. Cell phones are made of some of the worst natural materials such as copper, plastic, and some non-biodegradable components that can boost the greenhouse effect while the phones are no longer in operation. There are five suggested guidelines to achieve green IOT and minimize carbon footprints shown in Figure 10.4.

1. Minimize the network size: Decrease the size of the network by positioning nodes effectively and employing ingenious routing methods. This means high-end savings in electricity.
2. Use Selective Sensing: In this particular case, collect only the data needed. A lot of resources can be saved by removing additional data sensing.

Figure 10.4 Recycling principal for green IOT.

3. Use of Hybrid Architecture: The use of active sensors will minimize energy usage for a variety of tasks in an IOT network.
4. Making Policy: Develop efficient policies to reduce smart building energy consumption. Policies can have a significant effect on electricity usage and substantial energy efficiency can also be achieved.
5. Intelligent Trade Offs: In order to conserve resources such as compressive sensing and data fusion, we should prioritize costs intelligently and encode our communication in certain cases. Trade-offs shall be picked according to a given situation.

10.6   Green IOT Architecture of Urban Climate

The bright future of green IOT will transform our intelligent world to a better, greener, more prosperous and sustainable world. The most interesting fields concentrate on greening such as green connectivity, green networking, green architecture, green deployment, green IOT services,

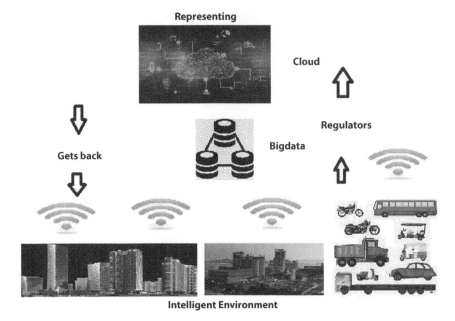

Figure 10.5 Green IOT architecture of urban climate.

green implementations, network management, smart objects, and green localization.

There are several problems in green IOT when it comes to transitioning from IOT to green IOT. They can be based on various criteria including being software based, hardware based, routing algorithm based, policy driven recycling, and so on. Designing a green IOT is possible from viewpoints that achieve outstanding efficiency and high levels of consistency. Supporting the greening of IOT is effective and efficient by defining suited strategies for optimizing QOS parameters. Moving for greening IOT would take less electricity, searching for new opportunities, and minimizing the harmful effects of IOT on human health and the environment. Green IOT will then make a major contribution to a sustainable green and intelligent world. For the purpose of carrying out energy-balancing for the promotion of green connectivity between IOT devices, the energy harvesting of radio frequencies must be considered.

They should be built in such a way as to conserve electricity. Hardware based computing may include processors, cameras, servers, ICs, RFIDs, etc. Cloud-oriented computing can be oriented, virtualization, data centers, etc. and can be based on smart policies.

10.7   Challenges of Green IOT in Urban Climate

Green IOT technology is still at its development. There are several problems in green IOT when it comes to transitioning from IOT to green IOT. There is a huge amount of scientific effort to move towards green technologies, but there are also a lot of hurdles and obstacles that need to be discussed.

- Incorporation of energy savings by IOT
- The architecture is designed to achieve an acceptable degree of efficiency
- Technology should be green in order to reduce its effect on the environment
- Performance of green IOT with models of energy consumption
- Context-awareness of the energy-efficient IOT system
- Both technologies and protocols used for communicating can be used effectively with less energy usage
- Reducing the complexity of green IOT networks
- Trade-off between efficient dynamic spectrum sensing and effective spectrum regulation
- Effective IOT energy mechanisms, such as wind, solar, vibration, and thermal to make IOT very promising

10.8   Discussion & Future Research Directions

The bright future of green IOT will transform our future world into a better, greener, high QOS, socially prosperous, and economically sustainable world. The most interesting fields on greening are green connectivity, green networking, green architecture, green implementations, advanced RFIDs and sensor networks, mobility and network management, and cooperation between homogeneous and heterogeneous networks.

The following research areas need to be addressed in order to establish optimal and efficient IOT greening solutions.

1. Designing green IOT is possible from viewpoints that achieve outstanding efficiency and high levels of consistency. Supporting the greening of IOT is effective and efficient by defining suited strategies for optimizing QOS parameters.

2. The transfer of data from the sensor to the mobile cloud is more valuable. A Wireless sensor network and the smart phone cloud combine with the sensor-cloud. This is a hot and promising IOT greening technology.

3. M2M connectivity plays a vital role in reducing toxic pollution and electricity use. To allow automated systems, intelligent machines need to be smarter. In the case of traffic and taking necessary and prompt steps, the wait to automate the system should be minimized.

4. Moving for greening IOT would take less electricity, searching for new opportunities, and minimizing the harmful effects of IOT on human health and the environment. The green IOT will then bring a major contribution to a sustainable, intelligent, and green world.

5. For the purpose of carrying out energy-balancing for the promotion of green connectivity between IOT devices, the energy harvesting of radio frequencies must be considered.

10.9   Conclusion

There are many advantages to the tremendous technical development of the 21st century. The growing demand for high technology innovations is accompanied by intentional e-waste and harmful emissions. The ICT revolution has qualitatively improved the IOT greening potential. With the help of ICT technology, all the things around us will become smarter to execute complex tasks individually. In our article, we survey the most important technology used for green IOT. We recognize how to keep our climate and community smarter and greener. We suggest future recommendations for the successful and productive improvement of green IOT-based applications.

References

1. Akkaya, K., Guvenc, I., Aygun, R., Pala, N., & Kadri, A. (2015). IoT-based occupancy monitoring techniques for energy-efficient smart buildings. *2015 IEEE Wireless Communications and Networking Conference Workshops, WCNCW 2015*. https://doi.org/10.1109/WCNCW.2015.7122529

2. Aslam, S., Ul Hasan, N., Shahid, A., Jang, J. W., & Lee, K. G. (2016). Device centric throughput and QoS optimization for iots in a smart building using CRN-techniques. *Sensors (Switzerland)*. https://doi.org/10.3390/s16101647

3. Baliga, J., Ayre, R. W. A., Hinton, K., & Tucker, R. S. (2011). Green cloud computing: Balancing energy in processing, storage, and transport. *Proceedings of the IEEE*. https://doi.org/10.1109/JPROC.2010.2060451

4. Caragliu, A., del Bo, C., & Nijkamp, P. (2011). Smart cities in Europe. *Journal of Urban Technology*. https://doi.org/10.1080/10630732.2011.601117

5. Farahnakian, F., Ashraf, A., Pahikkala, T., Liljeberg, P., Plosila, J., Porres, I., & Tenhunen, H. (2015). Using Ant Colony System to Consolidate VMs for Green Cloud Computing. *IEEE Transactions on Services Computing*. https://doi.org/10.1109/TSC.2014.2382555

6. Foteinos, V., Kelaidonis, D., Poulios, G., Vlacheas, P., Stavroulaki, V., & Demestichas, P. (2013). Cognitive management for the internet of things: A framework for enabling autonomous applications. *IEEE Vehicular Technology Magazine*. https://doi.org/10.1109/MVT.2013.2281657

7. Karakus, C., Gurbuz, A. C., & Tavli, B. (2013). Analysis of energy efficiency of compressive sensing in wireless sensor networks. *IEEE Sensors Journal*. https://doi.org/10.1109/JSEN.2013.2244036

8. Kiourti, A., Lee, C., & Volakis, J. L. (2016). Fabrication of Textile Antennas and Circuits with 0.1 mm Precision. *IEEE Antennas and Wireless Propagation Letters*. https://doi.org/10.1109/LAWP.2015.2435257

9. Lin, Y. H., Chou, Z. T., Yu, C. W., & Jan, R. H. (2015). Optimal and Maximized Configurable Power Saving Protocols for Corona-Based Wireless Sensor Networks. *IEEE Transactions on Mobile Computing*. https://doi.org/10.1109/TMC.2015.2404796

10. Liu, Y., Weng, X., Wan, J., Yue, X., Song, H., & Vasilakos, A. V. (2017). Exploring data validity in transportation systems for smart cities. *IEEE Communications Magazine*. https://doi.org/10.1109/MCOM.2017.1600240

11. Lopoukhine, N., Crawhall, N., Dudley, N., Figgis, P., Karibuhoye, C., Laffoley, D., Miranda Londoño, J., MacKinnon, K., & Sandwith, T. (2012). Protected areas: Providing natural solutions to 21st Century challenges. *Sapiens*.

12. Miorandi, D., Sicari, S., De Pellegrini, F., & Chlamtac, I. (2012). Internet of things: Vision, applications and research challenges. In *Ad Hoc Networks*. https://doi.org/10.1016/j.adhoc.2012.02.016

13. Moreno, M. V., Úbeda, B., Skarmeta, A. F., & Zamora, M. A. (2014). How can we tackle energy efficiency in iot based smart buildings? *Sensors (Switzerland)*. https://doi.org/10.3390/s140609582

14. Namboodiri, V., & Gao, L. (2010). Energy-aware tag anticollision protocols for RFID systems. *IEEE Transactions on Mobile Computing*. https://doi.org/10.1109/TMC.2009.96

15. Nandyala, C. S., & Kim, H. K. (2016). Green IoT Agriculture and Healthcare Application (GAHA). *International Journal of Smart Home*. https://doi.org/10.14257/ijsh.2016.10.4.26

16. Sample, A., Yeager, D., Powledge, P., & Smith, J. (2007). Design of a passively-powered, programmable sensing platform for UHF RFID systems. *2007 IEEE International Conference on RFID, IEEE RFID 2007*. https://doi.org/10.1109/RFID.2007.346163

17. Shuja, J., Bilal, K., Madani, S. A., Othman, M., Ranjan, R., Balaji, P., & Khan, S. U. (2016). Survey of techniques and architectures for designing energy-efficient data centers. *IEEE Systems Journal*. https://doi.org/10.1109/JSYST.2014.2315823

18. Sun, C. (2012). Application of RFID Technology for Logistics on Internet of Things. *AASRI Procedia*. https://doi.org/10.1016/j.aasri.2012.06.019

19. Sun, K., & Ryoo, I. (2015). A study on medium access control scheme for energy efficiency in wireless smart sensor networks. *International Conference on ICT Convergence 2015: Innovations Toward the IoT, 5G, and Smart Media Era, ICTC 2015*. https://doi.org/10.1109/ICTC.2015.7354625

20. Wang, C. X., Haider, F., Gao, X., You, X. H., Yang, Y., Yuan, D., Aggoune, H. M., Haas, H., Fletcher, S., & Hepsaydir, E. (2014). Cellular architecture and key technologies for 5G wireless communication networks. *IEEE Communications Magazine*. https://doi.org/10.1109/MCOM.2014.6736752

21. Yang, X., He, X., Yu, W., Lin, J., Li, R., Yang, Q., & Song, H. (2015). Towards a low-cost remote memory attestation for the smart grid. *Sensors (Switzerland)*. https://doi.org/10.3390/s150820799

22. Zamora-Izquierdo, M. A., Santa, J., & Gómez-Skarmeta, A. F. (2010). An integral and networked home automation solution for indoor ambient intelligence. *IEEE Pervasive Computing*. https://doi.org/10.1109/MPRV.2010.20

23. Zanamwe, N., & Okunoye, A. (2013). Role of information and communication technologies (ICTs) in mitigating , adapting to and monitoring climate change in developing countries. *International Conference on ICT for Africa*.

24. Zhu, C., Leung, V. C. M., Shu, L., & Ngai, E. C. H. (2015). Green Internet of Things for Smart World. *IEEE Access*. https://doi.org/10.1109/ACCESS.2015.2497312

11

Analysis of Human Activity Recognition Algorithms Using Trimmed Video Datasets

Disha G. Deotale[1]*, Madhushi Verma[2], P. Suresh[3], Divya Srivastava[2], Manish Kumar[4] and Sunil Kumar Jangir[5]

[1]CSE Department, G.H. Raisoni Institute of Engineering and Technology, Pune, India
[2]CSE Department, Bennett University, Greater Noida, UP, India
[3]TATA Motors Limited, Global Delivery Center, Pune, MH, India
[4]BME Department School of Engineering and Technology, Mody University of Science and Technology, Rajasthan, India
[5]CSE Department, School of Engineering & Technology, Mody University of Science and Technology, Rajasthan, India

Abstract

Recognition of human activities from a video sequence requires the system to perform multiple computations on the inputs. These computations range across pre-processing, segmentation, feature extraction, key-frame selection, feature selection, classification, and post-processing. All these steps require sophisticated image and video processing algorithms that work in tandem to get the final resultant output. In this chapter, the readers will be able to understand the different algorithms used for recognition of human activities from a video dataset. This chapter also analyses an in-depth case study which will take them through all recognition steps using an example-oriented approach. Using the study done in this chapter, readers will be able to design and develop their human activity recognition algorithms and tune their accuracies as per the application of these algorithms. This chapter also summarizes some of the most frequently used algorithms in this field and suggests methods to improve them. A convolutional neural network-based architecture is studied in this chapter which will assist researchers in designing and developing any human activity recognition system with high accuracy performance.

*Corresponding author: disha.deotale21@raisoni.net

Prateek Agrawal, Charu Gupta, Anand Sharma, Vishu Madaan, and Nisheeth Joshi (eds.) *Machine Learning and Data Science: Fundamentals and Applications*, (185–214) © 2022 Scrivener Publishing LLC

Keywords: Video, human activity, classification, machine learning, trimmed, recognition, feature, image

11.1   Introduction

Recognition of human activities from an input image or video data requires many operations to work in tandem. These operations must be designed with reference to the desired activities to be recognized and must be optimized for each of these activities. For instance, to recognize sports-based human actions (running, climbing, shooting, etc.), operations of segmentation and feature selection must be properly tuned to obtain a high value of accuracy, while for recognition of office-based human actions (sitting, standing, talking, etc.), the operations of key-frame selection and classification must be designed with the utmost efficiency. A sample support vector machine-based classification algorithm can be observed from Figure 11.1.

From the given figure, it can be observed that the process requires the following blocks to be designed for effective operation:

- The video source is the main source of information from where activity related data is captured and given to the system for processing. Usually, videos can either be

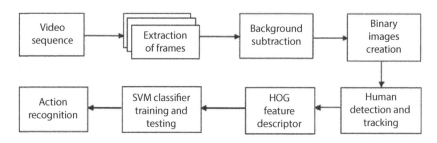

Figure 11.1 SVM-based classifier for human activity recognition.

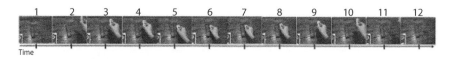

Figure 11.2 Cell phone cleaning trimmed video sequence.

○ *Trimmed videos* wherein the videos are already pre-processed and trimmed to particular activities. These videos are captured directly from the source and are cut into different sequences by manual observation. A sample video sequence of cell-phone cleaning can be observed from Figure 11.2 and this kind of video has a single activity running throughout the entire video.

○ *Untrimmed videos* are videos wherein multiple activities may or may not occur in the entire video sequence. Usually, these videos are taken directly from the source event and are fed to the system. Processing these videos requires an additional post-processing layer which summarizes the presence of different activities in the videos together. This summary assists in recognition of the presence of different video events in the entire video sequence. Figure 11.3 showcases an untrimmed video sequence which consists of different human activities like drumming, arranging things, bookbinding, etc. Such videos can be used for recognition of untrimmed video activities.

• These trimmed/untrimmed videos are given to a frame extraction unit. Here, the input video frames are extracted and clustered to arrange similar-looking frames together.

Figure 11.3 Example of untrimmed video.

The clustering process is done to make sure that videos belonging to one kind of activity are clubbed together to facilitate further processing. All the clustered frames are stored into lists which are indexed by the cluster numbers.

- Background subtraction or segmentation (in general) is a process via which the input image is analysed and divided into foreground and background regions. The background detection process requires some level of complexity as it needs to differentiate between the objects of interest and the background of the image. To perform this task, algorithms like salience map detection, frame sequence detection, temporal analysis, etc. are used. These algorithms allow the system to be fully automated and remove the background from the images. Recently, algorithms like depth analysis for background subtraction have been proposed, which utilize multiple image data to evaluate object depth and then extract the given regions of interest from the input image.

- Once the required regions are extracted, then features are extracted. These features can be either texture-based, colour-based, edge-based, or other domain-based (like frequency, wavelet, cosine, etc). All these features are required for just one task, which is to represent the entire image in the form of numerical values. These numerical values must be distinctive enough for each image sequence and must have a high degree of differentiation between images of different gestures. To make sure that these features are properly varying between different gestures, researchers have figured out feature selection methods. These methods are based on feature variance and different methods like principal component analysis (PCA), linear discriminant analysis (LDA), etc. have been proposed for the same purpose. The feature selection unit ensures that the different image sequences are represented with a lesser number of features. It also ensures there is limited redundancy during feature processing, thereby improving the accuracy of classification and reducing the delay needed for classification.

- Once the features are extracted, then the keyframe extraction process is followed. This process allows the system to reduce the number of images needed for performing the classification. Algorithms like histogram-based keyframe selection, threshold-based keyframe selection, etc.

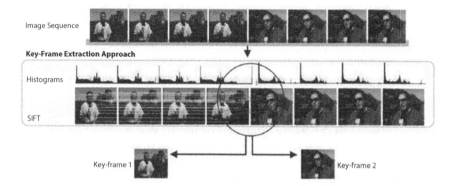

Figure 11.4 Keyframe extraction example using histogram features.

are used for this purpose. Based on these algorithms the input frames are reduced in number, therefore the algorithm requires a smaller number of computations for finding out the final gesture. An example of key-frame extraction can be observed from Figure 11.4 wherein the changes in the feature points are tracked and, based on these changes, keyframes are extracted from the image.

- Keyframes are those frames where the changes in the input are very apparent and these changes can be either in terms of statistical features or visual appearances. Using a key-frame extraction engine is optional, but can significantly reduce the computational load on the processing unit and must be used for high-speed classification applications.
- The selected features from the key-frames are given to a final classifier. The classifier can either be based on support vectors, decision trees, random forests, Naïve Bayes, neural

Table 11.1 Summarized output from post-processing layer.

Activity type	Frame numbers	Total frames
Running	1-10, 26-30	15
Walking	31-40, 56-70	25
Jumping	11-25, 41-55	30
	Total	70

networks, or linear co-operators. All these classifiers have different performances for different datasets. A comparative analysis of these classifiers is done in the next section of this chapter.

- Once the classification process is completed, then a post-processing layer is applied. This layer performs the task of aggregating extracted classes and summarizing the obtained class with the frame number. For instance, if frames 1 to 10 belong to a running class, 11 to 25 belong to a jumping class, 26 to 30 again belong to a running class, 31 to 40 belong with a walking class, 41 to 55 belong to a jumping class, and 56 to 70 belong again to the walking class, then the post-processing layer will output as shown in Table 11.1.

From the results, it is evident that the post-processing layer can summarize the results obtained using the given classifiers. Once the post-processing layer output is obtained, then further analysis can be performed on it based on the system application. For instance, if a system wants to evaluate the average percentage of time for which a runner jumped during the sporting event, then using the example in Table 11.1, it can be concluded that the runner jumped for 43% of the entire sporting event video. Using this analysis, further optimizations to real-time runner's performance can be done. To further understand the performance of the human activity recognition algorithms, the next section enlists some of the most recent state-of-the-art algorithms in the given field. Readers can use the knowledge from the next section to develop their classification algorithms.

11.2 Contributions in the Field of Activity Recognition from Video Sequences

Recently, various researchers have applied different types of algorithms to improve the efficiency of activity recognition from a video sequence. These algorithms vary regarding the application of feature extraction, feature selection, classifiers used, and post-processing used. For the readers to understand the performance of these algorithms, the Table 11.2 can be referenced. Using this table, readers can evaluate the best performing algorithms for the given application type and apply that algorithm of their activity recognition system.

Table 11.2 Comparison of different human activity detection algorithms.

Algorithm & application	Features extracted	Details	Accuracy (%)
Convolutional Neural Network (CNN) with TDMap [1] CNN with HoG & TDMap [1] Human Pose Detection (Boxing, Carrying, Jogging, Walking, Running, Handwaving, Hand Clapping, Digging, and Throwing)	Histogram of gradients (HoG) combined with temporal difference map (TDMap)	Initially, silhouette extraction is done to find out the presence of the human body in the given video. Then, HoG is used along with TDMap to evaluate the different features of the body. These features are combined with CNN to evaluate the accuracy of human pose detection. These poses are combined to perform video summarization as well.	99% 98%
Learning Semantic Descriptions [2] Human actions like still arm, free swing arm, torso leaning, etc.	Visual word histogram	An attribute model is created which utilizes different visual word histograms to differentiate between different human actions. Each of these attributes is assigned to an attribute interaction model and this model can provide a probability for each human action. These probabilities are combined to find the final human action.	91%

(Continued)

Table 11.2 Comparison of different human activity detection algorithms. (*Continued*)

Algorithm & application	Features extracted	Details	Accuracy (%)
Non-Local Neural Networks (NLNN) [3] Human body recognition	Gait features along with region segmentation are used	The work is divided into 3 parts wherein non-local features are extracted first, followed by relationship establishment between randomly selected gait energy maps, and this relationship is evaluated between different gait energy maps and human postures. Finally, a 2-class classifier is utilized to find whether the given input belongs to a particular human body posture or not.	93%
Template Matching [4] Human activities like walking, kicking, boxing, etc.	Adaptive background subtraction with silhouette distance signals	Silhouette distance signals are combined with adaptive background cancellation to find out the edge-based final templates of the image for a given gesture.	76%

(*Continued*)

Table 11.2 Comparison of different human activity detection algorithms. (*Continued*)

Algorithm & application	Features extracted	Details	Accuracy (%)
		These templates are matched using a template matching algorithm. The final template matching algorithm can be improved with the help of advanced machine learning classifiers like CNN, Support Vector Machine (SVM), kNN, etc. to further improve the accuracy of classification.	
PCA-based Template Matching [5] Human activities like walking, kicking, boxing, etc.	Adaptive background subtraction with silhouette distance signals and principal component analysis (PCA)	Silhouette distance signals are combined with adaptive background cancellation to find out the edge-based final templates of the image for a given gesture. The templates are given to a PCA unit to detect the final features for each of these templates.	85%

(*Continued*)

Table 11.2 Comparison of different human activity detection algorithms. (*Continued*)

Algorithm & application	Features extracted	Details	Accuracy (%)
		These features are matched using a template matching algorithm. The final template matching algorithm gives good accuracy when compared to [4], but can be improved with the help of advanced machine learning classifiers like CNN, Support Vector Machine (SVM), kNN, etc. to further improve the accuracy of classification.	
CNN with GEI [6] Walking style detection	Gait Energy Images (GEI)	The input video is given to a gait detection algorithm which is followed by finding out gait energy images (GEI). These images are then evaluated using CNN to identify the walking style of the person. Based on the walking style, it is possible to identify a set of persons whose data has been sufficiently trained into the system. Videos of the person at different angles are taken to identify the performance of the system.	98%

(*Continued*)

Table 11.2 Comparison of different human activity detection algorithms. (*Continued*)

Algorithm & application	Features extracted	Details	Accuracy (%)
Long-Short Term Memory (LSTM) [7] Sports activities detection	Single Frame Representation Model	The input video streams are given to a Single Frame Representation Model to form different representations from the input video. These representations are then given to an LSTM based CNN network. The representations assist in finding out the position of the person at different kinds of angles and thereby evaluating the gestures for a given application. Pre-processing is done using the optical flow method, which is followed by a pair of CNNs which act as 2 class classifiers. The outputs of these CNNs is given to a global average and global max layer to find the feature representation of the images. Finally, an LSTM is generated to classify between 1 of N gestures.	93.3%

(*Continued*)

Table 11.2 Comparison of different human activity detection algorithms. (*Continued*)

Algorithm & application	Features extracted	Details	Accuracy (%)
CNN [8] Walking postures	3D gait features	The input videos are given for the evaluation of 3D gait features. Each of these features is given to a CNN for the final evaluation of walking patterns. These walking patterns apply to both marker-based and markerless applications. The main reason for improved accuracy, in this case, is the presence of marker-based 3D imagery, which can train the neural network with utmost accuracy.	98%
SVM with NN [9] General human body gestures	Skeletal Joint Dynamics and Structural Features	Video datasets from KTH, UTKinect, and MSR Action3D are used to evaluate Skeletal Joint Dynamics and Structural Features. These features are given to a multi-class SVM, which uses Structural Features	90%

(*Continued*)

Table 11.2 Comparison of different human activity detection algorithms. (*Continued*)

Algorithm & application	Features extracted	Details	Accuracy (%)
		using joint angles and Temporal Features using joint displacement vector to train 2 different SVMs. Outputs of the SVMs are given to a neural network which is based on score fusion. The fused score from both the networks is used for final classification of human body gestures.	
kNN [10] Random forest [10] LSTM [10] Standing, Walking, Eating, Calling, Lifting, Handclapping, Sitting	Depth information from 3D RGB depth sensor	The input video is captured using a 3D RGB depth camera. The information from this camera is fed into a Haar-wavelet transform (HWT) wherein information preservation is done before reducing data size. Finally, an averaging algorithm is used for finding out the final reduced features. These features are given to a kNN classifier for final classification.	97.8% 98.1% 99.1%

(*Continued*)

198 Machine Learning and Data Science

Table 11.2 Comparison of different human activity detection algorithms. (*Continued*)

Algorithm & application	Features extracted	Details	Accuracy (%)
NN with Hidden Markov Models [11] Sports gestures evaluation	Curvature scale-space features	The input videos are given to evaluate curvature scale-space features. These features represent the input gestures into curves, which can then be analysed to find the final gestures. Trained NN and HMM models are used for the final classification process.	90%
Statistical classifier [12] Panic detection from crowd videos	Single motion field	The input images are given to a motion estimator, followed by a feature extraction unit to find the single motion fields, then using a statistical classifier the features are classified into 1 of N panic detection classes. These classes are then optimized into finding out panic behaviours as a post-processing task.	98%

Table 11.2 Comparison of different human activity detection algorithms. (*Continued*)

Algorithm & application	Features extracted	Details	Accuracy (%)
Fuzzy SVM [13] Violation detection	Multiple modal features	The input video is given to an optical flow pre-processor, which produces an optical flow image. This is followed by finding out a statistical optical flow histogram of the images, followed by finding the optical flow histogram of the entire video. These histograms are given for dimensionality reduction. The final features from PCA are given to a fuzzy SVM classifier to find any violation detection in the video. Replacing fuzzy SVM with CNN can result in better accuracy for the given system.	91.8%
One-class SVM [14] Multiple events in videos	Histogram of Gradients	The video sequences are pre-processed for noise removal, followed by feature extraction using HoG method. The extracted features are given to multiple one-class SVM classifiers to identify	97.4%

(*Continued*)

Table 11.2 Comparison of different human activity detection algorithms. (*Continued*)

Algorithm & application	Features extracted	Details	Accuracy (%)
		if the particular video frame belongs to a given class. Finally, a voting engine is employed to find the final class from the given set of classes. It can also be observed that the input video sequences are processed using optical flow techniques and histogram of gradients are evaluated for each of the frames. The HoG features are given to multiple SVM classifiers and then, by using a novel voting mechanism, they are combined to get the final activity class.	
SVM [15] Crowdsourced human behaviour detection	Histogram of Gradients	The video sequences are pre-processed for noise removal and then are segmented into different blocks. This is followed by feature extraction using the HoG method. The extracted features are given one-shot SVM classifiers to identify if the particular video frame belongs	86%

Table 11.2 Comparison of different human activity detection algorithms. (*Continued*)

Algorithm & application	Features extracted	Details	Accuracy (%)
		to a given class (human or non-human). Finally, clustering is applied to evaluate the presence of human regions in the image. Each of these human regions is then given to another HoG descriptor which is followed by a final SVM classifier to obtain the category of action in this video frame.	
YOLO v3 [16] Vehicle-mounted applications of human activity detection	Windowed colour, texture, and shape	Videos captured from vehicle-mounted cameras are directly given to a YOLO (You Look Only Once) object detector. This detector uses a combination of cascade object detection along with machine learning classifiers to get the final object type. The classifier is tuned for obtaining the final class for activity detection and due to the mobile YOLO implementation, it can be mounted on a Raspberry Pi-based kit to get the final results.	91.27%

(*Continued*)

Table 11.2 Comparison of different human activity detection algorithms. (*Continued*)

Algorithm & application	Features extracted	Details	Accuracy (%)
3D CNN [17] General human activity detection	Learning Spatiotemporal Features, Windowed colour, texture, and shape	The input video sequences are given to a segmentation layer, wherein different human postures are extracted. These postures are scaled and given to a 3D CNN where each dimension is responsible to classify one particular angle of the input object. All the dimensions are combined to produce the final resulting class for the given human activity dataset.	80%
Vector Space Analysis [20] General Human Activities	Directionality-based feature vectors	Initially, background subtraction is performed which is followed by silhouette detection. This is then followed by feature vector extraction and normalization. Finally, vector space analysis and temporal smoothing are applied to obtain the final human activity.	91%

From the table, it can be observed that CNN based algorithms outperform other implementations of human activity detection. Moreover, the review done in [18] and the studies found in [19] also confirm the same. It can also be observed that methods like SVM and random forest also provide good classification performance and can be used for real-time human activity detection systems. Some authors recently developed various object recognition and human activity recognition applications using deep learning, video processing, and computer vision methods [21–26].

11.2.1   Activity Recognition from Trimmed Video Sequences Using Convolutional Neural Networks

Profound net engineering enlivened by the VGGNet CNN model is talked about in this section. It utilizes the unpredictable component extraction and choice capacities of the VGGNet model and consolidates them with the productivity of highlight extraction methods like GLCM, edge maps, and colour maps. The design outline of the proposed profound net classifier can be seen in Figure 11.5. The examined design has the accompanying squares:

- Image division utilizing various levelled k-Means bunching
- Feature extraction utilizing GLCM, colour guides, and edge maps
- Feature choice utilizing head segment investigation
- Concatenation layer to join these highlights as pixel levels and annex them into the picture itself
- VGG Net model for preparing and assessment

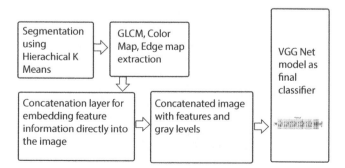

Figure 11.5 Overall block diagram.

The division layer utilizes progressive k-Means bunching that works utilizing the accompanying advances:

a) Divide the picture into 2 groups utilizing k-Means bunching
b) Evaluate the number of comparable pixels in each bunch
c) Discard the group with a higher number of comparative pixels and utilize the other bunch as the fragmented picture

When the sectioned locales are gotten, at that point apply dim level-co-event grid (GLCM) to the leaf picture. Apply the GLCM to every one of the 3-measurements and consolidate the highlights into a solitary vector exhibit. GLCM of a picture is fundamentally a mix of various dim level measurements and was defined by Haralick. It utilizes second request measurements to discover relations among surfaces and the general dim degree of the picture. To create GLCM, Haralick dissected that second request probabilities were adequate for human separation of the surface. All in all, GLCM could be registered as follows. Initially, a unique surface picture D is re-organized in picture structure (suppose the picture name is G) with fewer dark levels, Ng. Normally, the incentive for Ng is 16 or 32. After this, the GLCM measurements are assessed by assessing every pixel and its neighbour, characterized by removal d and point ø. At dislodging, d could take an estimation of 1,2, 3..., n, while a point ø is restricted 0 degrees, 45 degrees, 90 degrees, and 135 degrees. The GLCM P(i, j|d,ø) is a subsequent request joint likelihood thickness work P of dark level sets in the picture for every component in the co-event network by separating each worth Ng. After playing out every one of these means, the last dark level co-event framework is found and its inward measurable segments are assessed utilizing the accompanying conditions:

$$\text{Energy: } \sum_{i,j} P(i,j)^2 \tag{11.1}$$

$$\text{Entropy: } -\sum_{i,j} P(i,j)\log P(i,j) \tag{11.2}$$

$$\text{Homogeneity: } \sum_{i,j} \frac{1}{1+(i-j)^2} P(i,j) \tag{11.3}$$

$$\text{Inertia: } \sum_{i,j} (i-j)^2 P(i,j) \tag{11.4}$$

$$\text{Correlation: } -\sum_{i,j} \frac{(i-\mu)(j-\mu)}{\sigma^2} P(i,j) \qquad (11.5)$$

$$\text{Shade: } \sum_{i,j} (i+j-2\mu)^3 P(i,j) \qquad (11.6)$$

$$\text{Prominence: } \sum_{i,j} (i+j-2\mu)^4 P(i,j) \qquad (11.7)$$

$$\text{Variance: } \sum_{i,j} (i-\mu)^2 P(i,j) \qquad (11.8)$$

$$\text{where } \mu = \mu_x = \mu_y = \sum_i i \sum_j P(i,j) = \sum_j j \sum_i P(i,j)$$

$$\text{and } \sigma = \sum_i (i-\mu_x)^2 \sum_j P(i,j) = \sum_j (j-\mu_y)^2 \sum_i P(i,j)$$

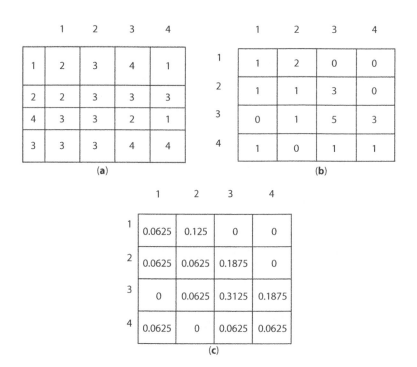

Figure 11.6 (a) Image matrix. (b) Co-occurrence matrix. (c) Actual GLCM values.

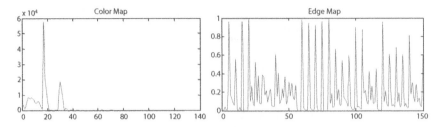

Figure 11.7 Colour map and shape map of image under test.

Figure 11.6a showcases an input image matrix, while Figure 11.6b showcases the evaluated GLCM components (as described previously). These components are given a normalization unknit wherein the final GLCM values are evaluated. These values are showcased in Figure 11.6c.

A shading map is characterized by the variety of shading levels (joined dark levels) in the information picture. These shading levels are framed by consolidating the red, green, and blue groups of the picture pixels. Because of this mix, a last estimation of shading is acquired, which is plotted on the X hub, and afterwards, the number of pixels of that specific worth are checked and plotted on the Y pivot. This structures the shading guide of the picture, while the edge map is the likelihood of edge event (edges are discovered utilizing vigilant edge administrator) on the specific pixel esteem as shown in Figure 11.7. These guides are valuable in discovering the highlights of the information picture.

All 3 highlights are joined together to structure an ideal descriptor for the leaf picture. These highlights are completely fit for recognizing the various sorts of video type. Every one of these highlights is attached to the picture itself on the red band (if the band is not applicable here, any band can be utilized by keeping different groups as zeros). Because of this affix activity, these highlights are likewise considered during the step-based element extraction and choice of the VGGNet CNN. When the highlights are extricated, at that point, a key segment investigation-based motor is utilized to separate significant highlights. To lessen the highlights, this work utilizes PCA. PCA is utilized so the general element vector can be diminished and just ideal highlights are accessible for characterization. This helps with decreasing the preparation delay and improving the general precision of order. The accompanying highlights are assessed in this work:

- Colour map of the input image
- Edge map of the input image
- GLCM features for the input image

Table 11.3 Features evaluated for each feature extraction technique.

Feature vector	Number of features	Components per feature	Total features
Edge Map	128	128	16384
Colour Map	256	1	256
GLCM	128	128	16384
		Total	33024

Table 11.3 demonstrates the number of features evaluated for each of the feature extraction techniques when an image size of 128x128 is taken for comparison.

Thus, a total of 33K features are evaluated for each input image. Most of the feature values are repetitive and can be reduced to a much lower number. Thereby, initially, a variance calculation is done for these features. The variance is not calculated within the features of the same image but across different images of the entire training set. The following formula is used to evaluate variance for each of the 33K samples:

$$V_i = \sqrt{\frac{\left(f_i - \dfrac{\sum f}{N_t} \right)^2}{N_t - 1}} \tag{11.10}$$

where, V_i is the variance of the ith feature (i goes from 1 to 33k), f_i is the value of the feature, and N_t are the total number of feature values for the given feature in the training set. Once the variance for each of the 33k features is obtained, then eigenvalues are obtained for these vectors. The variance is plotted on an XY axis, where the X-axis is the feature number and the Y-axis is the variance of the feature. For simplicity, consider that there are 6 features for which the variance is plotted, as shown in the Figures 11.8, 11.9 and 11.10.

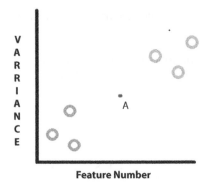

Figure 11.8 Sample 6 features plotted against variance.

The value 'A' is the mean between these points. Now, we evaluate the best fit line between these points, which aims to reduce the distance between these points, and showcase the line as follows:

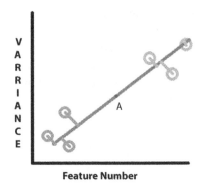

Figure 11.9 Best fit line between points.

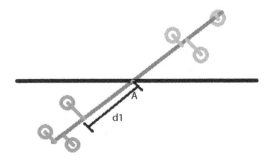

Figure 11.10 Axis coinciding with mean value.

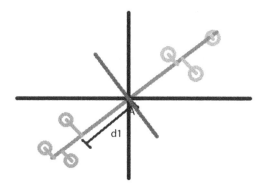

Figure 11.11 Orthogonal axis to feature vector d1.

The axis is shifted on the point A so that point A and the origin of the axis are coinciding with each other. This helps in evaluating the Eigenvalues.

Find the distances d1, d2, d3, d4, d5, and d6 using Pythagoras theorem and mark the values d1 to d6 as the eigenvalues of the features. Now, shift the axis making it orthogonal to d1 and evaluate the other feature vectors from d11, d12, d13, d14, d15, and d16, as shown in the following figure (the red line is the orthogonal line):

Similarly, the axis is made orthogonal to each of the features and the following matrix is evaluated:

$$
\begin{matrix}
d1 & d11 & dn1 \\
d2 & d12 & dn2 \\
dn & d1n & dnn
\end{matrix}
$$

The matrix consists of all the eigenvalues (or principal components) of the features. A singular value decomposition (SVD) is applied to these features and a single decomposed value is found for the given matrix.

$$SVD = \sum d_i * \sigma_i * f_i \tag{11.11}$$

where d_i is the eigenvalue, σ_i is the variance of the feature, and f_i is the feature vector value. All the positive values from these SVD values are considered for feature evaluation, while negative or zero values are removed. For our training set, the total number of features was reduced from 33K to approximately 8000 when using PCA, thereby improving the system speed and accuracy of classification. Using this PCA analysis, the features are embedded into the image itself and are given to CNN for classification. The CNN architecture can be observed in Figure 11.12, wherein an input size of 224 is taken, followed by sizes of 112, 56, 28, and 14 and finally a 7x7 window is used for final comparison.

Once these features have been evaluated, then the VGGNet convolutional neural network (CNN) training process is performed for the features and the body gesture types which are present in the input dataset. To recognize the body gestures, a multi-layered convolutional neural network with one input layer followed by five hidden layers and one output layer is designed and illustrated in Figure 11.12. The architecture starts with

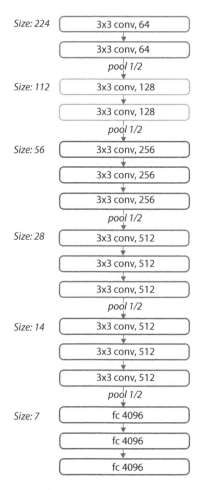

Figure 11.12 VGGNet CNN Architecture.

resizing the images into 224x224 dimension, followed by 2 convolutional layers of size 3x3 (stride). This helps to reduce the size of the image vector to 112x112, which is again followed by a series of convolutional layers and max-pooling layers that reduces the size of the image to 14x14x512. Finally, 3 fully connected layers are used which allow the system to classify the body gestures into one of the following categories: running, walking, jumping, sitting, standing, etc. These images were taken using a customized dataset because of its extensiveness of testing. The result evaluation on different kinds of videos can be observed in Table 11.4, wherein the CNN based models outperform other models of classification.

Table 11.4 Comparison of different activity detection algorithms.

Algorithm & Application	Accuracy (%)
Convolutional Neural Network (CNN) with TDMap [1]	99%
CNN with HoG & TDMap [1]	
Human pose detection (boxing, carrying, jogging, walking, running, hand waving, hand clapping, digging, and throwing)	98%
Non-Local Neural Networks (NLNN) [3] Human body recognition	93%
CNN with GEI [6] Walking style detection	98%
CNN [8] Walking postures	98%
KNN [10]	97.8%
Random Forest [10]	98.1%
LSTM [10]	99.1%
(standing, walking, eating, calling, lifting, handclapping, sitting)	
Statistical Classifier [12] Panic detection from crowd videos	98%
One-class SVM [14] Multiple events in videos	97.4%
The case study discussed in this chapter General human activity detection	98

From the results, it can be observed that the proposed CNN provides sufficiently high performance in terms of accuracy and can be used for any real-time detection of activities from different datasets.

11.3   Conclusion

In this chapter, readers were able to understand the concepts of video-based human activity detection and study different algorithms used for the same purpose. From this study, it is evident that the CNN-based human activity recognition systems outperform other systems by more than 10% in terms of the general accuracy of classification. A case study is done which allows the readers to go in-depth and understand the steps needed for the classification of human activities. From the case study, it is also evident that CNN, when combined with PCA, can produce a high-performance human activity detection system which can be used for customized and standard datasets.

References

1. Wang, X., & Yan, W. Q. Non-local gait feature extraction and human identification. *Multimedia Tools and Applications*, (258). https://doi.org/10.1007/s11042-020-09935-x, 2020.
2. Fu, Y., *Human Activity Recognition and the Activities Holter*, 2016.
3. Elharrouss, O., Almaadeed, N., Al-Maadeed, S., Bouridane, A., & Beghdadi, A. Combined multiple action recognition and summarization for surveillance video sequences. *Applied Intelligence*. https://doi.org/10.1007/s10489-020-01823-z, 2020.
4. Singh, M., Basu, A., & Mandal, M. K. , Human activity recognition based on silhouette directionality. *IEEE Transactions on Circuits and Systems for Video Technology*, 18(9), 1280–1292. https://doi.org/10.1109/TCSVT.2008.928888, 2008.
5. Bhuyan, M. K., *Computer Vision and Image Processing. Computer Vision and Image Processing*. https://doi.org/10.1201/9781351248396, 2019.
6. Beddiar, D. R., Nini, B., Sabokrou, M., & Hadid, A., Vision-based human activity recognition: a survey. *Multimedia Tools and Applications*, 79(41–42), 30509–30555. https://doi.org/10.1007/s11042-020-09004-3, 2020.
7. Shreyas, D. G., Raksha, S., & Prasad, B. G., Implementation of an Anomalous Human Activity Recognition System. *SN Computer Science*, 1(3), 1–10. https://doi.org/10.1007/s42979-020-00169-0, 2020.

8. Tammvee, M., & Anbarjafari, G., Human activity recognition-based path planning for autonomous vehicles. *Signal, Image and Video Processing.* https://doi.org/10.1007/s11760-020-01800-6, 2020.

9. Takahashi, M., Fujii, M., Shibata, M., & Satoh, S., Robust recognition of specific human behaviours in crowded surveillance video sequences. *Eurasip Journal on Advances in Signal Processing, 2010.* https://doi.org/10.1155/2010/801252, 2010.

10. Torres, B. S., & Pedrini, H. Detection of complex video events through visual rhythm. *Visual Computer, 34*(2), 145–165. https://doi.org/10.1007/s00371-016-1321-1, 2018.

11. Yuan, C., & Zhang, J., A novel violation detection method of live video using fuzzy support vector machine. *Journal of Ambient Intelligence and Humanized Computing,* (0123456789). https://doi.org/10.1007/s12652-020-02613-8, 2020.

12. Shehab, D., & Ammar, H., Statistical detection of panic behavior in crowded scenes. *Machine Vision and Applications, 30*(5), 919–931. https://doi.org/10.1007/s00138-018-0974-3, 2019.

13. Roh, M. C., Christmas, B., Kittler, J., & Lee, S. W., Robust player gesture spotting and recognition in low-resolution sports video. *Lecture Notes in Computer Science (Including Subseries Lecture Notes in Artificial Intelligence and Lecture Notes in Bioinformatics), 3954 LNCS,* 347–358. https://doi.org/10.1007/11744085_27, 2006.

14. İnce, Ö. F., Ince, I. F., Yıldırım, M. E., Park, J. S., Song, J. K., & Yoon, B. W., Human activity recognition with analysis of angles between skeletal joints using an RGB-depth sensor. *ETRI Journal, 42*(1), 78–89. https://doi.org/10.4218/etrij.2018-0577, 2020.

15. Muralikrishna, S. N., Muniyal, B., Acharya, U. D., & Holla, R., Enhanced Human Action Recognition Using Fusion of Skeletal Joint Dynamics and Structural Features. *Journal of Robotics, 2020.* https://doi.org/10.1155/2020/3096858, 2020.

16. Kwolek, B., Michalczuk, A., Krzeszowski, T., Switonski, A., Josinski, H., & Wojciechowski, K., Calibrated and synchronized multi-view video and motion capture dataset for evaluation of gait recognition. *Multimedia Tools and Applications, 78*(22), 32437–32465. https://doi.org/10.1007/s11042-019-07945-y, 2019.

17. Li, X., & Chuah, M. C. (2018). ReHAR: Robust and Efficient Human Activity Recognition. *Proceedings - 2018 IEEE Winter Conference on Applications of Computer Vision, WACV 2018, 2018-January,* 362–371. https://doi.org/10.1109/WACV.2018.00046, 2018.

18. Elharrouss, O., Almaadeed, N., Al-Maadeed, S., & Bouridane, A., Gait recognition for person re-identification. *Journal of Supercomputing,* (0123456789). https://doi.org/10.1007/s11227-020-03409-5, 2020.

19. Wang, L., Tan, T., Ning, H., & Hu, W. (2003). Silhouette Analysis-Based Gait Recognition for Human Identification. *IEEE Transactions on Pattern Analysis*

and Machine Intelligence, 25(12), 1505–1518. https://doi.org/10.1109/TPAMI.2003.1251144, 2003.

20. Dedeoğlu, Y., Töreyin, B. U., Güdükbay, U., & Enis Çetin, A., Silhouette-based method for object classification and human action recognition in video. Lecture Notes in Computer Science (Including Subseries Lecture Notes in Artificial Intelligence and Lecture Notes in Bioinformatics), 3979 LNCS, 64–77. https://doi.org/10.1007/11754336_7, 2020.

21. Gurpreet Kaur, Prateek Agrawal, "Optimisation of Image Fusion using Feature Matching Based on SIFT and RANSAC", Indian Journal of Science and Technology, 9(47), pp 1-7, 2016.

22. Prateek Agrawal, Vishu Madaan, Dimple Sethi, Naveen Kundu, Sanjay Kumar Singh, "X-HuBIS: A fuzzy rule based human behaviour identification system based on body gestures", Indian Journal of Science and Technology, 9(44), pp 1-6, 2016.

23. Prateek Agrawal, Ranjit Kaur, Vishu Madaan, Sunil Babu Mukkelli, Dimple Sethi, "Moving Object Detection and Recognition Using Optical Flow and Eigen Face Using Low Resolution Video", Recent Advances in Computer Science and Communications, 2020, 13(6), pp. 1180–1187 DOI: 10.2174/2213275911666181119112315.

24. Prateek Agrawal, Deepak Chaudhary, Vishu Madaan, Anatoliy Zabrovskiy, Radu Prodan, Dragi Kimovski, Christian Timmerer, "Automated Bank Cheque Verification Using Image Processing and Deep Learning Methods", Multimedia tools and applications (MTAP), 80(1), pp 5319–5350. DOI:10.1007/s11042-020-09818-1.

25. Prateek Agrawal, Anatoliy Zabrovskiy, Adithyan Ilagovan, Christian Timmerer, Radu Prodan, "FastTTPS: Fast Approach for Video Transcoding Time Prediction and Scheduling for HTTP Adaptive Streaming Videos", Cluster Computing, pp 1-17. DOI: 10.1007/s10586-020-03207-x.

26. Vishu Madaan, Aditya Roy, Charu Gupta, Prateek Agrawal, Anand Sharma, Christian Bologa, Radu Prodan, "XCOVNet: Chest X-ray Image Classification for COVID-19 Early Detection Using Convolutional Neural Networks", New Generation Computing, pp. 1-15. DOI: 10.1007/s00354-021-00121-7.

Solving Direction Sense Based Reasoning Problems Using Natural Language Processing

Vishu Madaan[1], Komal Sood[1], Prateek Agrawal[1,2*], Ashok Kumar[3], Charu Gupta[4†], Anand Sharma[5] and Awadhesh Kumar Shukla[1]

[1]*School of Computer Science Engineering, Lovely Professional University, Phagwara, Punjab, India*
[2]*Institute of ITEC, University of Klagenfurt, Wörthersee, Austria*
[3]*Department of Physics, K.S. College, Laheriasarai, Darbhanga, Bihar, India*
[4]*Department of Computer Science Engineering, Bhagwan Parshuram Institute of Technology, New Delhi, India*
[5]*Mody University of Science and Technology, Lakshamangarh, Rajasthan, India*

Abstract

Direction reasoning has gained more attention in the field of reasoning. Qualitative representation, reasoning of direction, and distance relationship are recognized as a theme related to information management, planning, and services. Analytical geometry is used as a mathematical tool to represent both direction and distance relationship. The analysis of directional relation is based on the measuring of angles. An angle model is not described as a case of calculating different directions. In this chapter, a novel natural language processing based approach is proposed to solve the direction sense reasoning problems. This chapter concentrates on a directional relationship of objects, the distance between objects, and calculates the distance between the starting and ending travel points by the object. As it is working with the Cartesian points, we referred to a mathematical model to describe the positions and calculations.

Keywords: Natural language processing, direction sense based reasoning, distance relation, direction relation

Corresponding author: dr.agrawal.prateek@gmail.com
†*Corresponding author*: charugupta@bpitindia.com

Prateek Agrawal, Charu Gupta, Anand Sharma, Vishu Madaan, and Nisheeth Joshi (eds.) *Machine Learning and Data Science: Fundamentals and Applications*, (215–230) © 2022 Scrivener Publishing LLC

12.1   Introduction

Representation and reasoning of spatial relationships are issues that scholars are concerned with within surveying and mapping, geography science, and computer science. Spatial relations, including distance relation, direction relation, and topology relation, essentially show limits between spatial data in different levels, where distance relation is strongest and direction relation is stronger. A study on representation and reasoning of spatial relations was mainly focused on single spatial relations before. Still, the distance relation and direction relation are combined to form the integrated Model to ensure the only representation of spatial relation and veracity of spatial reasoning. There are many investigations and it is seldom they study the combination between the distance relation and direction relation [1]. Distance relation and direction relation describe different perspectives of positional relation, respectively. The distance intervals are used to describe how relatively far or near between the primary object and another object are in the distance relation. The direction of an object is calculated as per directions mentioned, i.e., north, east, west, south, or in a relation between directions, i.e., which described the angle through which the object wants to travel is northeast (NE), northwest (NW), southeast t(SE), or southwest (SW). The object who wants to move in which direction and through which degree is mentioned in Figure 12.1. Qualitative distance is the natural language that describes distance intervals. The ratio of adjacent distance intervals is constant so that reasoning results are robust when distance intervals are magnified or shortened in the same ratio. Direction relation, which is determined by the primary object, reference object, and one reference point, is used to describe the relative orientation relation between the primary object and the reference object. In two dimension spaces, the primary direction is described by degrees (0°, 45° ...). A qualitative value corresponding can also describe it to the direction region obtained by the projection or cone-shaped systems. In general, the distance and direction relations are integrated to describe positional relations well. Figure 12.1 shows the diagrammatic view of a direction identification compass to understand the direction sensing concept [2].

The positional relation is qualitative when the distance or direction relation is qualitative. The method that combines qualitative distance and direction relations to describe the relative relation between the primary object and reference object is called the qualitative representation of positional relation. Given three objects, A, B, and C, based on positional relations between primary object B and reference object A, and positional

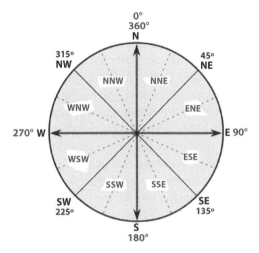

Figure 12.1 Directions identification compass.

relations between primary object C and reference object B, the positional relation is between primary object C and the reference object. A can be reasoned and this is called qualitative reasoning of positional relation. The description and reasoning of positional relation in the three-dimensional space is an important issue that must be resolved. The qualitative presentation and reasoning of positional relation in the three-dimensional space is studied with the space division method in the projection system based on `analytic geometrics [5].

12.2   Methodology

As per the direction sense constraint, one must have to face the problems regarding directions (east, west, and north, south) evaluation. Problems can be in clockwise or anti-clockwise directions evaluation, or it can occur when we have to work upon evaluating the person's direction while moving in any of the directions mentioned in Figure 12.1. During direction sense, one must also identify the starting positioning and after following the path, reach a positioning, i.e., the final point. Also, one can find the path that comes under a full scenario. The best method used to illustrate the scenario of solving direction sense reasoning is Natural Language Processing (NLP). NLP is a field of computer science, artificial intelligence, and linguistics concerned with the interaction between computers and human (natural) languages. NLP is used to describe the facts and rules of a given problem [3].

12.2.1   Phases of NLP

Reasoning problems include the step by step approach to reach the desired goal like Morphological Analysis Part, Syntax Analysis Part, Semantic Analysis Part, and Pragmatic Analysis [4]. Morphological analysis includes finding tokens, Syntax Analysis includes generation of a Tree, and Semantic Analysis includes verifying the meaning of tokens as well as sentences. Pragmatic Analysis includes verifying the working of syntax, as well as Semantic Analysis, or to identify the whole processing of syntax as well as the semantic part [5]. Tokens help in designing the tools and the Tree gives a step-by-step approach to reach a goal that is easily understandable by everyone. Figure 12.2 shows the step by step approach for working on the Phases of Natural Language Processing.

a. Morphological Analysis

Morphological Analysis is used to find out all the tokens which are used for solving the problems of direction sense reasoning. The lexical analysis helps to supply these tokens to another portion to make it more suitable to solve any problem. Each word from the sentence is divided into tokens. It does not matter if there is any meaning for this token or not; it is all calculated in another section as shown in Table 12.1 and 12.2. These tokens help in syntax analysis to make a view as a tree and helps in generating code in the remaining portions.

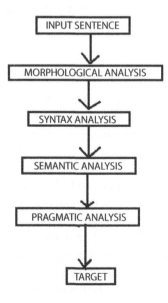

Figure 12.2 Phases of natural language processing.

b. Tokens

Table 12.1 Distribution of tokens.

Distance	Noun phrase	Noun	Verb	Proposition
Kilometer (km)	a-z or A-Z	he	is	to
Meter (m)	Name	she	am	of
Centimeter (cm)	Man	it	are	towards
	0-9		was	after
			were	in

Table 12.2 Distribution of tokens.

Direction	Verb phrase	Compound	Determinant
EAST	STARTS	AND	A
WEST	GO	THEN	AN
NORTH	WENT	AGAIN	THE
SOUTH	TOWARDS	FINALLY	
EAST-SOUTH	DISTANCE	LITTLE FURTHER	
EAST-NORTH	WALKS	AFTERWHILE	
WEST-SOUTH	WALKING		
WEST-NORTH	TURNS		
SOUTH-EAST	TURNED		
SOUTH-WEST	COVERED		
NORTH-EAST	FACING		
NORTH-WEST	DROVE		
CLOCKWISE	MOVING		
LEFT	TRAVELS		
RIGHT			
ANTI-CLOCKWISE	`		

c. Syntax Analysis

With the help of tokens, which are found during the lexical analysis, syntax analysis generates a syntax tree that gives the overview of the whole project, which is going to be done in further parts [6]. In short, Syntax Analysis gives a structural view of a given problem and also gives the way to solve it out. Syntax Analysis helps to give the idea, or we can say it helps to give the stepwise way to solve a problem easily shown in Figure 12.3. This part is easily understandable by all the persons who are new to this project.

a) **Syntax tree:**
NP = NOUN PHRASE
VP = VERB PHRASE
V = VERB
C = COMPOUND
DET = DETERMINANT
DIR = DIRECTION
P = PROPOSITION

PATTERN FOR GENERATING SYNTAX TREE:
[SENTENCE [NOUN PHRASE [C][NP1 [DET][NP2 [N][NP]]]]
[VERB PHRASE [VP1 [V][VP]][DIS][VP2 [PP [P][DET]][DIR]]]]

b) **GRAMMAR:**
SENTENCE = NOUN PHRASE/ VERB PHRASE/ NILL
NOUN PHRASE = C / NP1 / NILL
C = AND/ THEN/ AGAIN/ FINALLY/ LITTLE FURTHER/ AFTER WHILE/ NILL
NP1 = DET / NP2/ NILL

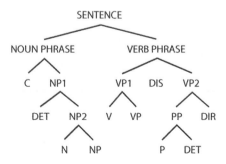

Figure 12.3 Syntax tree.

DET = A/ AN/ THE/ NILL
NP2 = N / NP/ NILL
N = HE/ SHE/ IT/ NILL
NP = NAME/ MAN/ NILL
VERB PHRASE = VP1/ DIS / VP2/ NILL
VP1 = V / VP/ NILL
V = IS/ AM/ ARE/ WAS/ WERE / NILL
VP = STARTS/ GO/ WENT/ TOWARDS/ DISTANCE/ WALKS/ WALKING/ TURNS/ TURNED/ COVERED/ FACING/ DROVE/ MOVING/ TRAVELS/ NILL
DIS = (0-1000) M/ KM/ CM/ NILL
VP2 = PP/ DIR/ NILL
PP = P/ DET/ NILL
P = TO/ OF/ TOWARD/ AFTER/ IN/ NILL
DET = A/ AN/ THE/ NILL
DIR = EAST/ WEST/ NORTH/ SOUTH/ EAST-NORTH/ EAST-SOUTH/ WEST-NORTH/ WEST-SOUTH/ NORTH-EAST/ NORTH-WEST/ SOUTH-EAST/ SOUTH-WEST/ LEFT/ RIGHT/ CLOCKWISE/ ANTICLOCKWISE/ NIL.

d. Semantic Analysis

Semantic Analysis is used to identify the actual meaning of all the tokens as well as sentences. Semantic Analysis is also used for checking grammatical errors while generating any sentence. Using a simplified form of logic for grammar and lexicon can be expanded for capturing some semantic information. The following Table 12.3 represents some Semantic Rules applied under the syntax as well as morphological phase:

Table 12.3 Semantic rule.

Syntactic rule	Semantic rule
Sentence → Noun Phrase, Verb Phrase	apply Verb Phrase (NP)
Verb Phrase → Verb, Noun Phrase	apply a Verb (Noun Phrase)
Noun Phrase → Article, Noun	apply Noun (Article)
Noun Phrase → Article, Adjective, Noun Phrase	apply Adjective (Article) apply Noun (Article)

e. Pragmatic Analysis

Pragmatic Analysis is designed to disambiguate sentences that are not completely disambiguated under the syntax and semantic analysis phases. Pragmatic Analysis interprets the result of the Semantic Analysis Part like we have in the sentence "Large Cat is running". The semantic analysis could not identify the Large Cat, so it takes both as keywords, not their actual meaning; Pragmatic Analysis interprets the sentence and makes the actual meaning of that keyword.

12.3　Description of Position

12.3.1　Distance Relation

In the geographical space, $d\ (A,\ B)$ is the distance between the primary object B and reference object A. According to the $d(A,B)$ length, the distance is divided into several intervals such as $(a0,a1]$, $(a1,a2]$, $(a2,a3]$, $(a3,a4]$, $(a4,a5]$, …. and so on. According to these intervals, primary objects and reference objects are used and the length ratio k of neighboring distance intervals is constant. The distance should satisfy three conditions:

    (1) Distance Range should be monotonously increasing
    (2) Distance Range is greater than current distance
    (3) Absorb Law,

where the means to absorb law is that a[i] follows a[j], which means a[i], the starting point is always following the a[j] reached point.

12.3.2　Direction Relation

Based on the projection method, the space for the reference object placed in the direction relation is divided by the six planes:

    i. $\pi\ X\text{max}: x\text{max} = \max\{xA \mid (xA, yA, zA) \in A\}$,
    ii. $\pi\ X\text{min}: x\text{min} = \min\{xA \mid (xA, yA, zA) \in A\}$
    iii. $\pi\ Y\text{max}: y\text{max} = \max\{yA \mid (xA, yA, zA) \in A\}$,
    iv. $\pi\ Y\text{min}: y\text{min} = \min\{yA \mid (xA, yA, zA) \in A\}$
    v. $\pi\ Z\text{max}: z\text{max} = \max\{zA \mid (xA, yA, zA) \in A\}$,
    vi. $\pi\ Z\text{min}: z\text{min} = \min\{zA \mid (xA, yA, zA) \in A\}$

Six planes are divided into three dimensional spaces as north (N), east (E), West (W), South (S), northeast (NE), northwest (NW), southeast (SE), and southwest (SW). Six planes also considered the directions through which movement is done as Up, Down, Left, Right, Clockwise, or Anticlockwise.

12.3.3 Description of Combined Distance and Direction Relation

The combined position is described by the qualitative distance and direction relation with the format that the qualitative distance is former and direction relation is latter, that is, $d\ AB\ dir(A, B)$, where $d\ AB$ is distance between the primary object A and reference object B and $dir(A, B)$ is the direction relation between the primary and reference objects. In the above mentioned absorb law in section distance relation, i refers to the dimensions and j refers to the directions. The dimensions and directions are mentioned in Section 12.3.2. Based on the positional relation between primary object A and reference object B and the positional relation between primary object B and reference object C, the positional relation between primary object A and reference object C can be inferred as shown in Figure 12.4.

$$dABdir(A,B) \land dBCdir(B,C) \rightarrow dACdir(A,C)$$

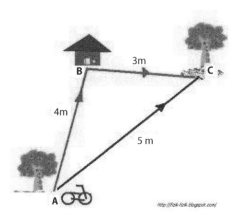

Figure 12.4 Relation between distance and direction.

12.4 Results and Discussion

This paper tells about what type of outcome is overcome. The result of direction sense reasoning is described on the basis of position, the path traveled by the object, and under which direction it traveled and calculates how much distance it travels from starting point to endpoint. All such types of problems are going to be solved using this concept.

The result of direction sense reasoning is described on the basis of the position of an object, the path traveled by the object, under which direction it traveled from starting point to the endpoint, and also in which direction the object is facing now, as being discussed above. Problems regarding direction constraints are going to be solved by using the concept mentioned above. Direction Sense Reasoning is the concept used to evaluate the directions (EAST, WEST, NORTH, SOUTH, NORTHEAST, NORTHWEST, SOUTHEAST, and SOUTHWEST). In this concept, problems come regarding the movement of a person in different directions. A person's movement is starting from one direction and then changes the path, i.e., in the Left/Right or in any other direction mentioned above. I have set the range of project "5," i.e., a person starts his journey from one particular point towards four directions, i.e., EAST, WEST, NORTH, SOUTH, then he wants to move left/right, after that turns left/right, again turns left/right, then at last moves left/right or in any other direction from position 2. Finally, one must want to evaluate in which direction is he now. This tool is working from range "2" to range "5". The Direction Sense Reasoning Concept helps to find out the problem regarding the above-mentioned problem, just like the same whole problems are mentioned and evaluating the solution for that. Direction relation, which is determined by the primary object, reference object, and one reference point, is used to describe the relative orientation relation between the primary object and the reference object. The qualitative presentation and reasoning of positional relation in the three-dimensional space are studied with the space division method in the projection system based on the analytic geometrics.

In my report, I have completed the task up to range 5 in different directions. I have made different combinations, followed by a pattern of directions. Whatever pattern I am going to follow is clearly mentioned in the following Table 12.4:

Table 12.4 Range distribution.

Range	Number combinations	Direction	Description
2	24	ALL	_____
3	48	ALL	_____
4	224	ALL	Direction must start from (EAST||WEST||NORTH||SOUTH) then either follows the pattern (LEFT||RIGHT) or any direction from 8.
5	64	FOUR (EAST||WEST||NORTH ||SOUTH)	Direction must start from (EAST||WEST||NORTH||SOUTH) then only follows the pattern of (LEFT||RIGHT)

12.5   Graphical User Interface

The GUI of this application is designed using Microsoft Visual Studio 2010. Different panels like Home Page, Login, Registration, and Get Direction are designed to be interacted with. We used Microsoft SQL Server 2008 to create a knowledge-base which stores the whole processing of the proposed tool. Whatever the functioning performed with this tool, it comes under this section. We divided the whole performance into different modules to fetch the value from the database or to store the value in the database. As a user uses the Registration Panel, the entirety of the entered information is stored under the table of registration so that it can be accessed for further login processing. As the user uses the Login Panel on the front end, all the values used for login are fetched from the registration panel. This will work only if the user uses the Registration Panel. As users use the Get Direction Panel from the front end, values are fetched from the table mentioned in the database. In short, whatever the functioning is going to perform with this tool regarding login, registration, and Get Direction is stored or fetched from this database. An SQL Server performs the Knowledge Base for this tool.

Home Page: On the Home Page, I have mentioned the instructions which are going to follow while using this tool. All the instructions need to be followed before starting to work with this tool as per Figure 12.5.

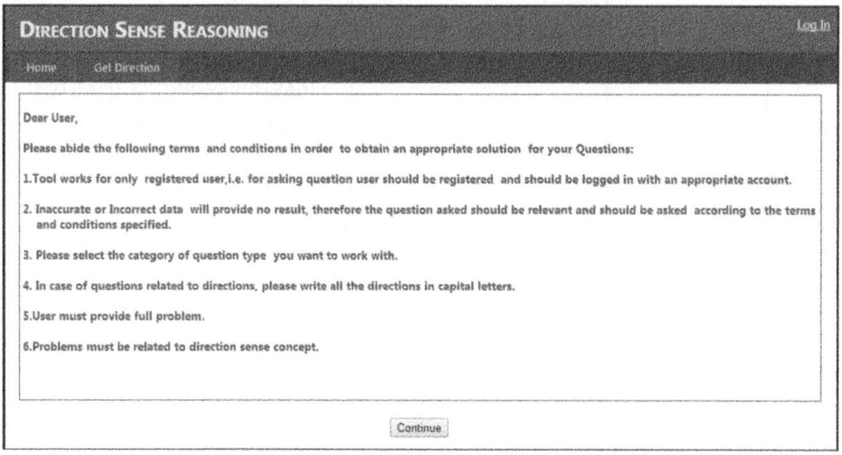

DIRECTION SENSE REASONING   Log In
Home   Get Direction

Dear User,

Please abide the following terms and conditions in order to obtain an appropriate solution for your Questions:

1. Tool works for only registered user,i.e. for asking question user should be registered and should be logged in with an appropriate account.

2. Inaccurate or Incorrect data will provide no result, therefore the question asked should be relevant and should be asked according to the terms and conditions specified.

3. Please select the category of question type you want to work with.

4. In case of questions related to directions, please write all the directions in capital letters.

5. User must provide full problem.

6. Problems must be related to direction sense concept.

Continue

Figure 12.5 Home page of direction sensing application.

Login: The user needs to login before starting the use of this tool. If the user does not login first, then the tool is not going to work. The login page is shown in Figure 12.6.

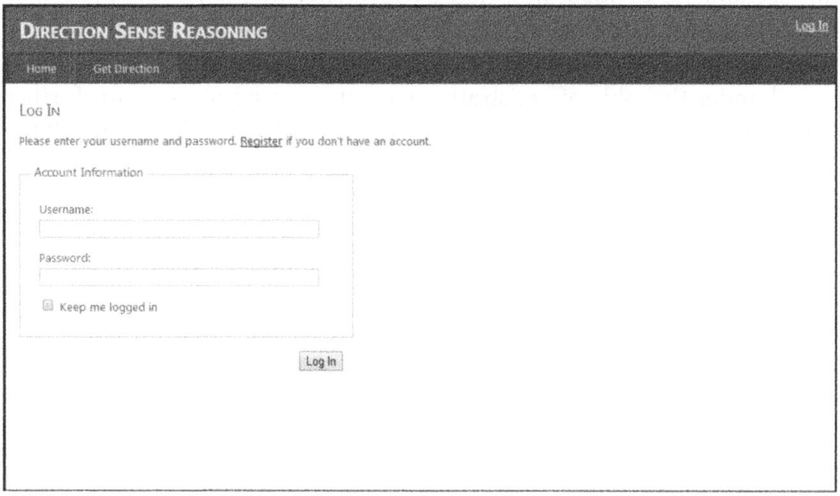

DIRECTION SENSE REASONING   Log In
Home   Get Direction

LOG IN

Please enter your username and password. Register if you don't have an account.

Account Information

Username:

Password:

Keep me logged in

Log In

Figure 12.6 Login page of direction sensing application.

Registration

The tool is valid only for registered users. In registration, the user needs to fill in some basic information about themselves as shown in Figure 12.7. After registration, by use of login the user can use the tool.

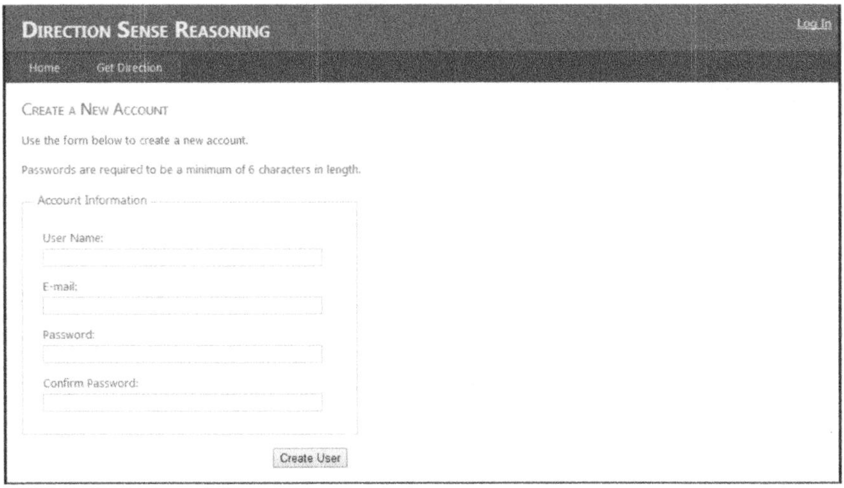

Figure 12.7 Registration page of direction sensing application.

Get Direction

The Get Direction Panel is the main part where the tool is going to work. Questions are entered in this panel and the solution is gotten according to the problem as shown in Figure 12.8a and 12.8b.

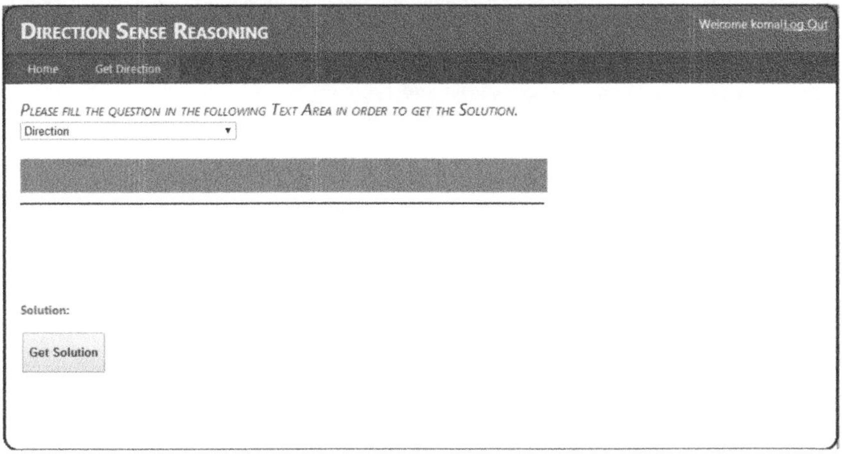

Figure 12.8a Get direction panel of direction ssensing application.

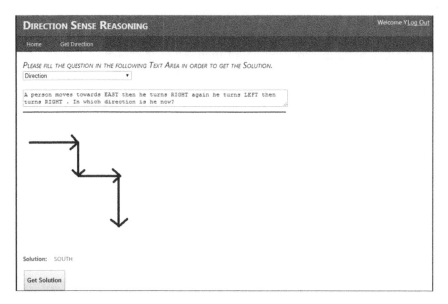

Figure 12.8b Get direction panel of direction sensing application.

If the user entered the wrong question or without reading instructions, the user is going to use the tool and it will give an error, i.e., the wrong question is entered. An error message appears on entering the wrong question as shown in Figure 12.9 and 12.10.

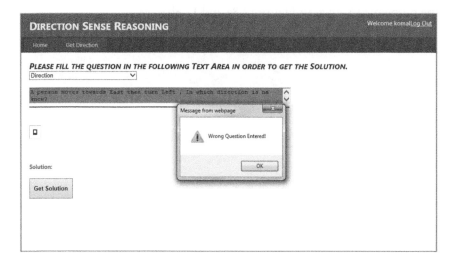

Figure 12.9 Error with input.

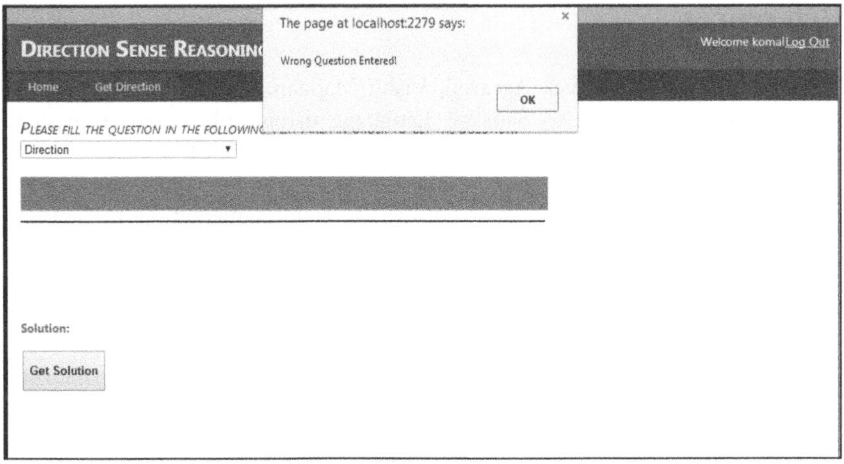

Figure 12.10 Error reflecting message on Giving Input of Wrong Question.

Tools work only for the registered user, i.e., for asking questions the user should be registered and logged in with an appropriate account. Inaccurate or incorrect data will provide no result. Therefore, the question asked should be relevant and should be asked according to terms and conditions specified. In case of questions related to directions, please write all the directions in a capital letter. The user must provide the full problem to get the solution. The problem must be related to the direction sense concept. Users must enter in which Direction it might start, i.e., EAST/WEST/NORTH/SOUTH, then follow the pattern according to data mentioned in the table discussed above.

Conclusion

For better learning and understanding of reasoning based problems, this natural language processing based tool is developed. The tool accepts every kind of reasoning problem by getting the meaning of the problem statement. The tool is provided with a user-friendly GUI that asks for a problem statement that undergoes all phases of NLP, draws the direction diagram, and finds the solution.

References

1. Neha Bhadwal, Prateek Agrawal, Vishu Madaan, "A Machine Translation System from Hindi to Sanskrit Language using Rule based Approach", Scalable Computing: Practices and experiences (SCPE), vol 21, issue 3, pp 543-554, Aug 2020.
2. Prateek Agrawal, Leena Jain, "Anuvaadika: Implementation of Sanskrit to Hindi translation tool using Rule-based approach", Recent Patents on Computer Science, 12(2), pp. 1-23, Bentham Science Publisher, 2019, DOI: 10.2174/2213275912666181226155829.
3. Leena Jain, Prateek Agrawal, "English to Sanskrit Transliteration: an effective approach to design Natural Language Translation Tool", International Journal of Advanced Research in Computer Science (IJARCS), 8(1), pp. 1-10, Feb 2017.
4. Prateek Agrawal, Vishu Madaan, Nandini Sethi, Vikas Kumar, Sanjay Kumar Singh, "A Novel Approach to Paraphrase English Sentences using Natural Language Processing", International Journal of Control Theory and Applications, 9(11), pp 5119-5128, 2016.
5. Leena Jain, Prateek Agrawal, "Text Independent Root Word Identification in Hindi language using Natural Language Processing", International Journal of Advanced Intelligence Paradigm (IJAIP), vol 7, issue3-4, pp 240-249, Inderscience Publications, 2015.
6. Neha Bhadwal, Prateek Agrawal, Vishu Madaan, "Bilingiual Machine Translation System Between Hindi and Sanskrit Languages", 3rd International Conference on Advances Informatics on Computing Research (ICAICR'19), pp. 312-321, Jul 2019, Springer CCIS.

Drowsiness Detection Using Digital Image Processing

G. Ramesh Babu*, Chinthagada Naveen Kumar and Maradana Harish

ECE Department, Raghu Engineering College (Autonomous), Visakhapatnam, Andhra Pradesh, India

Abstract

Car accidents and related forms of accidents are the major cause of death, where approximately 1.3 million innocent people die every year. Many of them are due to the drowsy state of the driver. High-speed highway roads reduce the margin of error for the driver. A large number of people who drive for long distances every day and night usually go through the problem of extreme tiredness and may easily fall sleep for some while. To prevent people from such accidents, this system has been proposed to alert the driver if he feels drowsy. Facial detection is being used in this system with the help of image processing where images of the driver's face are captured using a camera. The algorithm in this system helps to detect the symptoms of driver fatigue earlier, which can prevent an accident by cautioning the driver by an alarm. In this driver drowsiness detection method, following the face detection step, the most effective facial components are extracted and tracked in video sequence frames.

Keywords: Driver drowsiness detection, accidents, image processing

13.1 Introduction

Drivers usually get tired due to continuous driving for a long time, especially heavy vehicle drivers, resulting in driver fatigue and drowsiness, which leads to an accident causing a number of deaths. Each country has

---

Corresponding author: drgramesh24@gmail.com

Prateek Agrawal, Charu Gupta, Anand Sharma, Vishu Madaan, and Nisheeth Joshi (eds.) Machine Learning and Data Science: Fundamentals and Applications, (231–244) © 2022 Scrivener Publishing LLC

its own stats for accidents that occur due to driver fatigue. According to the road ministry's data, 467,044 road accidents were reported in India in 2018, an increase of 0.5% from 464,910 in 2017 [1], that took thousands of people's lives because of sleepy drivers. A survey revealed that 60% have driven while feeling sleepy and 37% of people admitted that they actually fell asleep while driving in the past year. Driver drowsiness detection is still under research [2] in order to reduce the number of accidents. Computer vision research has designed a system which is dedicated precisely to detecting human blinks. There are many ways to detect the drowsiness, such as Image Processing, EEG, Vehicular based measures, and Subjective measures. In the present system, we have chosen an Image Processing Based technique as it is a non-instrumented technique that does not require the driver's interaction with the machine. Here, the camera transmits real-time driver's data and determines drowsiness using the trained models of closed and opened eyes which are implemented using python. The focus of the system is based mainly on whether the eye is Closed or Open in all the consecutive frames. The proposed system works on a collected dataset with a very good accuracy.

13.2   Literature Review

One of the main causes for accidents in our country nowadays is drowsiness of the driver. In order to avoid heavy loss of life, technological methods must be developed to notice a driver's temporary state and warn him before he sleeps. In 2014, Nagajyothi and Geethu Mohan proposed a drowsy driver detection system that uses eye OPEN or CLOSE state in a facial image to detect drowsiness by using Matlab. Murugan *et al.* proposed a system in 2015 [3] which makes use of EEG signals to detect the driver's drowsiness using ADS1299 which is a cost effective and low power consumption model.

A system capable of detecting the drowsiness of a driver is provoked by the respiration captured by means of cameras and was proposed by Jose Solaz *et al.* in 2016. In 2017 [6], H.M. Chandrasena and D.M.J. Wickramasinghe used a sleepiness detection methodology which is a hybrid approach of eye membrane detection and pulse pattern detection to notice the temporary state of the driver. Puja Seemar and Anurag Chandna in 2017 [14] focused on a driver sleepiness detection system in an intelligent transportation system, where Raspberry pi is used to understand the unusual state of the driver. In their work, blink pattern and eye movements were transformed from 2D to 3D images using wavelet analysis.

R. Jabbar *et al.* in 2018 proposed a unique approach for time temporary state detection where deep learning methodology was used and enforced on humanoid applications with high accuracy.

13.3   Proposed System

The system proposed is a driver face tracking system which tracks the movement of eyes for the detection of a driver's fatigue and drowsiness using Python, Open CV, [3] and Keras, which will alert the driver when he feels sleepy. Some of the steps are shown in the flowchart shown in Figure 13.1.

The first step performed here is acquisition of image through the webcam by using Open CV for gathering images and loading them into a deep learning model that helps classify whether the eyes of the driver are Closed or Open. For the process of Face detection and Eye Detection we have used an algorithm called the Viola Jones Algorithm by taking its Haar Features

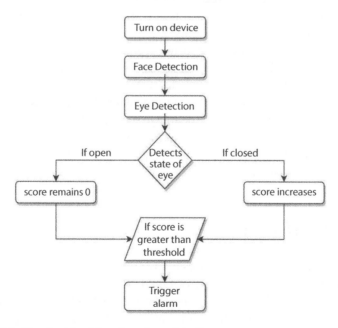

Figure 13.1 Flowchart for driver drowsiness detection.

Figure 13.2 Conversion of positive images to gray scale images.

and performing an adaptive boosting technique which is further described in the next section. Through the detection of faces in the image, a Region of Interest (ROI) has been created for better recognition of the face. The face captured is converted from color image to a gray scale image for calculating the threshold values and weights of each region shown in Figure 13.2.

The same process is performed for eye detection, but here eyes were selected from the ROI of the face and then fed [4] into the Classifier. The Classifier here means the cascaded images which are calculated. This Classifier compares extracted data with the dataset model which is initialized in the system and classifies the image state, giving the results whether the eyes were Closed or Open. At last, the score will be calculated through the threshold values [15]. The alarm starts ringing if the score increases and makes the driver alert.

13.4   The Dataset

In the dataset, the captured images of eyes are stored. Later, these are separated with labels as either Close or Open. The data does not contain any unwanted images. The data in the model consists of 7000 positive images of eyes under different lightning conditions and 5000 negative images. These trained images of respective weights and architecture were then attached to the file named models/cnncat2.h5.

13.5   Working Principle

13.5.1   Face Detection

Drowsiness detection using digital image processing has been developed using software machine vision based concepts [5]. In this, the system uses a web camera that directly catches and observes the driver's face movements in order to detect his drowsiness. In such a situation, if the driver is detected to be in fatigue a warning sound alert would be generated. This system deals with observing the eye's movement within the specific elements in the face. In this, the timer is set to 5 seconds which alerts the driver if he is asleep. Here, the face detection is done by the Viola Jones Algorithm. Some of the characteristics of this algorithm are as follows:

> Robust - It gives very low false-positive rate and very high detection rate
> Real time: For use in any real-world applications, at least 2 frames must be processed

The Viola Jones Algorithm consists of 4 stages:

- Haar Feature Selection
- Creating an Integral Image

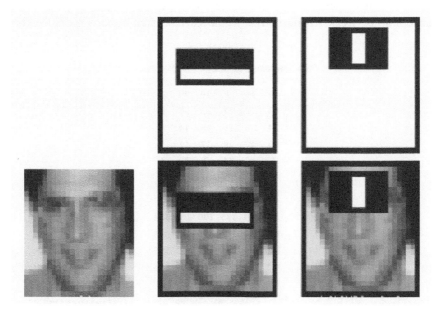

Figure 13.3 Selecting haar features using various haar techniques.

- Adaptive Boosting
- Cascading Classifiers

The first step is to collect the Haar Features from the image. This feature [6], shown in Figure 13.3, considers different adjacent rectangular regions at a particular location in the detection window. Later, the pixel intensities in each region are summed up and the difference between these sums is calculated.

In the **second step**, integral images are used to make this superfast. An integral image is a summed area table in a data structure and algorithm where the sum of values are generated quickly and efficiently in a rectangular subset of a grid.

Basing on these features, many features are found to be irrelevant. To overcome these features, a process named **Adaboost** is used to eliminate unwanted elements or features from the image.

The **third step** is to select relevant features from the image. Adaboost refers to a specific technique of coaching a boosted classifier in the form as

$$h(x) = \text{sign}(\sum_{j=1}^{M} \alpha_j h_j\ (x)) \qquad (13.1)$$

The **last step** is to form a classifier for several pictures, i.e., a Cascade Classifier. It consists of a set of stages where every stage is an associate ensemble of weak learners. The weak learners that square measure the

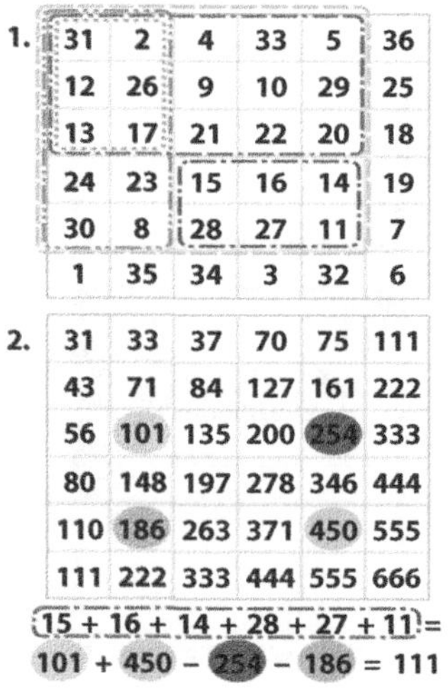

Figure 13.4 Calculating the algorithm from integral images.

input from the user square measure easy classifiers known as call stumps. Every single stage is trained employing a boosting technique. This technique trains an extremely correct classifier by taking the weighted average of the selected weak learners. Cascade Classifier [7] coaching needs a collection of positive samples and negative pictures as shown in Figure 13.4.

13.5.2   Drowsiness Detection Approach

a. Eye Detection

The calculation of eye state is considered after completion of face detection, as shown in Figure 13.5. The state is calculated by taking the eye aspect ratio which was defined to detect the eye's state, i.e., whether it is closed or open by using the scalar values. As the eyes are present at a particular place in the face, we limit our research in the areas of the forehead of the person and their mouth (i.e., by calculating its region of interest (ROI)). While driving, if the driver blinks or closes his eyes for some time or frequently, it means they are in a drowsy state. Hence, detecting the eye shape correctly to calculate the state of an eye is very essential. For every video captured, the eye landmarks were detected, as shown in Figure 13.6, between height and width of the eye. So, the EAR is given as follows:

$$\mathrm{EAR} = \frac{|p2 - p6| + |p3 - p5|}{2|p1 - p4|}$$

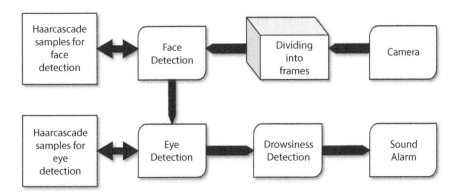

Figure 13.5 Diagrammatical approach for drowsiness detection process.

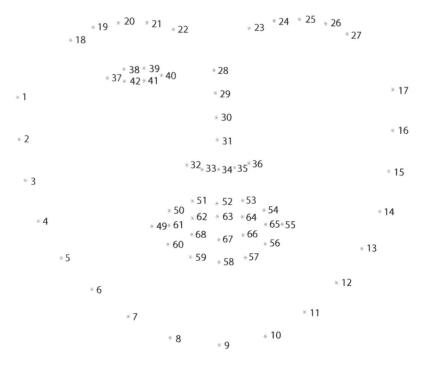

Figure 13.6 Facial landmarks on human face.

The approximate landmark values for the eye detection are:

Left Eye	37-42
Right Eye	43-48

The given equation shows the EAR formula [8] where 2D landmark locations are p1 to p6 and points p2, p3, p5, and p6 measure the height of the eyes and p1 and p4 measures width of the eyes in meters. The eye aspect ratio is a constant value when the eye is open, but declines consistently to 0 when closed, as shown in Figure 13.7a.

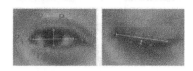

Figure 13.7 (a) Open eye with landmarks, (b) closed eye landmark.

$$EAR = x>0 \text{ ;eyes open}$$

$$x = 0;\text{eyesclose}$$

The EAR output variations throughout the eyes Open and eyes Close is unendingly determined. Throughout eyes Close, the EAR result is about zero, whereas throughout Open it is any range number that is x which is greater than zero. For detection of eyes, these eye states' square measure are fed through convolutional neural networks.

13.6   Convolutional Neural Networks

Convolutional Neural Networks [9], as shown in Figure 13.8, were specifically designed for recognizing images. They achieve this property by extracting options which rely solely on tiny sub-regions of the image. Data obtained is incorporated in the later stages to observe a lot of complicated options and, ultimately, to yield data concerning the image as a whole.

13.6.1   CNN Design for Decisive State of the Eye

To limit the complexness of the design, the CNN [9–12] solely uses a pair of convolutional stages (C1, C2) and sub-sampling layers (S1, S2). The primary stage shows non-linear template-matching with a fine abstraction resolution, bringing out basic options of the input image. The second stage acknowledges the specific abstraction mixtures of previous options, generating complicated options in a graded manner to produce completely different feature maps and extract the different options in layer C2. Each of these maps in layer C2 receives a distinct set of inputs from layer S1. The S2

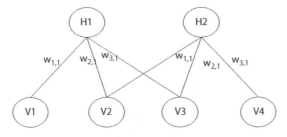

Figure 13.8 Every unit in layer H is connected by three similar weights to three units correspondingly in the previous layer (V).

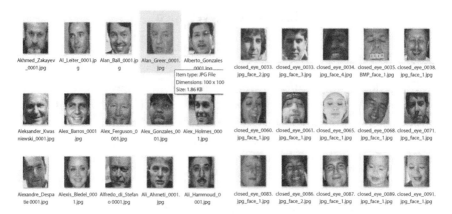

Figure 13.9 Samples of closed eye faces and open eye face images dataset.

layer is able to extract a series of disjointed options of lower dimensionality used in classification [13]. Therefore, layer C3 is a totally connected layer where every unit is connected to one map in layer S2 correspondingly. Finally, all the units in the C3 square measure are linked totally to make two outputs with softmax activation operate.

$$Y_k = \frac{e^{a_k}}{\sum_{j=1}^{2} e^{a}}$$

whereas k = 0 for eye pictures, k = 1 is for non-eye pictures, and Alaska is the output unit activation k, whereas wkj and wk0 are adjustable parameters for the output unit k, zj is the output for the hidden unit j in layer C3, and M is the variety of units in layer C3.

Here, the generalized performance of CNN depends on the number of training data. To add a huge variety of conditions, that is different head poses and face illuminations, simulated output images have been created and added to the original images. Some examples of the collected images are shown in Figure 13.9.

13.7 Performance Evaluation

In this section, performance of the proposed system is presented by performing an analysis of the obtained results. Firstly, the system collects real-time data, i.e., captures video of the drivers, as shown in Figures 13.10 and 13.11.

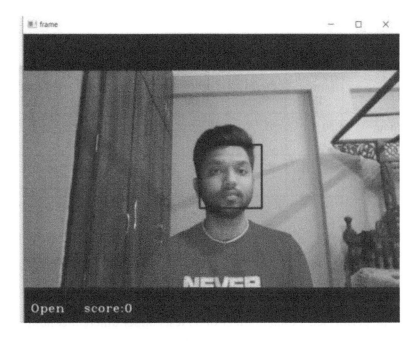

Figure 13.10 Results when eyes are open (without Spectacles).

Figure 13.11 Results when eyes are closed (without Spectacles).

Table 13.1 30 Tests under different conditions.

	Total tests		Detected correctly		Precision	
	Low light	Bright light	Low light	Bright light	Low light	Bright light
Without Spectacles	30	30	21	27	0.41	0.50
With Spectacles	30	30	19	24	0.38	0.44

It then determines the fatigue of the driver based on the EAR values that are computed based on the images captured by the user.

13.7.1　Observations

Here, we performed a total number of 30 tests under different conditions, as shown in Table 13.1. In these tests, our project is working perfectly under the bright conditions and is precise well, as high precision rate results in low false rate or low error rate.

13.8　Conclusion

In this paper, an eye blink detection algorithm was presented. We have suggested a better approach for driver drowsiness detection and alerting the driver to prevent accidents. It is a software build technique, so there would be no complications to perform it. Also, the process is non-invasive and continuously tracks the driver by keeping a track on the driver's eye movement.

References

1. A. Kumar and R. Patra, "Driver drowsiness monitoring system using visual behaviour and machine learning," ISCAIE 2018 - 2018 IEEE Symposium on Computer Applications and Industrial Electronics, pp. 339–344, 2018.

2. A. Gopal and V. Vineeth, "Driver Drowsiness Detection System," International Journal of Advances in Electronics and Computer Science, vol. 4, no. 3, pp. 101–104, 2017

3. B. Mohana, C. M. Sheela Rani," Drowsiness Detection Based on Eye Closure and Yawning Detection," International Journal of Recent Technology and Engineering (IJRTE), ISSN: 2277-3878, Volume-8 Issue-4, November 2019

4. G. Zhang, K. K. Yau, X. Zhang, and Y. Li, "Traffic accidents involving fatigue driving and their extent of casualties," Accident Analysis & Prevention, vol. 87, pp. 34–42, 2016.

5. Jang WoonBaek, Byung-Gil Han, Kwang-Ju Kim, Yun-Su Chung, Soon-In Lee, "Real-time Drowsiness Detection Algorithm for Driver State Monitoring Systems," 2018 Tenth International Conference on Ubiquitous and Future Networks (ICUFN), 2018.

6. Viola, Jones, Rapid object detection using a boosted cascade of simple features, Computer cool Vision and Pattern Recognition, 2001.

7. Li Cuimei, Qi Zhiliang, Jia Nan, Wu Jianhua, "Human face detection algorithm via Haar cascade classifier combined with three additional classifiers," IEEE 2017.

8. Kevan Yuen, Sujitha Martin and Mohan M. Trivedi, "Looking at Faces in a Vehicle: A Deep CNN Based Approach and Evaluation," 2016 IEEE 19th International Conference on Intelligent Transportation Systems (ITSC) Windsor Oceanico Hotel, Rio de Janeiro, Brazil, November 1-4, 2016.

9. Manu B.N, "Facial Features Monitoring for Real Time Drowsiness Detection," in 2016 12th International Conference on Innovations in Information Technology (IIT).

10. Kwok Tai Chui, Kim Fung Tsang, Hao Ran Chi, Bingo Wing Kuen Ling, ung Kit Wu, "An Accurate ECG-Based Transportation Safety Drowsiness Detection Scheme," IEEE transactions on industrial informatics, vol. 12, no. 4, august 2016.

11. Vishu Madaan, Aditya Roy, Charu Gupta, Prateek Agrawal, Anand Sharma, Christian Bologa, Radu Prodan, "XCOVNet: Chest X-ray Image Classification for COVID-19 Early Detection Using Convolutional Neural Networks", New Generation Computing, pp. 1-15. DOI: 10.1007/s00354-021-00121-7.

12. Prateek Agrawal, Deepak Chaudhary, Vishu Madaan, Anatoliy Zabrovskiy, Radu Prodan, Dragi Kimovski, Christian Timmerer, "Automated Bank Cheque Verification Using Image Processing and Deep Learning Methods", Multimedia tools and applications (MTAP). https://doi.org/10.1007/s11042-020-09818-1.

13. Charlotte Jacobé de Naurois, Christophe Bourdin, AncaStratulat, Emmanuelle Diaz, Jean-Louis Vercherde Naurois, "Detection and prediction of driver drowsiness using artificial neural network models" Accident Analysis and Prevention, 126, 95–104, 2019.

14. Chandrasena H.M, D.M.J. Wickramasinghe, "Driver's Drowsiness Detecting and AlarmingSystem". International Journal of Information Technology and Computer Science,Vol. 4, Issue 3, pp: 127-139, 2017.
15. Prateek Agrawal, Ranjit Kaur, Vishu Madaan, Sunil Babu Mukkelli, Dimple Sethi, "Moving Object Detection and Recognition Using Optical Flow and Eigen Face Using Low Resolution Video", Recent Advances in Computer Science and Communications, 2020, 13(6), pp. 1180–1187 DOI: 10.2174/22 13275911666181119112315.

Index

Also of Interest

Check out these other related titles from Scrivener Publishing

DATA MINING AND MACHINE LEARNING APPLICATIONS, Edited by Rohit Raja, Kapil Kumar Nagwanshi, Sandeep Kumar and K. Ramya Laxmi, ISBN: 9781119791782. The book elaborates in detail on the current needs of data mining and machine learning and promotes mutual understanding among research in different disciplines, thus facilitating research development and collaboration. *NOW AVAILABLE!*

MACHINE LEARNING TECHNIQUES AND ANALYTICS FOR CLOUD SECURITY, Edited by Rajdeep Chakraborty, Anupam Ghosh and Jyotsna Kumar Mandal, ISBN: 9781119762256. This book covers new methods, surveys, case studies, and policy with almost all machine learning techniques and analytics for cloud security solutions. *NOW AVAILABLE!*

COGNITIVE BEHAVIOR AND HUMAN COMPUTER INTERACTION BASED ON MACHINE LEARNING ALGORITHMS, Edited by Sandeep Kumar, Rohit Raja, Shrikant Tiwari and Shilpa Rani, ISBN: 9781119791607. The objective of this book is to provide the most relevant information on Human-Computer Interaction to academics, researchers, and students and for those from industry who wish to know more about the real-time application of user interface design. *NOW AVAILABLE!*

ADVANCED ANALYTICS AND DEEP LEARNING MODELS, Edited by Archana Mire, Shaveta, ISBN: 9781119791751. The book provides readers with an in-depth understanding of concepts and technologies related to the importance of analytics and deep learning in many useful real-world applications such as e-healthcare, transportation, agriculture, stock market, etc. *NOW AVAILABLE!*

Printed and bound by CPI Group (UK) Ltd, Croydon, CR0 4YY

27/10/2024

14580128-0001